Service Learning

*To my mother
Irene Margaret Boland Snyder
and to my father
Harold J. Snyder
They taught me how to be a lifelong learner.*

Service Learning

A Guide to Planning, Implementing, and Assessing Student Projects

Sally Berman

Skyhorse Publishing

Skyhorse Publishing books may be purchased in bulk at special discounts for sales promotion, corporate gifts, fund-raising, or educational purposes. Special editions can also be created to specifications. For details, contact the Special Sales Department, Skyhorse Publishing, 307 West 36th Street, 11th Floor, New York, NY 10018 or info@skyhorsepublishing.com.

Skyhorse® and Skyhorse Publishing® are registered trademarks of Skyhorse Publishing, Inc.®, a Delaware corporation.

Visit our website at www.skyhorsepublishing.com.

10 9 8 7 6 5 4 3 2 1

Library of Congress Cataloging-in-Publication Data
Berman, Sally.
Service learning: A guide to planning, implementing, and assessing student projects / Sally Berman.—2nd ed.
p. cm.
Includes bibliographical references and index.
ISBN 1-4129-3672-1 (cloth) — ISBN 1-4129-3673-X (pbk.)
1. Student service—United States. 2. Project method in teaching. 3. Active learning. 4. Multiple intelligences. I. Title.
LC220.5.B46 2006
361.3'7—dc22
2005032753

Print ISBN: 978-1-63220-570-4
Ebook ISBN: 978-1-63220-985-6

Printed in the United States of America

Contents

Sidebar Directory   xi

Preface   xiii
    About This Book   xiii
    How to Use This Book   xiv

Acknowledgments   xvii

About the Author   xix

Introduction   xxi
    What Is Service Learning?   xxi
    What Is the History of Service Learning?   xxi
    Why Do Service Learning?   xxii
    How Does Service Learning Work?   xxiv
    Who Are the Key Players in a Service Learning Project?   xxv
    How Do Students Benefit From Service Learning?   xxvi

1. The Fundamentals of Service Learning as a Curriculum Model   1
    How Does Service Learning Work?   1
        Selecting the Need for Service   2
        Assessing Risks: Establishing Protocols for Health and Safety   4
        Finding a Community Partner   5
        Reciprocity: The Community of Learners   7
        Aligning Service and Educational Goals   7
        Tapping Into Multiple Intelligences: Structuring Learning Teams   8
        Managing the Project   9
        Fostering Reflective Learning   11
    Assessment and Evaluation in Service Learning   12
    What About Challenges? How Can They Be Managed?   14
    Using the Project Ideas in This Book   17
        Tapping Into Multiple Intelligences:
            Managing the Management Plan   18

PART I: BASIC SERVICE LEARNING PROJECTS   21

2. Clean Streets, Green Streets:
    A Social Studies and Science Service Learning Project   23
    Description of the Project   23
        Keeping Records and Building a Portfolio   24

Assessing Risks: Establishing Protocols for Health and Safety 26
Selecting the Service Learning Focus: The Community Environment 27
Tapping Into Multiple Intelligences: Mapping Possibilities 29
Making Connections With the Community 30
Working With a Community Partner 31
Aligning Service and Educational Goals 32
Student Responsibilities and Curricular Areas 32
Reciprocity: The Community of Learners 33
Managing the Service Project: Clean Streets, Green Streets 35
Fostering Reflective Learning 35
Assessment and Evaluation 37
Elementary Reflective Log 39
Middle School Reflective Log 40
High School Reflective Log 41

3. **The Lending Locker:**
   A Health and Physical Education Service Learning Project 43
   Description of the Project 43
   Keeping Records and Building a Portfolio 44
   Tapping Into Multiple Intelligences: Let's Get Visible! 46
   Assessing Risks: Establishing Protocols for Health and Safety 48
   Selecting the Service Learning Focus: Sharing
   Fitness Equipment With the Community 48
   Making Connections With the Community 49
   Working With a Community Partner 49
   Aligning Service and Educational Goals 51
   Student Responsibilities and Curricular Areas 52
   Reciprocity: The Community of Learners 52
   Managing the Service Project: The Lending Locker 54
   Fostering Reflective Learning 54
   Assessment and Evaluation 54
   Elementary Reflective Log 57
   Middle School Reflective Log 58
   High School Reflective Log 59

4. **The Hygiene Tree: A Consumer Education and**
   Health Service Learning Project 61
   Description of the Project 61
   Tapping Into Multiple Intelligences: The Role of Rubrics 64
   Keeping Records and Building a Portfolio 65
   Assessing Risks: Establishing Protocols for Health and Safety 66
   Selecting the Service Learning Focus:
   Personal Hygiene Products for the Homeless and the Needy 66
   Making Connections With the Community 67
   Working With a Community Partner 67
   Aligning Service and Educational Goals 67
   Student Responsibilities and Curricular Areas 68
   Reciprocity: The Community of Learners 69

Managing the Service Project: The Hygiene Tree   71
Fostering Reflective Learning   71
Assessment and Evaluation   73
    Elementary Reflective Log   75
    Middle School Reflective Log   76
    High School Reflective Log   77

PART II: INTERMEDIATE SERVICE LEARNING PROJECTS   **79**

5. **Reading Pals: A Language Arts and**
   Life Skills Service Learning Project   **81**
   Description of the Project   81
       Keeping Records and Building a Portfolio   82
   Assessing Risks: Establishing Protocols for Health and Safety   85
   Selecting the Service Learning Focus: Reading
       Partnerships With the Community   86
       Making Connections With the Community   87
   Working With a Community Partner   88
   Aligning Service and Educational Goals   90
       Tapping Into Multiple Intelligences: Storytelling in Nature   90
       Student Responsibilities and Curricular Areas   90
       Reciprocity: The Community of Learners   92
   Managing the Service Project: Reading Pals   93
   Fostering Reflective Learning   93
   Assessment and Evaluation   95
       Elementary Reflective Log   97
       Middle School Reflective Log   98
       High School Reflective Log   99

6. **The Soup Troop: A Health and**
   Family Education Service Learning Project   **101**
   Description of the Project   101
       Keeping Records and Building a Portfolio   103
   Assessing Risks: Establishing Protocols for Health and Safety   103
   Selecting the Service Learning Focus:
       A Community Nutrition Project   104
       Making Connections With the Community   104
       Tapping Into Multiple Intelligences: Who's Got Rhythm?   106
   Working With a Community Partner   107
   Aligning Service and Educational Goals   107
       Student Responsibilities and Curricular Areas   109
       Reciprocity: The Community of Learners   109
   Managing the Service Project: The Soup Troop   110
   Fostering Reflective Learning   110
   Assessment and Evaluation   112
       Elementary Reflective Log   114
       Middle School Reflective Log   115
       High School Reflective Log   116

7. **Computer Tutors: An Instructional Technology
    and Language Arts Service Learning Project**   **117**
    Description of the Project   117
        Keeping Records and Building a Portfolio   119
    Assessing Risks: Establishing Protocols for Health and Safety   122
    Selecting the Service Learning Focus:
        Computer Education Partnerships   122
        Tapping Into Multiple Intelligences: Analyze, Prioritize   123
        Making Connections With the Community   124
    Working With a Community Partner   124
    Aligning Service and Educational Goals   125
        Student Responsibilities and Curricular Areas   125
        Reciprocity: The Community of Learners   127
    Managing the Service Project: Computer Tutors   127
    Fostering Reflective Learning   129
    Assessment and Evaluation   129
        Elementary/Middle School Reflective Log   131
        High School Reflective Log   132

PART III: ADVANCED SERVICE LEARNING PROJECTS   **133**

8. **The Voice of the People: A Social Studies
    and Library Technology Service Learning Project**   **135**
    Description of the Project   135
        Keeping Records and Building a Portfolio   138
    Assessing Risks: Establishing Protocols for Health and Safety   140
    Selecting the Service Learning Focus:
        A Community-Government Communication Pipeline   140
        Making Connections With the Community   141
    Working With a Community Partner   141
    Aligning Service and Educational Goals   143
        Student Responsibilities and Curricular Areas   143
        Reciprocity: The Community of Learners   144
    Managing the Service Project: The Voice of the People   145
        Tapping Into Multiple Intelligences: Storyboarding the Project   147
    Fostering Reflective Learning   148
    Assessment and Evaluation   149
        Elementary/Middle School Reflective Log   150
        High School Reflective Log   151

9. **Community Vision: A Visual Arts and
    Library Technology Service Learning Project**   **153**
    Description of the Project   153
        Keeping Records and Building a Portfolio   156
    Assessing Risks: Establishing Protocols for Health and Safety   158
    Selecting the Service Learning Focus: A Community Art Program   159
        Tapping Into Multiple Intelligences: Here's What You Missed   161
    Working With a Community Partner   162
    Aligning Service and Educational Goals   163

Student Responsibilities and Curricular Areas 163
Reciprocity: The Community of Learners 165
Managing the Service Project: Community Vision 165
Fostering Reflective Learning 165
Assessment and Evaluation 167
Elementary/Middle School Reflective Log 169
High School Reflective Log 170

10. **Main Street Gardens: A Science and Visual Arts**
Service Learning Project 171
Description of the Project 171
Keeping Records and Building a Portfolio 173
Assessing Risks: Establishing Protocols for Health and Safety 175
Tapping Into Multiple Intelligences: Give Your Body a Break 176
Selecting the Service Learning Focus:
Planting Local Color in the Community 176
Working With a Community Partner 177
Tapping Into Multiple Intelligences: Visual Patterning 179
Aligning Service and Educational Goals 179
Student Responsibilities and Curricular Areas 179
Reciprocity: The Community of Learners 181
Managing the Service Project: Main Street Gardens 181
Fostering Reflective Learning 182
Assessment and Evaluation 182
Elementary/Middle School Reflective Log 185
High School Reflective Log 186

Reproducible Masters 187

Bibliography 193

Index 197

Sidebar Directory

Tapping Into Multiple Intelligences

Structuring Learning Teams	8
Managing the Management Plan	18
Mapping Possibilities	29
Let's Get Visible!	46
The Role of Rubrics	64
Storytelling in Nature	90
Who's Got Rhythm?	106
Analyze, Prioritize	123
Storyboarding the Project	147
Here's What You Missed	161
Give Your Body a Break	176
Visual Patterning	179

Exemplary Projects

Foster Care Holiday Boxes	47
Writing and Sharing Science Books	86
Passing the Referendum	137
Northern Latitude Visions	157
School Gardens	175

Preface

ABOUT THIS BOOK

Human brains learn more, remember longer, and grow more connections when the learning occurs in a real-world setting (Diamond, 1988). Service learning projects such as those featured in this book offer students the opportunity to learn in both controlled classroom settings and the everyday world—within their communities. As service learning projects unfold, at times the teacher introduces students to facts, concepts, and skills in a controlled classroom setting. At other times, students do new learning or apply old learning by performing authentic community service. As students work in their communities, they discover the joy of helping community members and improving the neighborhoods and cities in which they live. They realize that their formal learning is giving them tools with which they can offer valuable contributions to their families and neighbors.

Using the approach in *Service Learning: A Guide to Planning, Implementing, and Assessing Student Projects*, the teacher helps students structure the service learning project so that service actions lead toward mastery of curriculum goals. A well-managed and rich service project will often align with goals in several content areas. Teachers from these different academic disciplines have a powerful tool for integrating their curricula if they choose to work together to web the service learning project through their content areas.

Studies show that quality design of service learning projects enhances student learning, and the factors that seem to matter most are strong alignment with standards, clear communication of goals, and extensive, direct contact with community members (Billig, 2004). Teachers and students need to examine curriculum standards for their classroom or content area to select appropriate service learning projects. Students need to work with community partners or volunteers as often as possible to strengthen their understanding of and empathy toward service recipients. These contacts often help students overcome negative stereotypes that they may have developed about people who are different from themselves.

To make sense of their experiences, students do reflective journal entries that focus attention on progress toward learning goals through the service learning experience. As students journal, they review content learning and the importance of performing civic service, and they often add graphics, images, illustrations, song or poem lyrics, and even musical notations to their journal entries to engage the intelligences through which they learn best. This reflection provides students with self-feedback about their service learning experience that helps them remember what they learned and value that learning more highly (Billig, 2005).

HOW TO USE THIS BOOK

The Introduction and Chapter 1 of *Service Learning: A Guide to Planning, Implementation, and Assessing Student Projects* presents the fundamentals of service learning as a curriculum model, detailing how service learning can be implemented. Chapters 2–10, grouped into Part I, "Basic Projects"; Part II, "Intermediate Projects"; and Part III, "Advanced Projects," are each devoted to a particular project and include the following elements:

- Description of the Project
- Assessing Risks: Establishing Protocols for Health and Safety
- Selecting the Service Learning Focus
- Working With a Community Partner
- Aligning Service and Educational Goals
- Reciprocity: The Community of Learners
- Managing the Service Project
- Fostering Reflective Learning
- Assessment and Evaluation

Some projects require independence of movement or physical strength or depth of background knowledge and skills that make them less suitable for younger students. With some modification, all of the projects are potentially usable by most teachers and students.

Included in the second edition are tips for tapping into multiple intelligences for each project. Each of Howard Gardner's eight identified multiple intelligences is targeted in at least two of the tips, which are drawn from the author's classroom experiences. These strategies work successfully with students from kindergarten through college, and using them gives learners the opportunity to learn in personally comfortable ways. Any of these strategies can be used successfully with any project to enhance its experiential nature and differentiated learning opportunities. In addition to the multiple intelligences tips, each project contains at least a few general pointers and background information that applies across all service learning possibilities. Alert readers will find useful nuggets in every chapter.

As teachers and students implement service learning in their classrooms, they need to begin building a master list of possible community service partners and Internet (Web site) addresses for a variety of service learning projects.

A search engine such as Yahoo! or Google leads to a number of different Web sites related to a given service learning topic. Many of these Web sites include references to community agencies or potential partners for projects.

To understand how to develop a management plan for a service learning project, a reader can cross-reference the section titled "Description of the Project" with the management plan grid provided in each chapter. Teachers need to spend some time examining the management grid for each project, which shows the actions of that particular service learning project, with the grid showing how the project aligns with typical goals in several different content areas. Teachers are encouraged to add to or revise the management plan that is included with a particular project. This strategic planning helps teachers effectively manage real-life service learning projects.

The feature in each chapter titled "Selecting the Service Learning Focus" includes a sample rubric that teachers and students can use to summarize their thinking about the specific service learning project at hand. Readers are encouraged to study these rubrics as samples, modifying them for use with their classes. See "Selecting the Need for Service" in Chapter 1 for detailed information about how to use the rubric. Each service learning project models the use of the rubric. Suggestions about possible community partners are included in each chapter. Teachers are encouraged to review the suggestions for potential community partners offered in each chapter and explore other options at their own discretion.

Service learning is a rich tool that gives students a unique opportunity to experience integrated content learning in the real world. Students often begin learning ideas and skills in content-specific classrooms, working toward a mastery of the vocabularies of the distinct disciplines. Students then experience the interconnectedness of the content areas as they participate in a particular service learning project. This reinforcement and feedback will help students learn the content better, remember it longer, and see its helpfulness to real life. Remember that the teacher helps students with this reinforcement and feedback by structuring reflective log entries that are task and age appropriate. Asking students to review specific content learning, the teacher often guides students in thinking about the different roles that they play as they work on the service project. In so doing, the teacher prompts students to self-evaluate their mastery of the content goals and to assess their efficacy as service providers.

The reproducibles at the end of this book include rubrics or observation checklists, which teachers and work site coordinators use to assess student work habits and teamwork. Students use these checklists to self-evaluate their own behaviors. Teachers are encouraged to use the writing evaluation rubric also included in the reproducibles section to evaluate students' written assignments, and they are also encouraged to give each student a copy of the rubric so that he or she has a tool to use for evaluating, polishing, and revising rough drafts of written assignments.

The nine service learning projects included in this book target goals in many different content areas and service sectors. Authentic learning targets for any school subject can align with carefully selected civic service projects; and teachers, administrators, and students can discover these alignments. Educators are encouraged to use their creativity and knowledge of their own disciplines to piggyback off these nine examples and develop their own community-specific service learning projects.

Acknowledgments

As I think about this revised edition of *Service Learning*, I need to say thank you to all of the old friends, the SkyLight people who meant so much to me, to the new colleagues, the Corwin Press people with whom I hope to build new friendships, and to the teachers and community volunteers who shared with me tales of their exemplary service learning projects.

First, the SkyLighters: My thanks go to Robin Fogarty, who invited me to write the book. Many thanks also go to Jean Ward, who contributed the idea for "The Voice of the People" service learning project and gave the manuscript its first SkyLight read-through. Thanks go to Sue Schumer as well, who guided the manuscript through production and final polishing. Her thoughtful work provided subtle changes in phrasing and flow that increased its value to all readers. The SkyLight writing model, like the SkyLight training model, demonstrated that no one of us is as skilled or articulate as all of us. We truly were a cooperative team.

Next, the Corwin Press people: Thank you to Cathy Hernandez, who patiently answered all of my questions and tolerated my display of "author's indignation." I appreciate your quiet tolerance and your advocacy for my ideas and ideals more than I can say. Thank you to Charline Wu, who guided me through the prepublication marketing protocols with warmth and collegiality. Thank you to Robert Holm who scrupulously edited each page and explained every change. I do appreciate your attention to detail and ability to smooth rough spots in the text while preserving my voice. Thank you to Diane Foster for guiding the work through the intricacies of production. To the others at Corwin Press, thank you for believing in this book and for giving me the opportunity to take a quality piece and make it even better. The Japanese word *kaizen*, meaning "continuous improvement," identifies a principle by which I live, and I appreciate the opportunity to strengthen the first edition of this work by adding some valuable elements, such as the tips for Tapping Into Multiple Intelligences.

And now the teachers and community volunteers: Thank you to Nicole Hite for taking time from her summer to answer questions about her service learning experiences. Carol Huntoon and Tammy Lancioni, friends and neighbors, thank you for giving me deeper insight into the service learning projects that engage students in our little community. Stephanie Smith, AmeriCorps volunteer, your in-depth, thoughtful comments enriched my understanding of the role of the community volunteer in service learning. And deep thanks to Gerard O'Brien, good friend and former colleague, for sharing your story that so closely aligns with "The Voice of the People," Chapter 8. All of your stories strengthen and enliven this book and provide other teachers with service learning models upon which they can build their own projects.

And finally, thank you to sweet partner Al and to the big sweet sea that is my source of calm, peace, and wonder.

All of us together made this book come alive.

PUBLISHER'S ACKNOWLEDGMENTS

Skyhorse Publishing gratefully acknowledges the contributions of the following reviewers:

Roxie R. Ahlbrecht, Second-Grade Teacher
Robert Frost Elementary, Sioux Falls, SD

Nicole Hite, Third-Grade Teacher
Temperance Road Elementary, Temperance, MI

Nathan Ivy, Service Coordinator
Irvington High School, Fremont, CA

Hollie Lund, Director, Center for Community Service-Learning
Assistant Professor, Urban and Regional Planning
California State Polytechnic University, Pomona, CA

About the Author

Sally Berman is an experienced, creative facilitator of interactive workshops during which educators learn how to create classrooms in which their students develop teamwork, cognition, metacognition, and self-evaluation skills. Sally developed and tested many of her ideas during her 30 years of science teaching at a large high school in the Chicago suburbs.

Sally received her AB in Chemistry and Mathematics in 1964 and her MS in Chemical Education in 1969. In the mid-1980s, feeling a need for professional rejuvenation, she embarked on a learning quest that led to work with a number of outstanding educators and theorists. A few of these were Jim Bellanca, David and Roger Johnson, David Lazear, and Robin Fogarty.

Using her newly acquired information, Sally created and led workshops and graduate courses for a variety of clients. She has worked with educators and industrial trainers from the United States, Canada, the Netherlands, Britain, Eastern Europe, and Australia.

Sally lives with Al, her best friend and husband of 35 years, near Ontonagon, Michigan, on the south shore of Lake Superior. They met when both were teaching at Palatine High School in Palatine, Illinois. Sally says, "It was love in the lounge!" Sally taught chemistry, and Al taught English and coached wrestling. Sally does not get up in the dark; she does, on occasion, stay up until dawn. She is sometimes compared with the Kay Thompson creation, Eloise.

Introduction

WHAT IS SERVICE LEARNING?

Service learning is in-context learning that connects specific educational goals with meaningful community service. Service learning projects include a dual focus: the goals of academic learning and the goals of authentic volunteer projects. Students learn course content, processes, and skills, strengthening their thinking skills as they develop empathy, personal ethics, and the habit of helping their communities. Doing service learning helps students understand their connectedness to and importance in their communities as they experience the role of service provider (rather than the role of service receiver).

John Dewey, William Kilpatrick, and other experts associated with the progressive education movement of the early 1900s argued that this experience helps students see the usefulness of their classroom learning in solving community problems (Titlebaum, Williamson, Daprano, Baer, & Brahler, 2004). More recently, Wigginton (1985), Goodlad (1984), and Boyer (1983) advocated using community service projects to promote social reform. As students do service learning projects, they not only experience learning, they experience a commitment to doing meaningful and authentic work, a sense of empowerment and joy in doing service that needs to be done, and a sense of community that results in providing help to others.

WHAT IS THE HISTORY OF SERVICE LEARNING?

In 1903, John Dewey with his students and colleagues published a number of papers that established the intellectual foundations of service learning. Dewey, a strong proponent of experiential education, went on to publish *Democracy and Education* (1916) and *Experience and Education* (1938) in which he stated that a person's permanent frame of reference for learning is the "organic connection between education and personal experience" (1938, p. 59), that the most important aspect of any experience was its agreeableness or disagreeableness, which formed the basis of its influence on later experiences, and that to learn from experiences, a person must reflect on them, and they must lead out into "an expanding world of subject matter" (1938, p. 59). Experience with its accompanying reflection, in other words, is the foundation of learning, and service learning immerses students in experiences and encourages them to reflect.

The establishment of the Peace Corps by President John F. Kennedy in 1961 and the creation of VISTA (Volunteers in Service to America) by President Lyndon B. Johnson in 1964 renewed enthusiasm for public service in the United States. In 1967,

Robert Sigmon and William Ramsey, educators who were working with the Manpower Development Internship Program in Atlanta, coined the term "service learning" to identify the essence of that program. The term, as the two educators explained it, implies a value consideration. It implies a link between authentic community service, intentional academic learning, and reflection. Service learning, as defined by Sigmon and Ramsey, has a value-added component because the learning takes place in the context of experience that makes a constructive, positive contribution to the community (Stanton, Giles, & Cruz, 1999). This definition is a key to clarifying service learning as a distinct curriculum model.

The National Student Volunteer Program, established in the early 1970s, began publishing *The Syntegist*, a journal linking academic learning and community service. In 1979, the NSVP, now named the National Center for Service-Learning, published Robert Sigmon's principles of service learning, which stressed the reciprocal nature of the experience. According to Sigmon, this experiential learning is "reciprocal": Both those who provide a service and those who receive it learn from the service. Unless that reciprocity exists, an experience is not true service learning. More recently, the term has been used with a variety of experiential education programs ranging from volunteer and community service projects to internships (Furco, n.d.). A thread that links Dewey with Sigmon and Ramsey and those who followed them is the need for structured time for reflection to, as Dewey would say, lead students out into an expanding world of facts, information, or ideas. For example, theorist David Kolb's learning cycle includes concrete experience and reflection (*Completing the Learning Cycle*, n.d.). Reflection is the key to making sense out of the experience.

At the historic Wingspread Conference, hosted in 1989 by the Johnson Foundation in Racine, Wisconsin, experienced service learning practitioners drew on what they had learned to draft *The Principles of Good Practice for Combining Service and Learning*. Teachers and other leaders of service learning projects have used these principles to develop effective programs and projects in their schools and communities. Other more recent milestones in the development of this experiential learning model include the endorsement of service learning by the Association for Supervision and Curriculum Development (ASCD) in 1993; the establishment in 1994 of the *Michigan Journal of Community Service-Learning* (the first refereed service learning journal that is committed to developing and sustaining the integrity of the model); the establishment of the AmeriCorps program in 1994, which provides many communities and schools with in-house service learning volunteers; the 1997 founding of the National Service-Learning Clearinghouse at the University of Minnesota; the first International Conference on Service-Learning Research in Berkeley, California, in 2001; and the adoption by several states and individual school districts of service learning requirements for graduation from middle or high school. Teachers who want more information about the history of this curriculum model or its principles and applications can find information online using Google or Yahoo! and the key words "service learning," "principles," "pioneers," and "history."

WHY DO SERVICE LEARNING?

Service learning strengthens students in many different ways. Students who learn to do for others rather than "being done for" by others become more self-confident and develop more self-esteem. They feel that they are useful members of the community who can identify problems, propose solutions, act independently in implementing solutions, and open themselves to new experiences and roles as they do so. Students gain self-respect as they develop the real-life skills of being on the job on time, having good attendance, and doing the work that they have promised to do (Billig, 2004). Often, as they discover that mistakes are opportunities for problem solving, brainstorming, and growth, students learn to treat others as they themselves want to be treated, to have empathy for the problems and concerns of others, and to defer gratification as they work toward long-term goals. Students who learn these components of emotional intelligence are more successful throughout their lives (Goleman, 1995).

Because service projects are done in conjunction with others in the community, students improve their communication and cooperation skills. As they work with people who represent a cross section of the community, they gain respect and appreciation for people from socioeconomic, ethnic, and cultural groups other than their own. They feel the inner joy, warmth, and satisfaction that come from giving to others and being accepted by others (Holdsman & Tuchmann, 2004). Service learning is brain-compatible learning. Because the learning is done in a real-world context, students' brains construct meaning from the learning and remember it effortlessly (Fogarty, 1997a). Students are able to recall the learning easily, especially when they revisit the original learning circumstances and locations. Furthermore, students experiencing service learning are able to update their learnings with little effort. The brain learns best when feelings are "in balance," and students feel happy, trusted, included, empowered, independent, and capable as they do service learning projects. These emotions trigger the mid-brain to produce a variety of hormones that brain researchers believe to be memory fixatives, so the positive emotions that the students feel result in more learning that is remembered longer (Jensen, 1996).

When asked about the impact of service learning on their thoughts, students in Saint Paul offered the following ideas:

- They learned how to network and how important networks are to everyday life.
- They realized how complex and interconnected issues can be.
- They discovered that they do have the power to change the world.

—(Johnson, M., 2001, p. 6)

In general, learners are motivated when they are given some choices about what to learn and how to learn it. Students doing service learning participate in choosing and managing the projects. They have some control over what service project they do, how the project is structured, when they work on it, and how long the project will last. Students, therefore, feel motivated to learn; these affirmative feelings lead to more effective learning of content as well as skill (Billig, 2004).

What about the belief, often stated as if it were fact, that residents in most communities want their schools to go "back to the basics" and take a traditional approach to teaching language arts, social studies, mathematics, science, and other content? A poll conducted in 2000 by Roper Starch Worldwide for the WK Kellogg Foundation and the Ewing Marion Kauffman Foundation found that while the vast majority of respondents want and expect schools to furnish students with the academic content, process, and skill knowledge that they need for future success, they also believe that schools need to link that academic learning to the skills that students need to be successful in the workplace and in their communities (*Service-Learning Delivers*, n.d.). When teachers or project leaders explain the philosophy and process of service learning to community residents, they support the model and recognize its benefits to the community, the service providers, and the service recipients. As the title of the National Service-Learning Partnership article says so well, "Service learning delivers what Americans want from schools."

HOW DOES SERVICE LEARNING WORK?

There is no one set formula for structuring successful service learning projects. Most projects do, however, share common elements. All of the service learning projects in this book include these elements:

1. *Selecting the need for service.* Before doing any detailed project planning, teacher and students need to gather information about the services that the community needs, the appropriateness of students helping with those services, and the interest that students have in the project. A rubric that students and teacher can use in evaluating these and other factors is included in Chapter 1. Students and teacher must put thought into selecting a project that balances student interest, community need, and authentic learning.

2. *Finding a community partner.* The teacher may be aware of some pro-education leaders of community service agencies. Students can ask their parents for information about possible community partners. When students are involved with contacting potential partners, participating in interviews, setting up schedules and agendas, and discussing responsibilities, they learn more about problem solving, decision making, and cooperative action.

3. *Aligning the service experience with educational goals.* Recent research indicates that one of the most important components of successful service learning experiences is strong alignment with curriculum standards (Billig, 2004). The teacher helps students maintain awareness of the content learning that is embedded in the service learning project. As students do reflective journal entries, the teacher focuses their attention on service goals and content standards.

4. *Managing the project.* Developing a project management plan is a complex process that requires creativity, flexibility, and common sense. Chapter 1 includes a detailed discussion of this process. When students and teacher plan together, the brainstorming is more likely to produce a comprehensive plan. Frequent assessment, review, and revision of the plan keep a project on course.

5. *Fostering reflective student learning throughout the project.* Each project in Chapters 2–10 in this book includes a portfolio list detailing tools and techniques

that students can use to document their actions and learning. As students do reflective journal entries, the teacher focuses their attention on service goals and content standards. Using these tools, students reflect on learning in many areas: academic content, processes and skills, community service, interpersonal understanding, and intrapersonal growth. Students can ask their parents for information about possible community partners. The more often students step back and reflect on what they are learning, what it means, and how it connects to new arenas, the richer the service learning experience becomes.

One benefit (to students of doing service learning) is that they became aware of their community. We are a very small school (approximately 275 students) where students are not often aware of their surroundings. The second benefit would be that they developed a sense of understanding and compassion. They were able to look outside their lives and realize some of the hardships that students face on a daily basis. The third benefit, and perhaps the most important, is that they became a part of the community. I can't express in words how enlightening it is to have students from a small community realize that they can become part of the "big picture." It's important for them to see that their voices matter and that they can make a difference in the lives of others.

—Stephanie Smith, AmeriCorps Volunteer, Ionia, Michigan

WHO ARE THE KEY PLAYERS IN A SERVICE LEARNING PROJECT?

Along with individual students and a teacher or project mentor, each service learning project involves some individual or agency from the community. Units of government such as the police department, the office of streets and sanitation, or the parks department often partner with students. Civic organizations such as a merchants' association, chamber of commerce, a municipal development authority, or a beautification agency are possible partners. Service organizations such as the Elks or Lions Club or a food pantry, soup kitchen, or homeless shelter are often willing partners. The partner may be a business entity like a local hospital or elder care home. Sometimes the agency participates in the project; at other times, it is an absentee manager. The agency sometimes helps students with funding, planning, and execution; at other times, it is simply the project administrator. The agency is involved in the project in various ways, depending on the nature of the project and the need for agency involvement.

At the beginning of the project, the teacher identifies the educational goals of the service learning project and the content concepts, processes, and skills that help students reach those goals. Also, the teacher discusses those goals, concepts, and skills with the students and structures the service learning project to ensure their safety. Teachers verify that adequate supervision is always available, and they make arrangements for students to be transported or escorted to and from the service site.

The teacher may look for parent volunteers who can provide transportation, or the teacher may arrange for school bus transportation.

Students work in teams of three or four at sites away from the school so that every student has a built-in buddy group. Because of the need to provide for the safety of the students, the teachers often prefer service projects that allow the entire class to stay together and work together, especially if students are younger.

The most amazing thing to me is how excited they are about it (service learning). They do one project and they immediately want to come up with another. They take the ideas and fly with them.

The biggest problem has been money. There have been some things we wanted to do that we just didn't have money for. Another teacher is going to help me apply for grant money. That will let us do some things we haven't been able to do.

—Tammy Lancioni, Teacher, Ontonagon, Michigan

HOW DO STUDENTS BENEFIT FROM SERVICE LEARNING?

Service learning experiences expand student learning of content information, life skills, and the service ethic. Brain research says that this kind of in-context learning is deep and is long remembered (Jensen, 1996). Students who do service learning projects demonstrate the increased self-confidence and self-esteem that result from responsible, ethical, independent action. Doing legitimate service projects in the community helps students feel useful (Goleman, 1995). A few generations ago, families needed the service contributions of children to get all of the household and farm work done. Now, with the different structure of today's society and many labor-saving devices present in modern homes, children may not be expected to do as many household chores to contribute to the day-to-day operation of the household.

Used as a curriculum model, service learning lets students have the experience of being needed. As students take on new roles, they become more willing risk takers. They open themselves to new experiences and people. They become more effective leaders, communicators, and teammates. Service learning projects help students develop an awareness and acceptance of others from different ethnic, national, or economic backgrounds. Students become more empathetic and less judgmental, accepting their own internal locus of control and being less likely to blame others or make excuses for shortcomings. They discover that mistakes lead to growth and learning. They grow through their experiences (Billig, 2004).

Service learning projects help students become better learners by enhancing their cognitive skills. Student reflection leads to deeper understanding and more genuine transfer of learning (Billig, 2004). Students become motivated to learn because they make many of the decisions about the service learning projects. This motivation leads to increased achievement among children, which leads to a belief in themselves as learners and a positive attitude toward learning. Students develop brainstorming and problem-solving skills as they work their way out of mistakes. Because service learning is learning in context, students remember what they learned better and longer, growing educated in the true sense of the word (Ammon, Furco, Chi, & Middaugh, 2002).

Another benefit of the service learning projects presented in this book is that they help students develop a social consciousness and social conscience. Students become more aware of community problems and their responsibility to help solve those problems (Billig, 2004). They recognize their responsibilities as citizens to vote in all elections and to hold elected or volunteer positions in the community. Furthermore, students learn that a community becomes stronger when all of its members work together to solve common problems and share resources, making a difference in building a safe, clean, orderly community. They grow connected.

The meaningful participation that students experience when they are partners in selecting and planning the service learning project helps them develop resiliency, which in turn aids their development into healthy, competent adults (Fredericks, Kaplan, & Zeisler, 2001). Students need to know that their voice is important to the service learning process. When they realize that their contributions are integral to the success of a project, they connect more strongly with it and are more likely to avoid risky behaviors such as substance abuse, misconduct, or dropping out of school (Billig, 2004).

One student in my class, who had behavior problems, was very worried about a family who needed help. I encouraged him to make a plan for positive action, and when the service learning project was successful, he commented on how good he felt, that he never thought he could do something that helpful or important. From that experience on, he was a great kid in class who was respected rather than resented by other kids in the class.

—Gerard O'Brien, Teacher, Palatine, Illinois

Finally, service learning helps students develop real-world skills. Students realize the importance of being on time, of being well groomed, and of being pleasant, polite, and professional in their dealings with others. They discover the importance of doing the job they promised to do, following the rules and directions. They learn to ask for help when they don't know what to do next and to offer help when they see that someone else needs it. Learning that self-evaluation is strengthening, students find that work can always be improved and that the world of work has its own rules, regulations, and expectations. Growing, responsible students become mature, responsible, ethical members of their communities. Figure 0.1 summarizes this and the other benefits of engaging students in service learning projects.

Figure 0.1 Benefits of the Service Learning Curriculum Model

Content learning

- In-context learning
- Enhanced learning (in breadth and depth)
- More enduring learning
- Transfer of learning to new situations

Personal development

- Perception of self as service giver
- Enhanced willingness to take risks
- Openness to new people and experiences
- Leadership, communication, and teamwork skills
- Exposure to and acceptance of different society groups
- Development of internal control
- More empathy—less judging

Cognitive skills

- Deepened understanding of concepts
- Enhanced transfer of learning
- Brainstorming
- Problem solving

Community connections

- Awareness of community problems
- Awareness of service organizations
- Enhanced civic responsibility

Life skills

- Knowing when to ask for help
- Knowing when to offer help
- Knowing how to find help
- Finishing a job that is started
- Following rules and directions
- Promoting personal safety
- Self-evaluating
- Deferring gratification
- Communicating clearly and precisely

The students discuss the project goals. They understand the goals well enough to be able to describe them to the community partner. They do appropriate project tasks identified by the community partner or themselves and communicate professionally with the community partner. The students learn how to assume different roles as they participate in the various projects suggested in this book. Students who are working in a community soup kitchen, for instance, learn to be cooks, servers, food buyers, or menu planners. Students who work in a sports equipment "lending locker" act as clerks, advertising specialists, or inventory managers. Students maintain personal awareness of the curricular goals and their progress toward reaching those goals. The students and the teacher use a variety of assessment tools, discussed in the next chapter, to verify that appropriate content learning is taking place.

The Fundamentals of Service Learning as a Curriculum Model

HOW DOES SERVICE LEARNING WORK?

There are many successful models for doing service learning. Robin Fogarty (1997b) suggests that they all have the following elements or steps in common:

- Selecting the need for service
- Finding a community partner
- Aligning the service experience with educational goals
- Managing the project or program
- Fostering reflective student learning throughout the process

The order of these elements often varies from project to project. The teacher may identify a curricular goal, such as learning the importance of exercising for fitness, and ask students to decide how they can help other children obtain specialized exercise equipment (i.e., ice skates or in-line skates) that children rapidly outgrow. Students and teacher discuss the value of "recycling" usable equipment through the community rather than letting it gather dust in the back of a garage. For another service project, a student may suggest that a local food pantry or soup kitchen needs more volunteers. Then the students and teacher identify nutrition and food preparation goals that tie content learning to volunteer work at a local community food pantry or kitchen.

All service learning projects in this book use the five elements mentioned above and serve to make community service projects the context for curricular learning. In addition, project (Chapters 2–10) involves teacher and students in a frequent review of both the service goals and the content learning goals to see how well students are meeting those goals. A chart showing such alignment is provided for each project.

Selecting the Need for Service

As students and teachers explore service learning opportunities, they begin by finding out what service needs exist in the community and how to go about offering their services. Students can discover what is already being done in the community by talking with their parents, teachers, neighbors, members of service organizations, and religious leaders in the community. Networking further, students can consult with the community relations contact person from a local hospital or elder care facility or from the police, fire, or community service department within the municipality. In addition, students can look for service organization announcements printed in the local newspaper or broadcast on the local television or radio station. Regularly watching the community "bulletin board announcements" that often are part of local-access cable television channels provides further leads on community needs.

As a result of such research, students are able to identify and locate

- Community food pantries or soup kitchens that need volunteers to make food baskets or prepare meals for the needy
- Hospitals or elder care facilities in the area that need volunteers to deliver mail or visit patients
- Municipal agencies that need help in keeping streets clean or parks landscaped
- Counseling services or help (phone) line services that need to have funds raised
- Child care agencies that need tutors

Students can also search the Internet for ideas about service learning projects. With adult supervision, students who use a search engine such as Google or Yahoo! and key words "service learning," "ideas," "projects," and "sources" find a wide variety of ideas for projects. Students also are able to find rich material about this model at Web sites for the National Service-Learning Partnership, Learn and Serve, and the National Service-Learning Clearinghouse.

Students and teachers will want to consider a variety of factors before deciding on a service learning project. These factors include interest in the project, need for the service, access to the service site or to necessary funds or materials, age appropriateness of the project work for the students, duration of the service learning project, and the availability of community support. A rubric, such as the one shown in Figure 1.1, can be very helpful to students evaluating the viability of a project. This form is duplicated for the teacher's convenience in the Reproducible Masters section at the end of this book.

To use the rubric for scoring, the teacher tallies all individual student rankings; then the students compute an average ranking for each of the factors or criteria. For example, if a class of 25 students rates a community soup kitchen project and if the teacher reports that 7 students said that they had *high* interest in the project, 15 students said their interest was *medium,* and 3 students rated their interest as *low,* students then do this set of calculations:

High = 7 students × 1 (ranking)	= 7
Medium = 15 students × 2 (ranking)	= 30
Low = 3 students × 3 (ranking)	= 9
Total ranking score	= 7 + 30 + 9 = 46
Overall ranking	= 46/25 = 1.8

The ranking is closest to *medium* interest in the project.

Students repeat the calculations for each of the other factors. Here are sample results for the soup kitchen project:

Interest	1.8
Need	1.1
Accessibility	1.0 (for an in-school soup kitchen)
	1.0 (for an off-site soup kitchen or food pantry with school bus to the site)
Appropriateness	1.3
Time Frame	3+ (all year)

As the teacher and students decide whether or not to do a project, they also will want to discuss the weight or importance of each of the various factors and criteria in the rubric. For the soup kitchen project, the students and teacher may decide that the most important factors are community need, access to the service site, and appropriateness ("fit" or alignment with service project goals and curricular goals). Note that in the scenario above, these three factors all have average ratings close to 1.0, which is the *best* overall rating that students can give. If students and teacher decide that a yearlong time frame really is best for this project because the longer time frame helps the students get feedback about their content and life skills learnings, the teacher and students decide to do the soup kitchen project.

Figure 1.1 Project Evaluation Rubric				
Proposed Project Title: _____				
Ranking / Criteria	**1** (high)	**2** (medium)	**3** (low)	**Comments**
Interest	High	Medium	Low	
Need	Great	Some	Little	
Accessibility	Easy	OK	Difficult	
Appropriateness	Good	Fair	Poor	
Time Frame	Just right	Somewhat rushed or prolonged	Much too rushed or prolonged	

The best piece of advice that I would give another teacher wanting to get started with service learning is to start small. After the students have had a chance to participate, they will be begging for more!

—Nicole Hite, Teacher, Temperance, MI

Assessing Risks: Establishing Protocols for Health and Safety

While teachers, parents, administrators, and students all acknowledge the benefits of service learning to everyone in the community, a primary concern is the safety and well-being of the students who provide the service. Students need to work in sites that are physically and emotionally as safe as possible. If the work site is some distance from the school, students need reliable, secure transportation. Teachers, community liaison persons, or project coordinators want to know that students have arrived safely at work sites, so communication procedures must be in place before students begin working at remote sites. When teachers want to bring outside speakers into the school, they first need to determine the legal requirements that those speakers must meet. Teachers and students need to plan carefully before they begin a service learning project so that they address concerns that all interested parties may have.

Each service learning project has its own safety and health concerns. Students and teacher, with input from administrators, parents, and community partners, need to develop a list of potential sources of injury, illness, or distress associated with the project. One way to develop and gather ideas is for students to discuss the issue with parents and other adults and for the teacher to talk with the administration and community partner. Students and teacher then have a class discussion during which they produce a list of concerns. During the advance planning for the project, teacher and students address each item on the list. From these discussions, they develop a set of health and safety protocols that students agree to follow when they do the project.

Common sense can guide the development of health and safety protocols, and resources available online also provide helpful tips. Doing an Internet search with the key words "service learning" combined with "risk," "safety" or "concerns" produces numerous results. Some service organizations, such as Lions-Quest, provide excellent online resources on this topic (Anderson & Witmer, n.d.). Many universities have service learning programs, and their Web sites include sections on risk management or health and safety. The most common suggestions include these:

- Selecting community partners carefully so that students work in lower-risk sites
- Giving students training—actual practice—in using all safety equipment
- Simulating accidents so that students have the physical experience of "first responding"
- Establishing communications procedures for students and partners (students need to notify teacher and partner when they leave school for a work site, and partners need to contact the teacher if the student does not arrive in a timely fashion)
- Involving all stakeholders in planning the project and the protocols for managing risks

Finding a Community Partner

The teacher and students contact appropriate community agencies or groups to ask if they are willing to be the community partner for the project. The teacher telephones each agency to explain the service project, establish agency interest, network with an agency person who can be the project liaison, and set up an appointment to discuss the project in more detail.

Typically, the agency wants to know the educational goals that are targeted by the project, how many students are involved, what kinds of work they are willing to do, and how the teacher and students see the project developing.

Preparing to be interviewed by the agency contact, the teacher and students prepare to answer questions:

- What is the goal of your service project?
- What will you be doing at the service site, and how often will you be doing it?
- What are you doing in school in relation to the project?
- Are you willing to do any job assigned to you?
- What jobs do you think we have?
- What do you need to do to complete each job?
- How long will we be working together?
- Are you willing to commit that length of time to doing the project?
- Could this be an ongoing project? In other words, do you want to "will" this project to next year's class?

For the soup kitchen project, the teacher and students prepare a script, such as the following, in case the agency contact or community representative (partner) asks for an explanation of how the project works and what specific goals are.

Interview "Script"

As we do this service learning project, we will be learning about the importance of good nutrition to overall physical and mental health. We will be learning about the food pyramid and using it to plan balanced body- and brain-healthy menus. In addition, we will be learning about food preparation and kitchen cleanup and practicing what we learn in a school foods lab. At the service site, we will use the skills that we have practiced in school to help with cooking and serving the food, cleaning up the kitchen, and storing leftovers.

We want to work in the soup kitchen for the entire school year, performing community service by helping prepare and serve two dinner meals a month. The school will provide bus transportation for students to and from the soup kitchen. To carry on the project, we will write a letter to next year's class encouraging them to continue school involvement with the soup kitchen.

As the relationship develops, a dialog is set up between the agency and the students with both sides involved in the planning and implementation of the project. In a successful service learning situation, the students, teacher, and community partner agree on how they can work together to help the students meet the curricular learning goals and the service goals. The teacher and community partner want to let the students plan and do as much of the project as they can. The more responsibility students have for the project, the more they learn and the more social growth they experience.

Reciprocity: The Community of Learners

The term *service learning* is used to describe a wide range of service and experiential learning projects. One of the earliest definitions, from Robert Sigmon, specified that service learning is reciprocal; both those who provide service and those who receive it learn from it (Furco, 2005). Students who provide services learn content and service information, processes, and skills throughout the project. Each of the nine projects that make up the bulk of this book contains a table showing the alignment among service actions and curriculum standards. That alignment is what makes these Service Learning (capital *S*, capital *L*) projects. Students who do projects like these make progress toward mastering grade-level or subject matter standards as a result of providing the service.

Recipients of the service learn a wide variety of things. Most recipients learn that the service providers, regardless of age, are capable, caring community members who want to help others. Other learnings flow from the content focus of individual projects. Teachers, parents, and community liaisons encourage students who are service providers to teach recipients what they are learning about reading skills, legislative processes, community action, nutrition, plant propagation, or mural design. As students learn the joy of giving to others, service recipients learn to see the students as valuable sources of knowledge, skills, and caring.

Aligning Service and Educational Goals

Because service learning projects include academic and service goals, the students and teacher must be certain that the goals are clearly stated and aligned with the academic and service project work. For example, the academic goals for students who work in food pantries (e.g., making food baskets) or in soup kitchens (e.g., making meals) include the ability to display the following skills and knowledge:

- Nutrients that are essential for good health and their effects on human physiology
- Strategies and guides for planning daily menus, such as the food pyramid
- Food preparation skills
- Metabolism of food and the effects of metabolism on factors like circulatory health, diabetes, and brain function

The service goals might include these understandings and skills:

- Identifying the needs of the community
- Planning and doing a service project that addresses those needs
- Acquiring and demonstrating curricular knowledge that aligns with the service learning project
- Seeing the value of school and community partnerships for service
- Demonstrating civic responsibility and ethical development by participating in the service learning project

Students transfer what they have learned about academic content, the community, and themselves as service providers by reflecting on the service learning experience. Life skills goals include caring for others, working on a team, and empathy for others. A chart showing alignment of service, life skills, and educational goals is provided for each project.

Teachers and students must be very clear about curricular and service goals and not lose sight of either. They must know the indicators that show that the students are learning the educational content and skills that align with the service and life skills goals for the project. They must be certain that specific, targeted academic learning is taking place and that students can transfer that learning, the service learning, and the life skills learning to new situations and apply them in new settings. The service project gives students the rich experiences that lead to lifelong learning of content, skills, and attitudes.

Because different students learn best in different ways, at different rates, and perhaps even on different days, teachers know that the best way to engage all students in learning is to differentiate instruction. The teacher structures lessons so that all students have opportunities to learn in ways that are personally comfortable and effective. The nine projects in this book use Howard Gardner's theory of multiple intelligences as a lens through which to sharpen the focus on differentiation. These service learning projects offer students a variety of experiences, and this invites engagement and participation. As they execute the service learning projects, students learn skills and content with the support and encouragement of teacher and teammates. It is not the purpose of this book to provide an in-depth discussion of differentiated instruction or the theory of multiple intelligences; teachers who use these service learning projects will find embedded applications in each project.

Tapping Into Multiple Intelligences: Structuring Learning Teams

The Interpersonal and Intrapersonal Multiple Intelligence

At the beginning of the school year, take some time to collect information about your students that signals their personal comfort zones. Use this information to assign students to cooperative learning teams. In every classroom, teachers find some students who are strong verbally and logically (these are often the high achievers), some who are comfortable visualizing and creating images, and others who have strong connecting and leadership skills. To maximize the synergy that teamwork creates, the teacher assigns one student with each of these strengths to each team.

To make the teams work, give each student an assigned role or job. Here are some ideas:

- The Correspondent: checks with teammates for understanding, makes a written record of team ideas, reports answers to the rest of the class (verbal/logical)
- The Conductor: keeps the team on time and on task, checks for progress toward completion of the task (interpersonal/leader)
- The Dry Cell: creates images or graphics, encourages and energizes the team using appropriate humor (visual/natural)

To facilitate the teamwork, coach students and give them practice in using cooperative teamwork skills. Here are some very helpful skills:

- Get into teams quickly and quietly.
- Stay together, physically and mentally.
- Use very quiet voices.
- Take turns contributing to the flow of ideas.
- Do a fair share of the work.
- Communicate for understanding.
- Use put-ups, not put-downs.

Students who work in cooperative teams, with guidance from the teacher, find that they produce high-quality work and learn more than they do when working alone. During the planning phase of a service learning project, students do much of their brainstorming in these teams. Students who brainstorm in teams contribute to class discussions freely and willingly because they have the power of the team behind them.

The Internet is an excellent source of information about cooperative learning. The teacher's commitment to this practice is the key to making it work.

Managing the Project

Managing the project involves three key components: preparing, monitoring, and evaluating. Once the teacher and students have selected a service learning project and aligned the service and educational goals, they need to pick a site for the service, plan what needs to be done and who does it when students are at the service site, arrange for students' transportation to and from the site, and plan adult (parent, community partner liaison, or other volunteer) participation in the project.

In a typical service learning situation, the teacher may decide to contact a site representative to set up an interview to discuss when the students can be at the site, how many students will be involved, and what they will be doing (what jobs need to be done to complete the project). The teacher will want to encourage the site representative to include students in this planning discussion. If the service learning project involves more than three or four students, the teacher often asks for parent volunteers who can escort students to the site and act as site facilitators. An adult from the site serves as the overall job coordinator. The students and teacher discuss the project in detail so that each student knows what to do at the site. The site representative and the teacher work together to help each student learn the skills and knowledge needed to do the job.

Monitoring the project includes observing students and helping them plan for future project work, troubleshooting and problem solving when things go wrong, giving feedback, reviewing the academic goals of the service learning project, reviewing and scoring curricular assignments, spot-checking the use of journals and logs, and encouraging ongoing student self-evaluation and reflection. Figure 1.2 is a guide that the teacher can use to assist the students in self-evaluation.

Adults from the site, volunteers, or parents can be particularly helpful in monitoring service project work. The monitoring work can become almost overwhelming for a teacher who is trying to do it alone. The teacher can use scoring devices such as rubrics to assess progress on curricular assignments, doing some concurrent

Figure 1.2   Sample Self-Evaluation and Reflection Guide

1. What was my best service action today, and what are my reasons for picking that action?

2. What was my most valuable insight from today's service, and what are my reasons for focusing on that insight?

3. What did I already know about today's content information? How is that prior knowledge connected to my new learning?

4. What are three other skills or pieces of content learning that I want to remember?

5. What service skill do I most want to improve the next time I do community service? Why is this skill valuable to me?

assessment of work (when appropriate, having students review the work of other students). If the students and teacher have done a thorough job of planning the project and defining jobs, the teacher and others can monitor service project work and academic work in a timely, effective manner.

The prompt feedback about progress toward curricular and project goals from self-evaluation and from adult observations helps students remember the overall project and academic goals and understand what they need to do to complete the service learning project and fulfill the academic learning goals successfully.

Students from Saint Paul made these points about having a voice in selecting and planning the service learning project:

- An idea that excites adults may not have strong appeal for students, and they need to feel excitement about their service learning project.
- They really like projects in which students do much of the decision making.
- They enjoy hearing ideas that other students have, and they feel excitement about the creativity that comes from brainstorming.

—(Johnson, M., 2001, p. 14)

Fostering Reflective Learning

Service learning projects must include student reflection on both the service experience and the academic learning. This reflection engages students in thoughtful remembrance that leads to heightened understanding of learning and relevant transfer of learning and skills.

Students use a variety of tools and strategies to record experiences and learning. They can use daily learning logs and journals to "ink their thinking," audiotapes to think out loud, and time sheets to keep a record of what they did and when they did it. Also, students may use the following opportunities for reflection:

- Peer-partner sharing sessions to free-associate and brainstorm, discovering the implicit meaning and value of student experiences
- Essays or visual graphics that demonstrate learnings

Students use reflective journals, interviews, and conferences as opportunities for reflection, revisiting their service project experiences, fitting the pieces together, and identifying areas of personal growth and change. By reflecting early and often, students give their brains the frequent, specific feedback that cements learning. They gain new insights each time they revisit their learning. They discover new ways to combine the academic, service, and life skills learning so that the whole of the learning is truly greater than the sum of its parts. Reflection deepens, broadens, and reorganizes learning and transfers it into unsuspected parts of students' lives (Sylwester, 1995).

Sample reflective journal pages, tailored for elementary, middle school, and high school students, are included for each of the service learning projects in this book. These journal pages or reflection log samples consist of reflection lead-ins that focus on the work that was done; the need for the work; progress the student made in reaching academic, service, and life goals; and transfer of the learning to new situations.

For maximum effectiveness, each student does a written reflection log entry after doing some major service project task. Students may also want to record impressions on audio- or videotape, associating project experiences with performances and creation of songs or poems; and they may want to use images or mind maps to create visual impressions of their learning. The reflective log is one way that students can give themselves immediate feedback about the details, meaning, and implications for the future of their service learning experience. Brain research experts say that this kind of reflection and feedback is vitally important to storing learning in the memory for future use (Jensen, 1995).

My students learned several things while completing service learning projects. The most beneficial were the following: all students (no matter their economic or academic status) working together for a common goal. The second is the self-confidence in themselves that they gained for having completed a project that helped their school community. And last, service learning projects made school "fun!" It took them beyond the four walls of the classroom.

—Nicole Hite, Teacher, Temperance, MI

ASSESSMENT AND EVALUATION IN SERVICE LEARNING

Assessment and evaluation of student work and learning on a specific service project must be planned before students begin working at the project site. Teachers and students will want to use a variety of authentic assessment tools to gather information about student learning during service projects, determining the final grade—as may be necessary—when the project is completed.

Observation checklists that detail on-the-job behaviors can be used to gather information about how often students contribute to the service project, how intently they are engaged in doing the work, how much work each student does, and how well each student works with members of the service project team. Both the teacher (or other adult sponsor) and the student fill out these checklists so that each can co-verify the other's observations.

Observation checklists can also be used to keep a record of punctuality, preparation for the job, consistency of work, and other specific behaviors that signal the student is achieving the goals of the project. Students and the teacher can brainstorm a list of behaviors and design these checklists before the service work begins. See Figure 1.3 for a sample observation checklist for a service learning project focused on work in a community soup kitchen.

Figure 1.3   Sample Observation Checklist: Working in the Soup Kitchen

Criteria \ Ranking	Awesome (5)	Acceptable (3)	Absent (0)	Comments
Observed actions				
Came prepared to work				
Worked smoothly with assigned team				
Focused on the task				
Accomplished the assigned work				

Because the most user-friendly checklists focus on no more than five behaviors, students and teacher often decide to develop two or three different forms. They agree to include an evaluation of performance as part of the students' final grades.

A rubric for evaluating teamwork during a project ("Evaluating Service") is offered in the Reproducible Masters section, along with a writing evaluation rubric.

Students answer content-knowledge questions during discussions, take traditional content-knowledge quizzes and tests, complete project activity logs, keep daily learning logs, write essays, create visuals and images, compose poems and lyrics, develop surveys for gathering information, collect and analyze ideas and facts, and demonstrate what they have learned by sharing portfolios. Each student compiles a project portfolio.

The most discouraging roadblock in working with service learning is finding the time to implement all of the steps in the process. I overcame this roadblock by making the service learning project a priority and trying to tie in other areas of my curriculum with the project.

—Nicole Hite, Teacher, Temperance, MI

Representative portfolios that show growth over time include these kinds of items:

- Performance (professionalism) checklists filled out by the student, teacher, and a representative-of-the-community partner for the project
- The student's daily learning log and service project reflective log
- Audio or video media on which the student has recorded insights, learnings, and reflections
- Rough and final drafts of essays
- Poems, song lyrics, or recordings of songs
- Graphics that represent a processing of content learning
- Quizzes and tests that demonstrate accuracy of content learning
- Photos of the student at the service project site
- Other artifacts that show what the student learned and how he or she learned it

The teacher uses a planner such as the one shown in Figure 1.4 to set up assessment plans for the project.

Students evaluate their own academic, service, and life skills learning throughout the project. When the project is completed, the teacher and each student have an evaluation conference during which they discuss a final grade; highlight the

Figure 1.4 Sample Planner: Assessing Soup Kitchen Learning

Quizzes and Tests	Feedback and Reflection
Food pyramid quiz	Journal/reflective project log
Diet and wellness quiz	Reflections on steps in project
Diet and brain function quiz	Record keeping
"Kitchen contagion" quiz	Self-feedback
Menu-scaling quiz	
Test 1 (topics?)	**Products**
Test 2 (topics?)	Breakfast menus (2)
	Lunch menus (2)
Checklists	Dinner menus (2)
#1	Food kitchen poster
#2	Food pyramid poster
#3	

student's most memorable academic, service, and life skills learnings; and set goals for future community service.

The assessment and evaluation techniques for service learning projects may sound complex. Such techniques, however, result in a more accurate picture of student learning than a simple paper-and-pencil test. Furthermore, these assessment and evaluation techniques mirror those used by managers in today's world of work. This authentic assessment and evaluation is one more way in which service learning helps prepare students to become effective members of society and the future workforce, and—just as important—responsible members of the local community.

WHAT ABOUT CHALLENGES?
HOW CAN THEY BE MANAGED?

Teachers who facilitate service learning projects with their students report several challenges to using this experiential curriculum model. These include the following:

- Time for planning and implementing the project
- Knowledge of techniques, strategies, and logistics
- Funds for materials, transportation, and incidentals
- Liability for student health and safety
- Transportation of students to and from the work site
- Assessment that demonstrates progress toward local, state, and national standards
- Student buy-in to learning while providing service to others

Challenges? Roadblocks? Just do it! It's important for kids to help others. To help with your time, provide time for kids to brainstorm their project and anticipate the challenges and develop plans to overcome the problems.

—Gerard O'Brien, Teacher, Palatine, IL

Here are some ideas for managing these challenges.

Time. Teachers need planning time, and administrators need to recognize this and provide teachers with inservice hours, workshop days, or subsidized summer preparation time. Planning time is an ongoing need; it must be provided each year or the quality of the service learning projects will suffer. Often teachers report that they receive planning time during the first year their school district commits to service learning and they receive no time in following years (Ammon, Furco, Chi, & Middaugh, 2002). Administrators need to remember that planning time is an essential component of the process and that they must make it readily available even for "legacy" projects that continue from one year to the next.

To make the introductory experience with service learning less overwhelming, teachers need to remember the KISS guidelines: They need to Keep It (the project) Short and Simple. Discomfort with change is part of the human condition. Teachers who begin with a short, simple project are more likely to experience successes from which they can learn and upon which they can build (Billig, 2005). A successful project is a great tool for building support among colleagues and administrators and encouraging the growth of service learning throughout a school district.

Knowledge. Teachers who receive carefully structured professional development before doing service learning projects report greater success and fewer problems (Ammon et al., 2002). Well-designed professional development courses and workshops provide teachers with strategies, insights, tools, and advice from practitioners. Because they gain insight into the service learning model and how it works, community partners also benefit from attending these professional development sessions (Holdsman & Tuchmann, 2004). The district administration needs to survey teachers to determine whether to use in-house experts in the field or outside consultants to lead the professional development program. Many districts find that using a blend of both works well. Outsiders provide an initial burst of energy and enthusiasm; insiders offer ongoing support, advice, and celebrations of success.

Funds. Doing a service learning project does require buying necessary materials, providing transportation to and from the work site, and paying for incidental expenses such as sun screen for students who are working outdoors, water or healthy snacks for students who are doing physically strenuous work, and other items that make students more comfortable on the job. Fortunately for teachers who want to do service learning projects, minigrants are available. Teachers need to prepare and submit grant proposals, and this encourages them to refine and tighten their project ideas (Holdsman & Tuchmann, 2004). Teachers need to remember to give the students a voice in the final planning of the project. If grant proposal deadlines fall during the summer recess, teachers and students work together after the start of school to finalize project selection and planning.

Some of the projects in this book suggest alternative sources for some funds. If costs are small, each student in a class may contribute a small amount toward the total needed. Parent groups often donate funds to support school projects, and community service organizations may have funds set aside for this purpose.

One final suggestion: In their quest to identify potential community partners, teachers often overlook the schools in which they work. Schools have many needs, from additional library books to hallway decoration to outdoor landscaping. Students who want to design and produce a mural as a visual-arts project can decorate a large white space in the school such as a hallway wall. Instead of working in a soup kitchen, students can help with food preparation in the school cafeteria. A creative teacher and his or her students can approach the school administration and say, "These are the learning standards we want our service learning project to target; how can we help the school and meet these standards?" In-school projects provide service and connect students and the school in ways that benefit both.

Liability. Teachers need to ask the school administration for information about a variety of liability concerns. Most districts have policies in place that address these issues. Teachers need to be sure that they follow established guidelines for the following:

- Working at remote sites. Most schools have policies regarding field trip parameters and protocols. Service learning trips off school grounds follow these policies.
- Acquiring transportation. School districts have lists of licensed transportation providers. Some districts have their own fleet of buses. Teachers use the approved transportation companies to move students to the work site and back to school. If the work site is close to the school, students may walk between the two.
- Supervising students. The required number of adult supervisors or chaperones is often stated as a ratio—a maximum number of students per adult. Teachers need to adhere to these policies, and they also need to be sure that adult supervisors have passed any required background checks before they are allowed to work with students.
- Taking steps in an emergency. Teachers need to know and follow school regulations detailing the protocols to follow in the event that a student becomes ill or is injured. All illnesses and injuries must be reported to the teacher by a student or adult supervisor.

Assessment. Assessing learning and determining grades require collection of information about all aspects of learning. Traditional report cards communicate content-learning results to parents. Results of service learning projects need to be shared with the administration, parents, the community partner, and other interested parties. To do this, the teacher and students can schedule a "celebration of learning" during which students report on what they did and what they learned about school subjects and being a service provider. These celebrations help to build community support for service learning in the schools.

> Doing this project helped me deal with some personal stress. I'm really proud of all of my classmates who care and want to help others.
>
> We didn't do all we set out to do. At first I thought we failed, but then I thought again and decided the project was a success because of what we did accomplish.
>
> This (providing service to the community) is the most important thing I've ever done.
>
> —Students, Palatine, IL

Student buy-in. Before doing their first service learning project, teachers report concern that students will not buy into the concept (Ammon et al., 2002). When they evaluate the effect of challenges after finishing a project, teachers often say that this was a nonissue. Students, once they are introduced to the process, are usually willing participants in service learning.

Making the experience participatory is key to keeping students involved. Students who help to select and plan projects see themselves as important stakeholders who have vested interest in the success of the project. As they move into actively providing service to others, students discover a sense of self-worth and dignity that flows from the ability to be of help to others. Teachers report that students' buy-in is greatest in projects when the students help to select and plan.

Support from the teacher and peers keeps students engaged. Cooperative learning teams play a huge role here. As students check in with their teammates each day and tell each other stories about experiences they had "on the job," they give each other encouraging words and celebrate mutual successes. Teachers and students review content learning standards, and students use tests, quizzes, rubrics, checklists, and other assessment tools to see how much progress they are making toward learning goals.

> I make clear my expectations (about contributing to the success of the project), and I lead the class to agreeing that service learning projects are cool and worthwhile. I give kids time to brainstorm so that they build the confidence they need to see the project through.
>
> —Gerard O'Brien, Teacher, Palatine, IL

USING THE PROJECT IDEAS IN THIS BOOK

Service Learning: A Guide to Planning, Implementing, and Assessing Student Projects features nine projects (Chapters 2–10), each focused on a specific service learning experience. Teachers are encouraged to skim through all nine to see what is available before selecting one or more for detailed investigation. The nine projects in this book vary in complexity, with the first three being fairly basic, the next three intermediate in complexity, and the last three rather advanced. Projects can be used as is or modified to suit various student needs—at the teacher's discretion. These service learning project ideas can also serve as models for teachers to use as they brainstorm new service learning projects—for themselves and for their students.

"Managing the Service Project" is a feature that gives teachers a grid format or chart for management planning that shows the entire service learning project at a glance. Teachers are encouraged to use this grid to do their initial planning, or to modify it to fit individual needs, rather than write their plans in paragraph form.

Tapping Into Multiple Intelligences: Managing the Management Plan

Visual, Logical, and Intrapersonal Multiple Intelligences

Do not overplan in advance. Because a person never knows what forks a road may offer or what roadblocks may present themselves, it is best to be open to change. Begin with the end in mind (Covey, 1989), and be flexible. Here are some tips:

Before beginning a management plan for phase 1 and after selecting the project, give each student 10 to 12 small sticky-notes. Build definitions for the terms *planning, monitoring,* and *evaluating.* Tell students, "If you want to come to class tomorrow prepared to help your team, you will think of at least three components of the service learning project that need to be done during each of these categories during phase 1 of the project." Ask for questions and check for understanding of the assignment.

The next day, before students arrive in class, tape three large sheets of chart paper on the wall. Label one "Planning," the second "Monitoring," and the third "Evaluating." Direct student cooperative learning teams to go through the sticky-note ideas that members have and weed out any duplicates. Then tell one person from each team, probably the Dry Cell, to place the unduplicated sticky-notes on the proper sheets of chart paper. When all of the sticky-notes are in place, read them aloud to students. Ask, "Is this where we want to keep these ideas? Do we need to rearrange?" Draw on your experience to suggest relocating any of the sticky-notes that seem to be out of place and ask students for permission to add sticky-notes of your own if you know that there are gaps in the plan that need to be filled. Leave the sheets of chart paper on the wall and make a small version of the plan. Setting up a table in a good word-processing program will give you a grid that you can use to do this. Duplicate the small version so that each student has a copy.

Repeat the process with the sticky-notes at appropriate times throughout the service learning project. Take down the sheets of chart paper only when that phase of the service learning project has ended. You and the students can save some time by moving sticky-notes from one phase of a project to another if the action on that sticky-note is repeated or if it was misplaced. Doing the planning this way gives students a genuine voice in planning the service learning project and enhances their roles as stakeholders.

Research shows that the brain responds well to patterned "maps" that show the big learning picture because initial stages of information processing seem to be parallel rather than serial (Jensen, 1996). Concrete visual images also promote more powerful thinking and reflection. The performance management grid (or another mapping tool that shows the entire management plan in a powerful graphic) is the most brain-friendly way for teachers to do their planning.

In the "Fostering Reflective Learning" section of each project, teachers find suggestions for reflective log lead-ins or sentence stems for elementary, middle school, and high school students. These specific lead-ins help students focus their thinking and writing, and the visual organization helps them do better, more reflective, deeper thinking about their learnings. The reflective log also provides a way for students to get immediate self-feedback after working on a service project. Project plans suggest that students share their reflections with peers in small-group discussions. This self- and peer feedback, brain research suggests, also helps students to mentally file the learning more effectively (Jensen, 1996).

The "Assessment and Evaluation" section of each project (or chapter) includes a list of the portfolio pieces for the project. Teachers will want to stress that each portfolio contains some pieces that are chosen by the student. One goal of a project portfolio is to allow the students to show growth over time. As students look at the personal artifacts that they have collected during the life of a particular service project, they reflect on the service learning (project) experience, select key portfolio pieces, reflect on their meanings, and visualize where their learning started—as well as how far they have come. Students give themselves another deep feedback experience that cements the academic, service, and life skills learnings that have occurred through immersion in the service project experience.

PART I

Basic Service Learning Projects

2

Clean Streets, Green Streets

A Social Studies and Science Service Learning Project

DESCRIPTION OF THE PROJECT

Students "adopt" a road by identifying a trouble spot in their locality, picking up litter from a selected stretch (several blocks in length) of a city street or a one- to two-mile stretch of highway. As they pick up the litter, they sort the paper, metal, glass, plastic, and "other" pieces into separate, labeled containers. Students weigh each container empty before the litter cleanup and full after the litter collection. To demonstrate their commitment to service, students collect litter from the same stretch of street or highway once a month for three months. If younger students are doing the project, the teacher designates a "clean streets" day during which the entire class participates in working together to clean up a single street or highway. If school policy permits this, the teacher assigns older students to work in separate small groups, and students and teacher locate a different cleanup site for each group. School field trip policy probably requires that each of the cleanup groups be accompanied by an adult supervisor or chaperone. The administration is the teacher's best source of information about these policies.

As students begin the project, the teacher assigns them to base teams of three. In the case of older students, the base teams are the cleanup teams. A base team is a group of students who work together for the duration of the project. Students begin their base-team work by doing trust-building activities and working together in class on project planning. For the life of the project, the base team is the student's "home base" for making plans, deciding on appropriate service action, brainstorming, debriefing, self-evaluating, and making special products. Students discuss reflective log entries with members of their base teams and make their initial portfolio presentations to their base teammates. The base teams become groups in which students feel comfortable sharing self-evaluations that include plans for future improvement, insights about themselves and their roles in the community, and AHA!s (great moments of revelation) about content learning. Furthermore, the base teams provide students with the frequent opportunities for feedback that their brains need to make sense out of their learning (Sylwester, 2000). Some of the other service learning projects included in this book suggest that students work in base teams to do some of the project work. The above is the working definition of *base team* that is intended throughout the book.

In their base teams, students develop a KND chart describing the litter problem in their community. The *K* stands for what students KNOW about the litter problem. The *N* represents what the students believe they NEED to find out about the litter problem. The *D* signifies what the students want to DO about the litter problem. The teacher leads a whole-class discussion to develop a master KND list on a large sheet of chart paper that is displayed in the classroom. Each Clean Streets base team uses this brainstormed chart to design a poster, song, poem, "commercial" skit, or comic strip promoting community awareness of the importance of picking up litter. A copy of this product becomes part of the individual student portfolio for the Clean Streets, Green Streets service learning project.

Before students clean up the highway or street, they write a paragraph describing its overall appearance and their feelings and thoughts about how the amount of litter that they see speaks to the degree to which the community is aware of the role played by litter in environmental quality. Students who choose to do so may substitute a visual representation of the street or a poem or song lyric for the written description. Each student keeps a cleanup log for the adopted street or highway. Each log entry includes the weight of each category of collected litter, the total weight of litter picked up, and the names of consumer products for which they find packaging—bags, wrappers, cans, boxes, or bottles.

Keeping Records and Building a Portfolio

As students observe such phenomena, they describe how much decay or decomposition they see for at least two selected objects from each litter category. A Venn diagram is a handy tool to use to compare and contrast the appearance of the litter piece with the appearance of its new counterpart. Students note how much time they spent picking up the litter from their adopted stretch of street or highway. Each student signs and dates his or her log entry for each pickup day. The comparison and cleanup log becomes part of each student's service learning project portfolio.

Back in the classroom, students calculate the percentage by weight of each of the separate categories of litter. They rate the ease with which the different categories of litter seem to decay. Students may decide on ratings like "decays quickly and easily," "shows signs of slow decay," and "decays very slowly or not at all." The teacher helps students find a spot where they can bury one object from each litter category in the ground and leave it in place for at least a month. At the end of the period, students dig up the objects and see how much each one has decomposed, and they use this information to confirm or revise their initial ratings of how easily each category of litter decomposes. After dividing the class into five large groups, the teacher assigns each group one category of litter: paper, glass, metal, plastic, or "other."

Each group writes and illustrates a brochure describing the litter category, the resources used in making the category of litter (metal ores, sand, limestone, crude oil, coal, wood pulp, animals, or vegetables), whether the resources are renewable or not, and the implications for producing a new supply of the material by recycling discarded consumer items or by using "new" supplies of the resource. Close to the end of this unit of study, each group presents its findings to the rest of the class. Each member of the group has a copy of the brochure in his or her project portfolio.

Next, each student looks for connections between his or her family's buying habits and those of the community by comparing the list of consumer products packages that were contained in the litter with a list of products purchased by the student's family. Students may choose to collect this information about products in a table such as the one that follows:

Product Type	Family Example	Litter Example
Candy	gummies	chocolate bar
Chips	nacho corn chips	rippled potato chips
Soft drink	cola	lemonade
Fast food	pizza slice	burger
Grocery bag	brown paper	plastic
Extra packaging	cotton balls	medicine box

Students use these connections to write essays, produce visuals, compose poems or song lyrics, or create videos explaining their personal connections to the litter that they are collecting. Base teams produce comic strips, songs, poems, or posters to help increase community awareness of the importance of keeping streets and highways clean by disposing of litter responsibly. Each member of a base team has a copy of the community awareness product to place in his or her portfolio.

Possible community partners for this service learning project are the state department of transportation, a county road commission, a city department of streets, or a regional sanitary district (which can provide information about landfills or recycling). Before the students and teacher interview a service partner, they will want to develop a list of the materials that students need to do this project, and they will want to decide which items the teacher and students provide and which materials they want to obtain from the community partner. A sample litter cleanup project materials list follows.

Items	Provider(s)
garbage bags	community partner or students
disposable gloves	community partner or students
scales	students
recycling bins	community partner
first-aid supplies	students
traffic cones	community partner
adhesive bandages	students
antiseptic hand cleaner	students
antiseptic wipes	students
safety vests	community partner

The community partner, teacher, and students need to negotiate what services or materials, such as garbage bags, disposable gloves, and antiseptic wipes, each party agrees to provide. Students need to know what kind of commitment the partner wants from them and what safety precautions they need to take to minimize the risks of accidents or injuries occurring while they pick up litter. The teacher contacts the sponsoring agencies by telephone and schedules a personal meeting between an agency liaison and the teacher and students. The meeting gives all parties the opportunity to connect and establish trust in each other. If transportation funding is not available, the teacher and students schedule their own transportation to and from the cleanup site. For this reason, younger students probably need to select a site close to the school. Older students may be able to provide personal transportation if school policy permits them to do so. Students also will want to find out where and how to dispose of the collected litter. If the litter is collected near the school, they may obtain permission to place it in trash or recycling containers at school. Students and teacher will want to maintain ongoing communication with the community agency that is sponsoring the project.

ASSESSING RISKS: ESTABLISHING PROTOCOLS FOR HEALTH AND SAFETY

Prudence dictates that the teacher and students take time to identify health and safety risks and establish procedures to safeguard against accidental injuries or illnesses. Students are working on streets and highways where they need to be aware of the threats posed by passing motor vehicle traffic. To increase their visibility, students need to wear safety vests of the type worn by road repair workers, vests made of neon-bright colors and containing reflective materials. To distance themselves from cars, trucks, and buses, students need to work outside of traffic lanes. The teacher and students study visual representations of traffic lane markings so that students are familiar with these, and the students and teacher agree on litter pickup procedures such as, "Stay on grassy surfaces only," or "Stay above the curb when working on city streets," or "Work only where adults say it's safe to be."

A wide variety of bacteria live on roadside litter, on vegetation, and in the soil, and students will want to avoid contact with these infectious agents. Students must be taught that before they begin to collect litter, they need to put on disposable gloves. If the gloves tear during use, students need to throw away the torn gloves, clean their hands with antiseptic hand cleaner or wipes, and put on new gloves. The teacher demonstrates a safe way to take off used gloves and place them in the trash. Students of all ages need to be reminded to avoid touching their faces while they are wearing the gloves. Face touching is an excellent way to introduce bacteria into the body.

Even when they handle litter carefully, students may suffer small cuts or scrapes. They need to know that washing with a copious amount of hot water and soap is the best way to clean out cuts. If they do not have access to running water, students need to know that cleaning the scrape with antiseptic hand cleaner or wipes helps until they get to hot water. Whether or not a cut or scrape is bleeding, after cleaning it out, students want to cover it with an adhesive bandage. Above all, the teacher emphasizes the need for students to report all accidents and injuries, no matter how small they might seem at the time. A twisted ankle or arm may result in a painful sprain.

An untended cut or scrape may become infected. The students' best defense is to be sure that the teacher knows about any and all accidents as soon as they happen.

The teacher needs to know if any students are allergic to insect bites, and students who need a medication to lessen allergic reactions need to have a supply of that product with them whenever they work out-of-doors. Students are more comfortable picking up litter when they are wearing "work clothes," baseball caps (to keep the sun out of their eyes and off their faces), and when they have drinking water available. Students and the teacher can stock a small cooler with bottles of water before leaving the school for the work site.

The "Making Connections With the Community" section of this chapter includes the suggestion that the teacher invite a representative from a city agency to come in to talk to the class. The teacher needs to check local school codes and state laws to see if the regulations require a visitor to a school to undergo a background check. Bringing in a speaker is a good idea, but the teacher needs to balance the benefits of a presentation by an outside expert against potential risk to students and legal requirements that must be met by the guest.

Students from Saint Paul appreciated working in well-structured, well-supervised teams. They had these very important comments to make about teamwork:

Teams need to be well supervised so that everyone is held accountable for doing his or her assigned task. Roles and duties must be laid out at the beginning of the project. If they are not, one or two people wind up doing most of the work.

Teamwork requires trust. It takes time to build relationships within the team and to establish a level of trust and dedication to the team. If the going gets rough, teammates who trust each other will "tough it out."

(Johnson, M., 2001, p. 12)

SELECTING THE SERVICE LEARNING FOCUS: THE COMMUNITY ENVIRONMENT

Conservation is a "big idea" theme that threads its way through the curriculum from kindergarten through college and beyond. Litter cleanup is a topic that makes the news many times a year in communities of all sizes and settings from megalopolises to wilderness villages. In introducing this service learning project to students, the teacher says that conservation of resources is a theme that reaches out to all content areas, involves skills such as public communication and teamwork, and has important implications for future generations. After this introduction, the teacher asks, "What are some service projects that need to be done in our community that could help us learn more about conserving resources?" The teacher suggests that students ask their parents such questions as, "When you read newspaper stories (or hear radio or television reports) about town council meetings, what town needs do you hear about that could be addressed by volunteers, and which of those volunteer services can help us learn about resources, conservation, and recycling?"

The teacher asks students to come to class with a list of ideas that the family brainstormed and build a master list of project ideas from those suggestions. If the teacher has a favorite idea, he or she may add it to the list of possible projects. The teacher introduces the idea with some explanation, for example: "A friend of mine who works for the city department of streets says that work crews are falling behind schedule for doing road repairs because they are spending so much time picking up litter. We could do a litter cleanup service project to learn about resources and recycling. Is this a project that the class would be interested in doing?"

Sometimes, a class continues or repeats a project that a previous class began. If a previous class started a tradition of doing litter cleanup, the teacher introduces it by saying, "Three years ago, the third-grade class became official 'Adopt-a-Highway' sponsors by volunteering to clean up the five-block stretch of Highway 26 that runs past the school and continues east to the town limits. Last year's class renewed the sponsorship by continuing the project. Does this year's class agree to continue the project? We're beginning to have a grade-level tradition going on here."

The class and teacher can evaluate the service learning project idea using a rubric such as the one shown in Figure 2.1.

Figure 2.1   Sample Project Evaluation Rubric: Clean Streets, Green Streets

Ranking / Criteria	1 (high)	2 (medium)	3 (low)	Comments
Interest	X			We would like to walk to school along clean streets. We can use the project to learn about resources and recycling.
Need	X			The department of streets can do road repair more efficiently if we help by picking up litter.
Accessibility	X			We can clean up the streets that are close to the school.
Appropriateness	X			We can pick up litter, follow health and safety rules, and teach community members about resources and recycling.
Time Frame	X			We can do litter pickup twice in the fall and twice in the spring.

One way to use the rubric is for each student to do an individual ranking of the factors. The teacher and students then tally the rankings, and students calculate an average ranking as discussed in Chapter 1. The teacher then leads a whole-class discussion to weigh the average rankings and decide whether the project enhances the content learning. When students are prompted to reflect on what the sentence "I like to see clean streets as I walk to school" means, the teacher asks, "What is your picture of clean streets? Can you begin to visualize that? How would you describe it to someone else? What would clean streets look like, and what would clean streets say to a stranger about the people who live in this community?" Students may not know what kinds of maintenance or road repairs the local department of streets routinely makes, why such work is necessary, or how much time road repair and maintenance require. To give students a deeper understanding of how their community functions, the teacher suggests that they contact the community agency and ask where they can find this information.

Tapping Into Multiple Intelligences: Mapping Possibilities

Visual, Logical, Interpersonal, and Intrapersonal Multiple Intelligences

Students participate most enthusiastically in service learning projects if they are given a voice in project selection. Here is a process that works very effectively to involve students in choosing a service learning project:

First: Give students an ill-structured problem statement and give them a few days to brainstorm ideas. Ask, "Are you familiar with national 'Make-a-Difference Day' on which individuals, groups of friends, families, or clubs perform a service that benefits the community?" Lead a discussion about Make-a-Difference Day.

Then: Ask students, "How can we make a difference that benefits our community?" Tell students when they need to be ready to discuss their ideas. On that day, tell students to share their ideas with members of their base teams, and ask each base team to pick its *one* favorite idea. Call on teams at random to contribute and explain their ideas to the rest of the class. Make a master list of ideas as teams contribute them.

Next: Tell students, "When we select our way to make a difference, we want to find a service project idea that connects to the curriculum. Your job is to brainstorm connections between your service idea and subject areas (language arts, math, social studies, science), processes (visual arts, music, physical education), and skills (all of the above and more). As we benefit the community, we're also going to be learning concepts, facts, processes, and skills." Teach students the basics of mind mapping (Buzan model, see more in Chapter 3) and tell base teams to mind map the learning connections to their service project idea. The center of the map is a visual representing the service project, and the "spokes" lead out to the curriculum connections.

Next: Ask base teams to present their mind maps to the rest of the class. Post mind maps on the walls of the room so that students can review each one.

Next: Do some homework. Dig out your grade-level or content area standards and evaluate the degree to which each project idea aligns with the standards. Identify and contact possible community partners for the projects. Tell students that you need to do this groundwork. Explain to them what you are doing and why it is necessary. On the basis of your research, identify two or three service learning projects that align well with standards and possess strong ties to a community partner.

Next: Present your results to the students. Tell students to evaluate the finalists using the project evaluation rubric (see Figure 2.1). Announce the date on which you and the students make the final project selection.

Next to last: On the due date, give base teams time to discuss their evaluations. Tell each team to select its number one service project. Then lead a whole-class discussion, polling the teams, to decide on the overall winner. Tell students that this will be the service project they do unless you encounter roadblocks that cannot be overcome.

Finally: Do more homework. Make final arrangements with a community partner, the school administration, and any other participating parties. Announce the final selection to the students and begin the project.

Making Connections With the Community

At this point, the teacher asks a representative from the department of streets to present a short talk addressing the work that the department does and the damage that may be done to cars and trucks or the accidents that occur when the work is not done. This community spokesperson may also address how litter pickup is handled when volunteers are not available. If a representative is not able to appear in person, the teacher asks his or her permission to record an interview and show the recording to the class. Hearing about street maintenance firsthand from someone who works at it makes that work come alive for students. Personal appearances give students an opportunity to ask questions and receive additional information, but state and local laws may discourage outsiders from visiting schools.

This is a good time for the teacher to tell students to inspect the streets near their homes to see if they are in good repair. He or she will post a large sheet of paper for students to use as a graffiti wall on which they record their neighborhoods' road repair needs. When students see that streets that are close to their homes have potholes that need filling or crumbling curbs, they become more aware of the problems that result from street crews having to pick up litter instead of fixing roads.

If this project continues community service that started in a previous year, the teacher asks the class to adopt the same street or highway that the original class did. In picking a street or highway, the teacher often will want to use a site that is close to the school to simplify transportation needs. He or she certainly will find it easier to have students walk out of the schoolhouse door and begin working right away than to arrange for a school or city bus or for parent chauffeurs to transport students to a distant site. By doing the work close to the school, the teacher can be the main adult supervisor for the project, knows there is parking available for parents or other adults who volunteer to help with project supervision at the school, and can have students do the work during the school day or right after school dismissal. This streamlines the project for everyone concerned.

Picking up litter is an activity that is age appropriate for everyone in the community. The more people who voluntarily pick up one misplaced piece of trash and put it in the proper place, the cleaner, more visually appealing, and safer the community will be for all of its members. The teacher will want to be certain that students are old enough to know and remember safety rules. Students who are working close to a busy street must wear bright-colored clothing and safety vests.

During the planning part of the project, they need to find a source of those vests. Local streets departments can direct the teacher to an adopt-a-highway office, which is a good source of these items.

For purposes of health and hygiene, it is strongly recommended that students also wear disposable plastic gloves (as well as regular work gloves) to protect themselves as they pick up trash. Plastic gloves may be purchased inexpensively at most discount stores. The teacher may want to request money ahead of time from the school to make this purchase or ask each student to contribute a small amount of money—perhaps one dollar or less—toward the purchase of a few boxes of gloves for the entire class to share. Grant money, if available, can be used to buy the gloves. Students need to take home permission slips allowing out-of-school activities (or field trips) for parents to sign, and only those students who return the signed forms to the teacher are allowed to participate in the project.

Students of all ages love to be outside when the weather is nice, and by scheduling pickups for the fall and spring, the teacher is giving him- or herself an opportunity to say "yes" when students ask, "Can we go outside today?" The teacher will want to schedule the pickup dates and announce them well in advance so that students can come to school dressed for street work. Remembering that the weather may be uncooperative, the teacher will definitely want to include a "rain date" in the schedule so that the pickup gets done no matter what the weather is like on the original date.

WORKING WITH A COMMUNITY PARTNER

The teacher telephones the municipal department of streets or other appropriate agency to explain the project and its curricular goals, request partnership in the project, and get information about adopting a street. This initial contact may be followed up by a visit to the appropriate office by the teacher and, time and laws permitting, a group of students. At this time, a department representative can become the liaison between the school class and the city agency.

Teachers and students who want to learn more about adopting a street or highway before finalizing their plans can find information at a number of Internet Web sites. A Google or Yahoo! search using the keywords "adopt a highway" or "community cleanup" gives them many results from which to choose. Teachers, parents, or other adult supervisors need to monitor student Web searches. Information is also available at local secretary of state offices located throughout a state. Addresses and telephone numbers for these offices are available in local and areawide telephone directories.

Teachers from Saint Paul say that it is much easier to pick one project and address many content areas with it than it is to do several projects that each address a different content area. Finding a project that threads through several content areas shows students that all learning is interconnected.

(Johnson, M., 2001, p. 13)

ALIGNING SERVICE AND EDUCATIONAL GOALS

As students do their Clean Streets, Green Streets service learning project, they keep a record of consumption of consumer products based on packaging they find on the roadway. All students look for familiar product packages in the litter and describe their personal connections to their community (social studies) by looking for similarities between what they find on the street and consumer products that they encounter at home. Once they have done this analyzing, students write descriptive essays (language arts) about those connections. A student may, for example, notice that several cardboard holders for single slices of pizza were picked up in the street and write, "We found four holders for pizza slices. Some people who walk near the school must really like to eat pizza. So does my family. We have it for dinner almost every Saturday night." Another student may write, "I picked up nine filters from cigarettes. My mom used to smoke. She quit two years ago, and she does not get as many colds as she used to."

Cataloging the litter from the streets gives students an opportunity to do "concurrent archaeology." The teacher can ask students to compare their collection of litter with an archaeologist's collection of artifact bits and pieces from former civilizations. The teacher says, "We use historic artifacts to try to reconstruct the day-to-day life of people in those civilizations. What could future generations conclude about our civilization from the bits and pieces of litter that we are collecting? How is our job similar to that of traditional archaeologists? Our conclusions are about our own society, so we'll call what we are doing *concurrent archaeology.*"

The teacher encourages students to see how they and their families connect with, contribute to, and are products of the society in which they live. Each student's written description of the personal connections that he or she finds between consumer products in the litter and his or her personal lifestyle are included in the project portfolio.

Student Responsibilities and Curricular Areas

Students who do litter pickup are also asked to develop a response to a local resources/recycling issue, such as using recycling to reduce the flow of garbage into a rapidly filling landfill (social studies) as they identify which categories of litter can be recycled. The teacher can call the regional sanitary authority, describe the service learning project, and ask for information about how often a new landfill facility needs to be opened to serve the area. Students can then use computational methods for solving problems with proportion and percentage (mathematics) to calculate what percentage of the litter that they picked up could be recycled and to estimate how many extra years of life the present landfill facilities would gain if the community developed an aggressive recycling program. Also, students can examine use of resources and land and environmental protection (social science; earth science) as the five materials teams investigate the resources that are used to produce metal, plastics, glass, paper, and "other," beginning to form opinions about whether it is better to produce these goods by using virgin (raw) resources or by recycling discarded material.

Students can plan and conduct a simple investigation (science) to determine which kinds of litter disappear through rapid decay or decomposition, and they can describe these changes in properties as chemical changes (science) when they summarize the results of their investigations. As they do all of their writing, they use appropriate grammar and sentence structure (language arts), and when they participate in class discussions about the nature of physical and chemical changes, they use precise vocabulary to convey meaning (language arts). Students demonstrate knowledge of ways to protect against infection (health) by discussing the reasons for using gloves as they pick up litter and washing their hands thoroughly when they are finished. They identify specific bacteria or other infectious organisms that could be living in the litter and describe the effects of these infectious agents on human health. They list ways to protect personal safety (life skills) on the pickup job.

Students who help clean the streets have identified a need of the community and actively participated in organized service that addresses that need (service skills). The teacher writes tests or quizzes and asks students to write, produce visuals, and discuss learning to demonstrate curricular knowledge that they developed and acquired through participation in service learning (service skills). In addition, every service learning project asks students to keep a reflective log in which they think and write about the significance of their service learning experience and its implications for themselves and the community (service skills).

Students frequently hear slogans and read bumper sticker sayings that reflect "big ideas" without knowing how those ideas apply to their lives. The Clean Streets, Green Streets service project can be used to teach students the meaning of such slogans as "Think globally, act locally." Throughout the life of the project, teachers can also focus student attention on some big concepts. *Change* is one of those concepts—change in attitudes (toward solid waste and its disposal, toward use of resources, or toward preservation of prairie and forest), change in the manner in which materials are made and then decompose, and change in habits (ranging from throwing all solid waste in the garbage can to sorting for recycling). *Conservation* is another big idea—conservation of matter as it changes appearance and form but not amount, conservation of resources through recycling, and conservation of habitat by leaving land unmined and undrilled with forests uncut. *Resources* is another huge idea—natural resources, production resources, economic resources, human resources, environmental resources, and so on.

Because the service project is extended over time, students have a chance to hook into some of the truly big ideas that are the "threads" that link all content areas together. The teacher could start things off by asking students, "How many of you have heard that we need to reduce, reuse, and recycle?" After getting a show of hands, the teacher might say, "What if I told you that the real challenge is to conserve, connect, and change? Can you define those terms for me?" The class could then do some brainstorming to develop initial definitions of those terms and pictures of what conserving, connecting, and changing look like and how they parallel reducing, reusing, and recycling. Over time, those definitions and pictures are revisited, enlarged, and modified to reflect what students are learning. See Figure 2.2 for a model alignment of service and educational goals.

Reciprocity: The Community of Learners

Throughout the life of the service learning project, from project selection to celebration of completion, students are encouraged to discuss the project with siblings, parents, guardians, and other community members. The teacher directs students,

Figure 2.2   Clean Streets, Green Streets: Aligning Service and Educational Goals

Major Subject	Learning Goals	Life Skills	Big Ideas	Service Actions
Social Studies	School/ community connections Local issues Use of resources	Offering help Listening Prioritizing	Think globally; act locally Identifying different kinds of resources— personal, natural, economic, etc.	Litter cleanup Awareness poster; song
Mathematics	Ratio and proportion	Comparing Computational skills	Proportion in different kinds of areas— measurements, representation, emotions, points of view	Calculating percentage
Science	Experimenting Conservation of matter Chemical and physical change	Observing Analyzing Problem solving	Conservation— It's nature's way! Conservatorship	Decay experiments Explaining recycling options Packaging investigation
Language Arts	Appropriate grammar Sentence structure Precise vocabulary	Explaining Summarizing Clarifying	Communication: "Seek first to understand" (Covey, 1989)	Reflective journal Writing essays Discussing learning with classmates and family

with appropriate supervision, to ask community retailers for permission to display their Clean Streets posters in windows or on bulletin boards. Many grocery stores have areas near entrances that are set aside for displaying community announcements. The teacher contacts service organizations in the community to ask for help in distributing materials that the students produce: Comic strips, lyrics to songs, poems, or other materials can inform the community what the students are learning about conserving, connecting, and changing. As they see the posters and talk about the project with the students, members of the community become more aware of the need to conserve natural resources, the importance of recycling, and the resourcefulness of the students. Communitywide commitment to keeping streets clean, decreasing solid waste, and increasing the amount of material set aside for recycling is a very realistic outcome of this service learning project.

MANAGING THE SERVICE PROJECT: CLEAN STREETS, GREEN STREETS

Before students begin the service learning project, the teacher and students need to make detailed plans for managing the project. Management ideas need to be outlined for the three phases of the project: planning, monitoring, and evaluating. The teacher organizes the management plan in a grid as shown in Figure 2.3. Content work focusing on recycling and resources is ongoing during the life of the project.

Successful management of the project depends on this plan. The teacher will find that the more completely he or she and the students make plans that pay attention to detail, the smoother the project runs. The teacher and students will want to do detailed plans for phase one and outline the rest of the phases to start with. Then, when phase one of the project is completed, they revise the outline and do the detailed plans for the next phase of the project. The teacher and students take advantage of this ongoing planning to reflect on the success of each phase of the project as it is completed, "tweaking" the management plan when the need for these revisions is fresh in their minds.

In general, planning the management of a service learning project follows these steps:

1. Develop an initial plan for the overall project.
2. Begin the project.
3. Evaluate the start-up; revise the plan for future use; revise the outline for the rest of the project as needed.
4. Begin phase two of the project.
5. Evaluate, revise, and continue.
6. Repeat the cycle until the end of the project.

FOSTERING REFLECTIVE LEARNING

Every student does a reflective journal entry after each litter cleanup. The vocabulary that the teacher uses to focus the reflections is age appropriate for the grade level of the students, and older students are encouraged to consider a greater variety of ideas

Figure 2.3 Management Plan: Clean Streets, Green Streets

Phase	Planning	Monitoring	Evaluating
1	Contact department of streets to confirm partnership and get "Adopt a Street" information. Select cleanup site. Write letter asking for parent helpers. Write project description for parents and students, plans for cleanup and reflection logs, assignments, and assessments.	Maintain contact with streets department liaison. Have students and families evaluate the need for litter cleanup.	Discuss student and family evaluations of project. Confirm project selection.
2	Discuss project with students. Hand out assignment sheet. Discuss "Look of Litter" writing assignment, cleanup and reflection logs. Send home letters to parents, including written permission slips and project calendars. Assign base teams. Begin resources and recycling unit of study. Confirm parent helpers.	Collect signed "field trip" permission slips. Make a list of parent helpers with phone numbers. Read and score "Look of Litter" essays. Confirm cleanup dates. Assemble cleanup supplies: bright vests, garbage bags, disposable gloves.	Revise calendar as needed. Do content-learning assessment: quizzes, tests, and class discussion.
3	Do first cleanup of adopted streets (with help from parents as needed). Do litter sorting and weighing. Assign materials teams and "New or Recycled Resources" brochure and presentation. Bury selected litter materials in ground to check on decay rates.	Spot-check cleanup logs. Students share log entries in base teams. Base teams plan poem, song, poster, etc. to promote community awareness of importance of cleaning up litter. Spot-check reflective logs.	Have students self-evaluate progress and discuss in base teams. Materials teams check accuracy of brochure information and develop three alternative answers to question, "Make from new or recycled material?" More content-learning assessment. Base teams share community awareness products with the whole class.
4	Do the second cleanup, litter sorting, and weighing. Materials teams continue researching resources and plan brochure presentation. Dig up buried materials to check decay rates. Review "Personal Connections to Litter" assignment. Check students' list of portfolio pieces.	Read and score "Personal Connections" essay. Check materials teams on presentation plans. Calculate litter totals for both pickups. Do percent calculations. Assemble and check portfolios. Do revisions/improvements of portfolio pieces. Spot-check reflective logs.	Evaluate math skills by giving students new numbers to add or use in percentage calculations. Materials teams do presentations—teacher and teams score presentations for accuracy. Students take paper-and-pencil test on "Resources and Recycling." Students and teacher concurrently evaluate content learning.
5	Do final cleanups. Celebrate project completion by writing a "will" asking future classes to continue the project. Share portfolios in base teams. Write whole-class letter to streets department liaison saying, "Thank you for your help." Students and teacher each write one goal for future personal service work.	"Eavesdrop" on portfolio sharing. Ask students to tell each other their greatest learning AHA!, their most burning unanswered question, what they liked most about the project, what they found least comfortable, what they felt they did best, and what they would do differently (and better) next time.	Students and teacher discuss project strengths and areas for improvement. Each person shares with whole class his or her greatest AHA! and personal goal for future service work.

than younger ones. The basic elements of all of the reflective logs focus on the same ideas: What is the need for the service? What did the student do well? What did the student learn about academic content and skills, life skills, and service skills by doing the community service? See the sample journal pages at the end of this chapter for strategies to prompt reflection. These models consist of sentence stems and open-ended questions about the Clean Streets, Green Streets service learning project. Students may create images, use graphic organizers, develop mind maps, or compose poems or song lyrics to focus their thinking before they write the log entries; learning to write clearly is a lifelong skill that students need to master.

The use of the reflective log or journal reinforces content learning and helps the students understand how they are helpful to their community as well as providing them with a tool to use to evaluate their personal strengths and determine areas for personal goal setting and improvement. It is one of the strategies that make service learning particularly valuable to students.

A student was asked by the local newspaper what made service learning different from things she did every day in school, and she said, "It didn't feel like we were learning. With so much time being given to testing, it was nice to do something fun and outside!"

Our community partner (Red Cross) also loved the service learning idea: "It was great. We loved being able to show the students around our facility and work together."

A recipient of our project stated: "It was nice to see the young people working together to help our community."

—Nicole Hite, Teacher, Temperance, MI

ASSESSMENT AND EVALUATION

The teacher assesses content learning using traditional tools such as class discussions, question-and-answer sessions, and paper-and-pencil quizzes and tests. She gives students a list of assignments that includes doing sketches of the work site before and after cleanup, writing an essay describing the safety precautions that students used during the cleanup and the importance of using those precautions, keeping a personal list of definitions and types of change and conservation, doing a storyboard that shows how litter builds up, and composing a poem or song lyric that expresses the safe feeling of clean streets.

Before students begin the writing assignments, the teacher gives them a rubric that is used to score the final draft of each assignment and shows them how it is used. The teacher does this by showing the students exemplars of excellent, acceptable, and unacceptable work with a chart that explains how these pieces were scored. Students can then use the rubric to self-evaluate the quality of their rough drafts and improve their own written work. A sample rubric for scoring student writing is included in the Reproducible Masters section at the end of this book.

Each student also assembles a project portfolio that includes written work, graphic work, the cleanup log, the reflective log, quiz or test scores, and other evidences of learning that complete the picture of the student's learning that resulted from the Clean Streets, Green Streets project.

Each student has the following specific portfolio pieces for this project:

- The cleanup log
- The reflective log
- Essay: "The Look and Feel of a Street That Is Littered"
- Decay rate investigation notes and findings
- Materials group brochure
- Base-team community awareness product
- Essay: "Personal Connections to Litter"
- Greatest AHA! and personal service goal
- Quiz and test scores
- Three other evidences of learning chosen by the student

The final three evidences are a required part of the portfolio and could include photos, audio- or videotapes, additional writings or visuals, or a list—developed individually or with the help of the class—of extension projects that are related to the Clean Streets, Green Streets service learning project.

Each student shares his or her portfolio with base teammates during the project celebration. This final feedback helps students realize how much they have learned about course content and themselves as service-givers by doing this project.

Elementary Reflective Log

My cleanup job today was . . .	My town feels safer because . . .
What I learned about • concurrent archaeology: • "natural" recycling: • doing community service:	What I did well was . . .
I "picked up" the following big idea: It's my favorite big idea because . . .	What I can do better next time is . . .

Middle School Reflective Log

Today's cleanup project involved . . .

My community is a better place because . . .

Here are my most important learnings about

- conservation and change:

- myself:

- doing community service:

My best actions and thoughts were . . .

Next time I want to improve . . .

High School Reflective Log

The conservation and change learning that I experienced today is . . .
About decay and different substances I learned . . .
The health and safety learning that I most want to remember is . . .
My greatest insight about the importance of clean streets is . . .
My feelings about my role as a member of this community are . . .
The personal strengths I brought to the project today are . . .
Next time I want to strengthen . . .

3

The Lending Locker

A Health and Physical Education Service Learning Project

DESCRIPTION OF THE PROJECT

Young children outgrow many pieces of athletic equipment before wearing them out. Students begin this project by soliciting donations of "pre-owned, yet usable" athletic equipment from other students in the school to obtain "stock" for a lending closet or "locker" of sports equipment. The contributions can include roller skates, in-line skates, ice hockey or figure skates, street or ice hockey sticks, bicycle helmets, protective knee and elbow pads, athletic shoes, baseball bats, and helmets or gloves for a variety of activities.

To facilitate the project, students put out a call for donated equipment by producing an advertising poster in which they explain to potential donors that the equipment they give to the project will be loaned free of charge to children who want to participate in a sport or activity but lack the necessary equipment. Specifying that any equipment that is donated must be in usable shape, the poster also advertises that any child who wants to borrow equipment may do so. The purpose of the locker is to extend the useful life of equipment that the original owner has outgrown, so anyone, regardless of family income, may borrow the equipment. The teacher gets permission to produce a supply of these posters—say, 100 of them—using school duplicating equipment. There are several potential sources of poster board including the school, the PTO, and community service groups. If the teacher has obtained a minigrant to fund the service learning project, he or she can buy poster supplies using grant money, or students may each contribute a small amount—say, 50 cents—toward purchasing these supplies. Students place these posters in classrooms in their school and on announcement bulletin boards in common areas such as the school attendance office and the cafeteria. Students ask local business owners or managers for permission to place posters in store windows or on store bulletin boards.

The teacher finds a community partner such as the park district, a community center, a recreation center, a community club, or an extramural program sponsored by the school itself that can give the students a facility in which they can sort, catalog, and store the equipment that they collect. The teacher or students also set up an electronic database that students use to inventory the donated items and to keep track of them once the lending locker begins loaning equipment. Once the partner and the site are in place and the database is ready for use, students begin collecting the equipment.

The teacher assigns students to base teams of four to six members. Each base team is in charge of a certain type of equipment. The students decide, for example, which team is responsible for each of the following categories of items: in-line and roller skates, hockey skates and sticks, protective knee and elbow pads, helmets, figure skates, baseball equipment, and so on. Each team has its own category of equipment that it inventories, cleans, and manages.

Keeping Records and Building a Portfolio

For each respective type of equipment, each team catalogs the items that are available using the electronic database. The catalog information includes a brief description of each item: the size of the item; its current condition; the name, address, and telephone number of the person who checked out the item; and the date that the item is due to be returned. The teacher and students can practice entering this information into the electronic database and printing copies of the database when the information from all of the teams has been recorded.

Students need to obtain boxes or bins to store sorted equipment by size and type, and the locker room needs some shelves. The teacher asks the community partner if it can provide these items. If it cannot, the teacher uses grant money to set up the locker room; if grant money is not available, the teacher asks the PTO, interested parents, or the school for help with funding. Locker room shelves that the teacher, students, school staff, parents, or community partner members build from supplies purchased at a home supply center or lumber yard often provide greater flexibility than prebuilt shelving units.

Each team takes its turn running the lending locker. The class uses new advertising flyers posted in classrooms in the school and in businesses around the community to inform other students and parents of the dates and times that the lending locker will be open for service. Students and teacher contact the local newspaper to ask about placing a community service advertisement. In many communities, businesses provide funding for this type of advertising so that nonprofit groups can advertise products or services at no charge to themselves. Children who want to check out equipment do so by coming to the locker room when it is open, selecting the equipment, trying it out for size, and signing a form promising to take care of the equipment. Here is a sample checkout form:

LENDING LOCKER EQUIPMENT CHECKOUT

Student's name: Date out:

Due in:

I promise to be careful with this equipment and to return it clean and in good condition.

Signed:

The students who are running the locker may decide that they want to have parents cosign with young borrowers so that the parents are aware of the terms of the equipment checkout. Equipment is checked out—much as a book is checked out from a library—for a specified length of time. The rental is renewable as long as the borrower can show the lending locker that he or she still has the equipment and is keeping it in usable condition. Children return borrowed equipment during the lending locker's regular "business hours." When equipment is returned, the students who are serving as lending locker clerks evaluate the condition of the item, update that information in the database, and change the checkout information to show that the item has been returned. The lending locker works in much the same way as "loan closets" that make expensive medical equipment available to senior citizens or hospice patients, and students will want to find out more about these loan closets before they begin the project.

The teacher can schedule a field trip to a local medical equipment loan facility or other type of lending agency or ask a hospice worker or nurse to come to school to explain the equipment loan program to the students. The teacher needs to ask school administrators about procedures for bringing guest speakers into the school. Students are often unfamiliar with the lending closet concept, and hearing about it from someone who works there or visiting a hospice lending closet helps students understand the functioning of such a facility.

Once the lending locker is set up and functioning, the teacher asks students to keep a log of television, radio, or print ads for athletic equipment that they see or hear over a period of one week and to collect at least 10 of the print ads. When students have collected the information, the teacher asks them to meet in their base teams to compile a master list of the products and brands that were featured in the ads and the fitness activities for which people use these products. Teams then compare the list from the advertising with the information from the locker room database, and each student writes an essay about the influence advertising has on the kinds of activities that locker room donors take part in and the equipment that they choose. Students often find that organizing their thoughts before they write using an outline or graphic organizer facilitates the writing process. Each member of a base team has a copy of the team's master list, the locker room database, and the comparison. The print ads, copies of the team master list of ads and the locker room database, and the essay become part of each student's project portfolio.

Tapping Into Multiple Intelligences: Let's Get Visible!

Visual, Kinesthetic, and Intrapersonal Multiple Intelligences

Because some students are more comfortable when working visually, spatially, or kinesthetically than verbally, ask students to organize their thoughts using a mind map. Use Tony and Barry Buzan's model of mind mapping (1994), which relies heavily on color and images or graphics and is light on words. (I tell students to think of a mind map as a "photo album for the brain" because they'll be using words to caption images rather than to represent all of the information.)

Students develop mind maps using a few basic rules:

- Start the mind map in the center of blank white paper.
- Start with an image that represents the title or overall theme of the mind map.
- Make branches, using thick lines or arrows, leading out from the center for each subordinate idea or theme.
- Do each branch in a separate, bold color.
- Write key words on lines, and use both capitals and lowercase.
- Remember those images. Represent subthemes and their details using images. Use as few words as possible; use them to "caption" images.
- Think outside the paper. You can't run out of room; if you get close to the edge of the paper, tape on another sheet.

Show students some examples of mind maps and do a practice one together. Then ask base teams to develop a mind map "just for fun." Themes like party foods, awesome presents, leisure activities, or in-style clothes liberate creativity and help students learn the mind mapping process. Once they have practiced the process, have them do a mind map to organize their ideas for an essay, such as the lending locker essay. Students who are comfortable processing verbally find that strength enhanced by the prewriting brainstorming; students who are more comfortable processing visually, spatially, or kinesthetically find that they write more easily when they do a mind map first.

During the course of the school year, each student sets a personal fitness goal and chooses activities to help him or her reach that goal. These goals and plans are discussed with members of the base team. Students evaluate their progress toward their personal fitness goals by analyzing their fitness test scores for indications of improvement, and they use this self-evaluation to revise their fitness plans as needed. The teacher selects a standard fitness test that uses indicators such as resting and active pulse rate, blood pressure, and percentage of body fat analysis to determine personal fitness.

As the teacher emphasizes the importance of having a fitness plan, community use of lending locker equipment shows students that many community members promote and participate in activities that promote wellness. Each student's personal fitness goals, plans, and revisions are included in his or her project portfolio.

Students keep lending locker reflective logs so that they have a record of their participation in and learnings from the project. Each student does a reflective log entry after designing the posters; distributing posters to school classrooms and community businesses; collecting, sorting, and cataloging equipment; and working as a checkout or checkin clerk at the lending locker. Student copies of the posters and the reflective log become part of each student's project portfolio.

Exemplary Project: Foster Care Holiday Boxes

This project engages middle school students in partnering with a local community agency to provide foster children with holiday presents. Stephanie Smith, an AmeriCorps volunteer who worked with the students, described the project:

> Our school, in cooperation with the local Family Independence Agency, participates in a "Foster Care Box" drive each year during the holiday season. Each classroom "adopts" one or more foster children who reside in our county and fills boxes with presents such as clothing, school supplies, games, and toys.

The project begins when the community partner provides students with "Santa Lists" from foster children. Each foster child is identified by gender and age only. The students then acquire funds in a variety of ways from direct fundraising to personal contributions. Students use their math skills to calculate the cost of obtaining the items on each list. Based on their totals and available funds, the students decide how many foster children they can sponsor. They then use the monies to purchase school supplies, toys, games, clothing, and other items for foster children.

The students also use their math skills to compute the amount of gift wrap needed to make the "care boxes" holiday bright. The community agency collects and distributes the boxes, and foster children write thank you notes to the students who participated in the project. The project is growing according to Smith, who explained,

> This project has become very popular in our school. The students are never required to continue it; however, they have chosen to continue it for the past three years. The first year we sponsored about 12 foster children, and this past year we were able to sponsor 29.

Describing the experience, Smith explained,

> In the beginning, the most discouraging roadblock was a lack of sensitivity for those involved in the issue. This roadblock was addressed several ways. Students researched the reasons behind children being placed in foster care and looked at the number of children who are in the foster care system. We also had a foster care mother come into the class, talk about her experiences, and answer any questions. We have found that at the middle school level, a lack of sensitivity is often a lack of awareness. Once students had the information along with real-life experiences, this project became not only a mission but a passion.

Smith explained how the students benefited from this project:

> At the middle school level, there is increased difficulty in connecting projects that students create to the curriculum. This project addressed surface area (covering the boxes with wrap), scale factor (scale drawings of designs to be put on the wrap), graphing and comparing local and national data, using data to make predictions, and population densities. The students learn and work with all these concepts and understand their place in a real-life context. It's funny how the top two benefits are never "We improved test scores" or "My students passed their standard." There's so much more to learning than paper, pencil, and book. The students can learn and be a part of the community.

ASSESSING RISKS: ESTABLISHING PROTOCOLS FOR HEALTH AND SAFETY

Some community members see the lending locker as an opportunity to clean out the garage, and they need to know that equipment that is donated must be usable. The teacher, adults from the community partner agency, parents, or older siblings will want to check all equipment for usability before accepting a donation. Helmets must have intact protective padding and straps, and they cannot be cracked. Gloves and pads must not have rips or tears, and they must have good life left in their cushioning material. Skates or shoes of any kind must be free of rips and holes and have strong laces and eyelets.

The teacher needs to check with the administration on all liability issues before he or she and the students plunge into this project. The school, teacher, and students will not operate the lending locker if it exposes them to personal liability for injuries that occur when borrowers are using the equipment. A separate and very important issue is liability incurred by bringing in outside speakers. Some states have laws governing visits to schools by outsiders, and teachers and administration want to be sure that they are not exposing students to unnecessary risk by bringing in "expert speakers."

The teacher or another adult needs to monitor students as they work in the lending locker. If students need to use ladders or step stools to access equipment, the teacher demonstrates and has students rehearse safe practices. The teacher also demonstrates safe methods of lifting heavy objects and gives students a chance to practice lifting with their legs, not with their backs. Each student worker needs to sign a statement agreeing to use donated equipment only with permission and supervision from the teacher or another adult. Accidents can happen when students decide to play with donated equipment that they are cataloging or storing, and the adult can provide first aid and obtain emergency help as needed.

SELECTING THE SERVICE LEARNING FOCUS: SHARING FITNESS EQUIPMENT WITH THE COMMUNITY

The teacher can create interest in this service learning project by asking students to brainstorm a list of physical activities that promote fitness and good health. Students usually include such activities as skateboarding; playing baseball, soccer, or hockey; running; riding a bicycle; in-line skating; and swimming in their lists. Then the teacher might ask, "Can you think of any roadblocks to doing any of these activities? What are some reasons why community members would not choose one of these activities as a way to maintain good fitness? Why might they want to donate equipment to the locker?"

As students brainstorm some answers to such questions, they list possibilities:

- Equipment is often expensive.
- People lose interest in an activity and do not use the equipment.
- Children outgrow equipment and do not receive new equipment that fits.
- Someone who is injured or ill may have restricted activity.

- Some activities are seasonal, so equipment is not used during several months of the year.
- Some activities are tailored to specific age groups.

Here is one scenario: A student says,

"My sister got a good bike helmet. She wore it two summers ago, and by this summer she outgrew it. My mom and dad don't want the garage filling up with stuff we don't use, and the helmet is just sitting there, and they don't like that."

Then the teacher asks, "Why can't you borrow your sister's helmet?"

The student says, "She's my little sister and her helmet is too small for me."

The teacher responds,

"Can you think of a way that we could help all of the students in the school have good athletic equipment AND get unused "stuff" out of people's garages? How could we help someone else use your sister's bicycle helmet that's now too small? Do you think this is something that our school community needs—a way for students to borrow sports equipment?"

Making Connections With the Community

At this point, the teacher goes on to explain to students that what he or she has in mind is a lending locker, run like a medical loan closet. The teacher asks students to discuss the idea with their families to find out if the adults in the community would be interested in the project. The teacher tells students that they will be charting their own fitness throughout the school year and that doing this project helps them maintain an awareness of the importance of being physically fit while doing something to encourage others to participate in healthy activities.

The class and teacher will want to evaluate the service project idea before they continue, using a rubric such as the one shown in Figure 3.1. Each student rates the factors individually; the teacher tabulates the responses; and students then calculate an average ranking for each of the factors. Students and teacher may agree to weight the factors for importance. For example, teacher and students often agree that a long or short project length is not as important a factor as community need, appropriateness to learning the curricular goals, and wellness.

WORKING WITH A COMMUNITY PARTNER

To obtain answers to important questions—like liability for injuries—the teacher discusses the idea for this project with the school principal before looking outside of the school for a community partner. Because this service learning project involves loaning athletic equipment to other students and community members and the goal is helping all students meet age-appropriate fitness standards and being aware of the importance of a lifestyle that promotes fitness, the school may decide to become the community partner for this project.

Ranking Criteria	1 (high)	2 (medium)	3 (low)	Comments
Figure 3.1 Sample Project Evaluation Rubric: The Lending Locker				
Interest	X			We could borrow equipment from the locker.
Need	X			Athletic equipment is very expensive, and lots of kids outgrow such purchases before they wear out.
Accessibility	X			We can use an old storage room in the community recreation center, right across the street from the school.
Appropriateness	X			We have the skills to do the work, and we need to meet fitness standards.
Time Frame	X			We'll open two afternoons a month. Each team will run the locker room twice during the school year. We'll all be busy during start-up, sorting, cataloging, and setting up the lending locker.

If school sponsorship is not viable for the lending locker project, the teacher can contact the community park district or recreation director, the community recreation center, or a community fitness club, asking one of these organizations to be the project partner. The teacher will want to inform the community agency that students need (a) a large room where they can store the athletic equipment, shelves, bins, or boxes for keeping the equipment sorted by type and size and (b) access to the lending locker storage facility. The community partner and the teacher will need to work out details about where the locker room will be, how students obtain access, and who supplies the bins, boxes, and shelves before finalizing the agreement. The teacher asks the community partner to select someone to be a liaison to the class during the course of the project. Students find that a community "closet" agency, such as a medical equipment loan agency, is a valuable advice-giving partner while they are running the lending locker. For more information about loan closets, students can go online and find Web sites using "loan closets" as the key phrase. The teacher, parents, or other adults will want to supervise students who are doing Internet searches.

The best piece of advice I can offer to teachers who want to get started in service learning is to get support. Get support from your building administrator, get support from a parent and/or volunteer to help monitor the students planning various activities, and most importantly, get support from your students by letting them create and plan the entire project. Your students have to be the bulb of the "flashlight" so to speak. You can turn on the switch, but without them the light will never come on. When the students are active planners, you'll see the light shine. When students are able to develop a project and see its positive impact, they become catalysts for change in so many ways.

—Stephanie Smith, AmeriCorps Volunteer, Ionia, MI

ALIGNING SERVICE AND EDUCATIONAL GOALS

Students who are involved in this service learning project are expected to meet age-appropriate, health-related fitness standards (physical education). The teacher gives each student an age-appropriate fitness test during each quarter of the school year to emphasize the curricular goal of maintaining age-appropriate fitness. Collecting the athletic equipment, sorting it, cataloging it, and taking a turn at running the lending locker help all students develop a greater awareness of a variety of activities that can promote fitness, and they see that these are activities that can be done by people of all ages.

As students gain access to athletic equipment through the lending locker, they often decide to select and participate in varied physical activities in order to improve physical fitness (the goal of physical education). Because students are doing activities—both in and out of school—to increase their overall physical fitness, these students are more aware of the link between personal "healthy behaviors" and individual well-being (the goal of a health and fitness program). As students look at the equipment that is donated to the lending locker, they write their project essays, linking product choice to advertising and identifying how the media influence health behaviors and choices. Students use mind mapping, graphic organizers, or outlines to organize the information before writing the essays.

Students demonstrate their ability to identify computers as tools for storing and accessing information and to use or prepare a database to enter and edit data and to find records (instructional technologies). Each student also writes using appropriate grammar, sentence structure, and precise vocabulary (language arts). This service project gives students an opportunity to practice and refine their computer and writing skills as they focus on physical fitness and its importance on personal wellness.

Student Responsibilities and Curricular Areas

Addressing another curricular goal, students can calculate the "value of service" of a piece of equipment (math). They can assign a dollar value to each piece of equipment, say, half the value of the new piece. If a new pair of in-line skates, for example, would cost $100, the students say that the value of the loaner skates is $50. The "value of service" is calculated using the following formula:

Value of equipment × number of times used = value of service

This valuation of service shows how much money members of the community save by using the services of the lending locker, and the number of times an item is used is an indicator of the community's commitment to reusing and recycling items.

In terms of service learning in general, the lending locker gives students an opportunity to identify the needs of the community. As students collect equipment, organize it, and run the locker room, they are performing meaningful service learning that demonstrates their understanding of community resources. Students are improving the quality of life in the community by making the athletic equipment available to other students, and they demonstrate that they realize the significance of their service learning experience through entries they write or sketch in their reflective logs.

As students manage the lending locker, they learn about the "big idea" of sharing. From the time that most students are old enough to play with others, adults in their lives encourage them to share what they have with others. As students see other students bringing good outgrown athletic equipment to the locker, they see the opportunities that sharing can give to other children and the community. The teacher may comment about how sharing is perceived in different cultures. For instance, traditionally the Navajo teach their children that sharing expands the spirit and hoarding narrows it. Students have an opportunity to experience empathetic and ethical growth as they run the lending locker.

From the time that students first hear about environmentalism, they are told that it is environmentally friendly behavior to "reduce, reuse, and recycle." The lending locker service learning project targets reuse. In doing the project, students are keeping used, outgrown, but still usable athletic equipment from going to a landfill. Items that are broken or "used up" are discarded, and this probably happens only after many children have used a piece of equipment. This kind of reuse is a fact of life in large families. Clothing, toys, and sports gear are passed from an older sibling to a younger one as a matter of course. In smaller families, this kind of reuse does not occur as easily or naturally. The lending locker is one way that students can learn to reuse and share by helping others find and borrow athletic equipment that can be a valuable community resource. For a summary of such project factors, see Figure 3.2 for a model alignment of service and educational goals.

Reciprocity: The Community of Learners

The lending locker benefits both students who contribute to or borrow from the locker and their families. Contributing families appreciate having an outlet for athletic equipment that is no longer used by any family members. Since the rapid growth of the environmental movement raised consciousness about the benefits of reusing and recycling, a large number of households have searched for ways to

Figure 3.2   The Lending Locker: Aligning Service and Educational Goals

Major Subject	Learning Goals	Life Skills	Big Ideas	Service Actions
Physical Education **Health**	Fitness standards Fitness planning Effect of behavior on health	Maintaining fitness through regular exercise	Sharing Reusing and recycling products	Personal fitness goals Personal exercise plan
Instructional Technology	Using a database	Identifying usefulness of computers to store information	Archival records	Maintaining a database inventory
Language Arts	Clear writing Precise use of language Narrative flow	Clear, precise communication	Importance of sharing Conserving by reusing and recycling products	Writing advertising Developing check-out form Checking in equipment in the lending locker
Mathematics	Inventory Classification Computation	Keeping accurate records Precision in calculating	Archival records Patterning	Doing and maintaining the inventory records Calculating the "value of service"

reduce the amount of solid waste that they produce. Adults in these families feel good about sharing unwanted items with other families in the community, and they appreciate the lessons in sharing that the lending locker teaches their children. Community residents, through this sharing, connect with each other in new, positive ways. They become more aware of the wants or needs of each other and more appreciative of the ways in which they can support each other. The rapidly accelerating pace of daily living often disrupts ties among neighbors, let alone among more distant community residents. The shared experience of the lending locker draws people back together.

Availability of equipment from the lending locker helps borrowers maintain exercise programs that are integral to healthy lifestyles. Adults as well as children may find some equipment that they can use. For example, some adults with smaller feet may be able to wear in-line skates or ski boots that no longer fit adolescent students. As family members see students keeping fitness logs, writing fitness plans, and analyzing the results of fitness tests, they become more aware of the importance of exercise in daily life. Many physicians say that the single most important contributor to overall health—the factor that lowers blood pressure, reduces blood sugar, burns calories, boosts the metabolic rate, improves the lipid profile, and improves cognition—is exercise. By modeling commitment to their exercise programs, students teach community members how to make exercise a part of their lives. Stephen Covey in *The Seven Habits of Highly Effective People* (1989) made "Sharpen the Sword" his seventh habit because he recognizes the importance of and need for regular physical exercise and reconnecting with community to overall physical and mental health.

MANAGING THE SERVICE PROJECT: THE LENDING LOCKER

Careful planning and management by the teacher are vital to the success of this service learning project. The teacher needs to pay attention to the site and preparation of the locker room or storage area, the accuracy of the information in the database, and staffing the locker room. The teacher also needs to keep the students focused on the curricular goal of maintaining and improving health and fitness. The management plan for the project needs periodic review and revision as the project moves along. One way to organize the management plan is shown in Figure 3.3.

FOSTERING REFLECTIVE LEARNING

Every student does a reflective log entry after planning and distributing both posters, collecting and cataloging equipment, helping to set up the locker room, and serving as a checkout clerk. The vocabulary that the teacher uses to focus the reflections is age appropriate for the grade level of the students; older students are encouraged to consider a greater variety of ideas than younger ones. The basic elements of all of the reflective logs focus on the same ideas: What is the need for the service? What did the student do well? What did the student learn about academic content and skills, life skills, and service skills by doing the community service?

For strategies to prompt reflections, see the reflective logs for the elementary, middle school, and high school levels at the end of this chapter. These models consist of sentence stems or starters and open-ended questions about the lending locker service learning project.

The use of the reflective log or journal reinforces content learning and helps the students understand how they are helpful to their community as well as their personal strengths and areas for personal goal setting and improvement. Reflection is one of the tools that make service learning particularly valuable to students.

ASSESSMENT AND EVALUATION

The teacher does some assessment of content learning using class discussions, baseteam sharing sessions, goal setting, and personal fitness planning. The teacher also evaluates physical fitness progress by giving each student a fitness test and discussing the results with the student. Before students begin the writing assignment, the teacher gives them a rubric that is used to score the final draft of each assignment.

Figure 3.3 Management Plan: The Lending Locker

Phase	Planning	Monitoring	Evaluating
1	Contact school principal to discuss partnership. Contact other community agencies as needed. Write letter explaining the project to students and parents, asking for parent volunteers to help in setting up and supervising the locker room or storage area.	Maintain contact with project liaison. Have students and families evaluate the need for a lending locker in the school community.	Discuss student and family evaluations of project. Confirm project selection.
2	Discuss project with students. Hand out assignment sheet. Discuss reflective logs. Plan "Call for Donations" posters. Send home letters to parents, including written permission slips and project calendars. Assign base teams. Begin focus on fitness. Give fitness test 1. Confirm parent helpers.	Collect signed parent permits. Make a list of names and phone numbers of parent helpers. Duplicate and display posters. Give first fitness tests. Set up electronic database for cataloging donated equipment.	Revise calendar as needed. Discuss importance of activity on fitness and wellness.
3	Collect initial equipment donations. Base teams sort and catalog. Organize locker room with help from parents. Plan "Lending Locker Schedule" poster. Assign media advertising survey. Students write personal fitness goals and plans. Do fitness test 2.	Duplicate and display posters. Open locker room for equipment checkout and checkin. Base do teams master list of ads; compare with database printout. Write "Influence of Advertising on Equipment and Activity Choice" essays. Spot-check reflection logs.	Read and score essays. Evaluate inventory—Is more needed? Evaluate condition of returned equipment.
4	Do follow-up fitness test 3. Continue equipment collection and cataloging. Continue lending locker operation.	Evaluate fitness scores for maintenance or improvement of fitness. Test electronic database skills by asking individual students to enter, revise, and find records.	Students evaluate fitness activity goals and plans with base teammates. Students revise plans to improve them. Evaluate operation of the locker room and condition of returned equipment. Give students feedback about their computer skills.
5	Do final fitness tests. Celebrate project completion by writing a "will" asking future classes to continue the project. Share portfolios in base teams. Write whole-class letter to community liaison saying, "Thank you for your help." Students and teacher each write one goal for future personal service work.	"Eavesdrop" on portfolio sharing. Ask students to tell each other their greatest learning AHA!, their most burning unanswered question, what they liked most about the project, what they found least comfortable, what they felt they did best, and what they would do differently (and better) next time.	Students and teacher discuss project strengths and areas for improvement. Each person shares with whole class his or her greatest AHA! and personal goal for future service work.

He or she shows them how the rubric is used to score written work and shares with them some writing exemplars so that students understand the rubric scoring of excellent, acceptable, and unacceptable writing. Students can then use the rubric to self-evaluate the quality of their rough drafts and improve their own written work. A sample rubric for scoring student writing is included in the Reproducible Masters section at the end of this book.

Each student also assembles a project portfolio that includes written work, graphic work, the reflective log, quiz and test scores, and other evidences of learning that complete the picture of the student's learning that resulted from the project.

Each student has specific portfolio pieces for this project:

- The reflective log
- "Call for Donations" poster
- "Lending Locker Schedule" poster
- Print advertisements for athletic products
- Base-team master list of advertised athletic equipment
- Essay: "The Influence of Advertising on Choices of Athletic Activities and Equipment"
- Results of fitness tests
- Personal fitness goal and plan, and revisions of the plan
- Greatest AHA! and personal service goal
- Three other evidences of learning chosen by the student

These last three portfolio pieces are required. They may include videotapes, photos, additional visual or writing products, interviews with athletes or fitness experts, or ideas for related service projects that the student has brainstormed individually, with his base team, or with the whole class.

Each student shares his or her portfolio with base-group teammates during the project celebration. This final feedback helps students realize how much they have learned about course content and themselves as service-givers by doing this project.

The teacher's goals for student fitness are realized if these students continue to participate in activities that promote age-appropriate fitness and general personal wellness. Establishing the habit of exercise when students are young is an effective way for teachers to reach these goals. Students who learn about fitness in the context of the lending locker service project are more likely to remember what they have learned longer and more effortlessly and to maintain good health habits.

Elementary Reflective Log

My lending locker job was . . .	This helps the lending locker project run smoothly because . . .

Here's what I learned about
 	
   • sorting/inventorying/clerking:
 	
   • myself:
 	
   • helping other students:
	What I did well was . . .

I want to share this big idea because . . .	What I can do better next time is . . .

Middle School Reflective Log

Today's lending locker job was . . .

I helped other students by . . .

Here are my most important learnings about my personal fitness plan and how it is working:

- Sharing, recycling, and me:

- doing community service:

My best actions and thoughts were . . .

Next time I want to improve . . .

High School Reflective Log

My new thoughts and feelings about sharing and recycling are . . .
My reasons for focusing on those thoughts and feelings are . . .
Some specific fitness skills I use well are . . .
Other ways that I can share ideas or products are . . .
Other times when I can recycle are . . .
My greatest insight about the importance of doing community service is . . .
My feelings about my role as a member of this community are . . .
The personal strengths I brought to the project today are . . .
Next time I want to strengthen . . .

4

The Hygiene Tree

A Consumer Education and Health Service Learning Project

DESCRIPTION OF THE PROJECT

As students do this project, they brainstorm a list of health care products that they consider to be necessary for good personal hygiene, obtain enough items of each product to make up 50 personal hygiene kits, package the personal hygiene kits, and put the kits in or on a "tree," a device for holding or displaying the kits. Students design and construct the display tree, and they place it with a local social service organization that distributes the hygiene kits to the homeless or to low-income community residents.

The teacher begins the brainstorm of health care products by asking students, "What personal hygiene actions or routines do you or adults in your family do every day?" Students probably include toothbrushing and flossing, bathing or showering, washing their hair, and shaving. The teacher then asks, "Are there special personal hygiene actions that you use occasionally, as you need to, say, in case you have an accident?" Students probably answer that they would want to use hydrogen peroxide to clean out a cut, antibiotic ointment to prevent infection, and adhesive bandages to protect cuts and sores. The teacher then says, "Let's look at our list of personal hygiene actions or routines and develop a list of the products that we use, regularly or as needed, for personal hygiene." Here is a sample personal and family hygiene list:

- Toothpaste
- Mouthwash
- Dental floss
- Bath soap
- Shampoo
- Conditioner
- Shaving cream
- Disposable shavers
- Hydrogen peroxide
- First-aid ointment or cream
- Adhesive bandages (plastic strips)
- Sterile gauze pads
- First-aid adhesive tape

In a typical scenario, the teacher asks, "Are there any items on the list that we want to omit? Do you have any ideas about shortening the list?" One student says that hair conditioner is not essential for personal hygiene. Someone else suggests that plastic adhesive bandages (plastic strips) come in packages that contain a variety of sizes, and people can often use large ones in place of the sterile pads and first-aid tape. Another student remarks that soap could be used in place of shaving cream. The teacher places a mark beside those items to indicate that they could be substituted for without sacrificing good personal hygiene. At this time, students also offer additions to the list, such as a tool for cleaning and clipping fingernails and a comb. Students negotiate including or removing items from the list; for example, about the shaving cream a student says, "Shaving cream really does protect my dad's face better than soap." The class revisits the list in a few days to do a final assessment and revision.

Each student makes a personal copy of the final hygiene product list to put in the project portfolio. Here is one example of a final list:

- Toothpaste
- Mouthwash
- Dental floss
- Bath soap
- Shampoo
- Shaving cream
- Disposable shavers
- Hydrogen peroxide
- First-aid ointment or cream
- Adhesive bandages—variety pack
- Nail clipper/nail file
- Comb

To focus on the importance of personal hygiene and its implications for wellness, each student then writes an essay describing his or her personal hygiene routine and practices. The teacher asks students to include both routine and nonroutine practices in the essay. The teacher says, "What do you really do if you get a cut? How does that help you? How does it help protect those around you?" The teacher suggests a variety of prewriting tools for organizing thinking and asks each student to place a copy of the prewriting organizer and the final essay in his or her project portfolio.

Once the hygiene products list is finalized, the teacher and students explore the possibility of the class assembling personal hygiene kits to give to the homeless or to low-income families in the community. The teacher and students contact local social service organizations and establish a partnership, and the social service agency locates and identifies the homeless or low-income residents who will receive the kits that the students make. Students who are members of religious congregations often have knowledge of outreach programs run by these establishments. In many communities, religious congregations cooperate with each other to provide services to the homeless, needy, or to senior citizens. Because these programs have an identified clientele, they can be excellent community partners for this service learning project.

The teacher and class discuss how to fund the project. In many instances, the teacher has applied for and received grant funding for the project prior to the start of the school year. If grant money is not available, each student makes a small contribution toward the purchase of the personal hygiene products. The Parent-Teacher Organization (PTO), an interested parents' group, or the school can often contribute funds to a hygiene tree project. In some cases, small groups of students volunteer to pool their funds to buy one or two of the products on the list. Students can ask parents who travel for business or pleasure to contribute the small bars of soap and bottles of shampoo that chain hotels and motels place in their bathrooms to The Hygiene Tree service learning project.

At this point, the teacher and students sometimes ask the school for permission to do some kind of fundraiser, such as a bake sale or an auction of personal services. When students are involved in raising the funds that are needed for the project, they become more aware of just how much money is really needed to provide these personal hygiene items for one person. If the class is making a large number of personal hygiene kits, students and teacher sometimes need to combine personal contributions, fundraising, and help from another source to pool all of the money that is needed for the project.

To decide how much money they need, the teacher and the students make a trip to a store that sells personal hygiene products. The teacher asks, "Where do you think we'll get the largest amount of product for our money? What kind of store do we want to visit?" Students probably suggest a large discount store. The teacher arranges for the whole class to visit the store together and asks that parents and other community volunteers coordinate student team efforts to collect price information. The teacher makes arrangements for a field trip to the store during school hours, if such arrangements work out with the store management and school administration. A model field trip plan follows:

Before making the store visit, students are grouped in teams of three and are given a copy of the personal hygiene products list. Roles are assigned as follows:

- One person in each team is the scout who locates the products in the store.
- A second teammate is the clerk who reads the price of a few different brands of each product aloud to his or her teammates.
- The third teammate is the bookkeeper who records the names and prices of the products on the team copy of the hygiene products list.

A parent or other adult supervisor escorts each team and helps younger students locate the aisles containing the products. The teacher encourages teams to try to find products that represent the best economy—the most "bang for the buck." Students want to price small plastic bags that can be used as the containers to hold the hygiene tree kits. The teacher makes a copy of the store products price list for each member of each team, and the store products price list is included in each student's project portfolio.

Tapping Into Multiple Intelligences: The Role of Rubrics

Logical, Verbal, and Intrapersonal Multiple Intelligences

Students produce their best work when they know in advance what excellent work looks like. They need information about the elements that make up the piece of work, whether it is an essay, a poster, a song or jingle, or any other performance or product. One information-gathering tool that teachers can build and share with students is a rubric that can be used to score individual or team products or performances. An advantage to making students part of the rubric-building process is that they buy into its use; they have ownership of the rubric. If brainstorming the rubric with students is seen as too time-consuming, the teacher can give each student a copy of a predesigned tool and say, "This is a rubric that I'm thinking about using to score your product/performance. Please look it over and be ready to offer opinions and suggestions about changes when you come to class two days from now." Giving students the opportunity to fine-tune the rubric is an alternative way of giving them some ownership.

- To design a rubric, first brainstorm a list of the important elements of the work, the elements that the teacher examines in determining the quality of the work. These "look-at" elements are called "criteria."
- Next, brainstorm brief descriptions of how these elements look when they are *excellent, acceptable,* or *unacceptable.* These descriptions are called "indicators," and it is important that they be stated as clearly as possible. Whenever possible, write indicators that are *quantitative.* Instead of saying, "Writing contains few misspellings," say, "Writing contains zero to two misspelled words."
- Arrange the elements in a grid with criteria listed vertically down the left side of the rubric and indicators listed horizontally across the top as shown below:

Indicators / Criteria	Excellent	Acceptable	Unacceptable	Absent

- Assign point values to the indicator categories if the rubric is used to score and evaluate (grade) a product or performance.
- Show students examples of work and how that work was scored using the rubric. Discuss the scoring so that students understand how it is done.
- Give each student a copy of the scoring rubric when making an assignment. Encourage them to use the rubric to self-evaluate initial versions of products or performances and revise work before it is submitted for grading.

When students know the "score" before they begin an assignment, they do better work, make better products, and present better performances *and* are more comfortable with the grading process. Rubrics demystify grading, and if grading is not mysterious, students do not complain that it is not fair.

Keeping Records and Building a Portfolio

Back at school, each team calculates the cost of making one personal hygiene kit and the cost of making 50 such kits. Each team includes sales tax in its calculations, using the sales tax percentage provided by the teacher. In order to arrive at a final cost for each kit, students need to decide how many people can use the products from one kit and the length of time that a kit is intended to last. Students need to know how long a bar of soap lasts if it is used by one person to take one bath a day. They want similar information about toothpaste, shampoo, and the other products that go into the kit.

For example, if students decide that they want each kit to last one month for one person, they then decide what size of each product would be the best value for such a kit and calculate the cost accordingly. During a whole-class discussion, teams compare their answers and discover the bottom-line cost for the kits. This tells students how much money is needed to make the personal hygiene kits. Each student includes a copy of the calculations in his or her project portfolio.

Students will also want to decide how to make the actual tree for displaying the kits. Do they want something that is shaped like a tree, or do they want to use a large box or bin that has the picture of a tree on the outside? The latter has the advantage of being fairly easy to take to the community partner site. If they decide on a tree-shaped display, they ask the teacher or a parent to make a tree out of strips of wood or cut a tree shape out of a piece of plywood. Members of the class then paint or decorate the wooden tree before using it to display the hygiene kits. Another alternative is to find a family that is willing to donate a used artificial evergreen tree on which students could hang the kits. Whatever the decision, students need to figure the cost of materials for the hygiene tree into the overall project cost.

Once the money has been acquired or raised, the teacher, parent volunteers, or students with adult chaperones visit the store and purchase the personal hygiene products and the small bags needed to make the kits. The teacher or parent volunteers provide the materials needed to make the tree. Students make up the hygiene kits, decorate or assemble the tree, and prepare the kits and the tree for delivery to the community partner. The teacher and students contact the partner to schedule a delivery date and time. Students, teacher, and adult chaperones take the personal hygiene kits to the partner's location. The partner then distributes the kits to homeless or low-income community residents who need the products.

Each student keeps a reflective log. He or she makes an entry after the initial hygiene product brainstorm, the visit to the store to get price information, the fundraising activities, the materials purchase, the assembly of the hygiene kits, and the delivery of the kits to the partner. Students share their log entries with members of their base teams so that they can give themselves and each other feedback to make their learning more meaningful and more permanent.

ASSESSING RISKS: ESTABLISHING PROTOCOLS FOR HEALTH AND SAFETY

Most school districts have established policies and procedures for field trips, and the teacher and students need to follow all such procedures during the trips to stores to obtain pricing information and the hygiene products. Adults who act as chaperones must meet all requirements for background screening. Students must know what to do in case they become accidentally separated from the group.

Before inviting a liaison from the community partner to come and speak to the class, students and teacher need to talk with the administration to learn about school policy, which may require that all outside visitors pass a background check before meeting with students on school grounds. Adult representatives from service organizations may already have this clearance; if they do not, they need to obtain it before they can meet with students in the classroom.

If students need to do painting to make the hygiene tree, they need to practice safe techniques for opening, mixing, and closing paint cans or for using spray cans. Students and teacher need to research pigments used to color paints to be sure that they are nontoxic. Water-based latex paints are better for indoor use because their fumes are less irritating. Proper cleanup of materials, surfaces, and hands is a must, and students need to wear clothing that covers as much skin as possible to minimize contact with paints and cleaners.

If the class receives an old artificial evergreen tree, the teacher or another adult needs to inspect the parts, looking for problems that could cause branches to fall off the tree or the tree to be unstable. No one wants a tree that is fully decorated with hygiene kits to fall and possibly hurt a passerby. Students need to use care when they insert branches into the tree trunk to avoid accidental cuts or punctures. As always, students must be told to report any and all accidents, however minor they may seem, to the teacher or an adult volunteer.

SELECTING THE SERVICE LEARNING FOCUS: PERSONAL HYGIENE PRODUCTS FOR THE HOMELESS AND THE NEEDY

As a possible scenario, the teacher may introduces the class to this project by saying,

> Last year, a person from a social services organization (e.g., Salvation Army, Red Cross, a veterans' group, Rotary Club, Lions Club, or other group) told me that many low-income families in our community were having a problem affording personal hygiene products. Because we study the importance of good personal hygiene to individual and community wellness, I suggested to last year's class that we make up kits containing personal hygiene products to distribute to low-income families through this social services organization. The class members said that this service learning project would reinforce their use of good personal habits and make a contribution to the community. This service project was done last year with positive results. The students thought that the project was so helpful that they wanted to pass it along to you, so they wrote a "will" doing just that. Let's discuss the possibility that you will continue the work that they started.

As students discuss the project, the teacher seriously considers any changes that this year's students want to make in the project. Several features that are already in place align strongly with goals; teachers do need to remember that students need to feel ownership in a service learning project in order to derive maximum learning from the experience.

Making Connections With the Community

At this point, students are given the assignment of determining just how great the need for this service is in their community. They are asked to discuss the project with their parents and to watch the local television newscasts, listen to local news on the radio, and read the newspaper for a two-week period, watching and listening for information about low-income families or the homeless. Students are directed to keep a record of what they learned about the problems of the homeless or low-income residents of the town, and they are encouraged to discuss with each other and the teacher what they learn from their parents and the local news media. If such arrangements can be made, a liaison from the social services organization that worked with the previous year's class comes to school and discusses the need for the project. At that time, students get information from the agency that is serving as the community partner.

The students and teacher evaluate the service learning idea using a rubric such as the one in Figure 4.1.

Each student individually ranks the criteria in the rubric, and then the teacher tallies the rankings. Students next compute an average ranking for each factor, as explained in Chapter 1. The class then weights the factors to determine the overall appropriateness of the project.

WORKING WITH A COMMUNITY PARTNER

The teacher and students contact social services organizations such as the Red Cross, Salvation Army, United Way, Catholic Charities, Jewish Community Servicers, Lutheran Child and Family Services, or service clubs such as the Rotary, Lions, Elks, Shriners, or Eagles to ask if the organization is willing to be the community partner for this service learning project. If a service organization or club is not interested in being the partner, it probably can suggest an organization or club that provides this type of service. Once the students and teacher have found a community partner agency, they will want to get the name of someone who can be the agency's liaison with the class.

Students and teachers who want to learn more about finding a community partner or get more information about doing a tree project may use a Web search engine to locate information. Key words like "mitten tree" or "St. Nicholas Project" used with Google or Yahoo! produce many Web sites with useful information. The teacher, parents, or other adult volunteers will need to supervise students whenever they do Internet searches.

ALIGNING SERVICE AND EDUCATIONAL GOALS

As students do this service learning project, their content work focuses on identifying important personal hygiene habits and the contribution that each habit makes to

| Figure 4.1 | Sample Project Evaluation Rubric: The Hygiene Tree |

| Ranking\
Criteria | 1\
(high) | 1\
(medium) | 3\
(low) | Comments |
|---|---|---|---|---|
| Interest | X | | | Good hygiene routines improve community wellness. |
| Need | X | | | Personal hygiene products can be too expensive for low-income families or the homeless to buy. |
| Accessibility | X | | | We can make the hygiene kits in class, and the teacher and parents or adults will help with visits to the store and the community partner site. |
| Appropriateness | X | | | We're never too young to practice good hygiene, and we can make up the hygiene kits ourselves. |
| Time Frame | X | | | This project can be done in two or three months. |

the wellness of the individual and the people around him or her. Because community wellness is so important, standards relating to this issue are threaded throughout grade levels and curricular areas.

Student Responsibilities and Curricular Areas

Students recognize issues related to personal and community wellness (consumer education), and they describe daily routines that affect personal and family wellness (consumer education). In addition, students analyze health information (health) and describe how the personal hygiene habits that they have identified as being important can promote good general individual health, helping to reduce the spread of certain contagious or infectious agents. Through their work with personal hygiene products, students show that they recognize the importance and function of health-promoting products (health). Also, they certainly are helping homeless and low-income residents of the community become aware of some of the health care services provided by social service organizations.

As students calculate the costs of the hygiene products kits, they compute with decimals, fractions, and percentages (mathematics) to determine how much of each product gives one person a one-month supply. Their writing shows that they can use appropriate paragraph and sentence structure and precise vocabulary (language arts) to communicate their ideas. As they do the project, students identify needs of the community and demonstrate civic responsibility (service learning). Making a hygiene tree aligns service to the homeless and low-income residents of the community with a wide range of curricular goals.

Medical advocates such as the Office of the U.S. Surgeon General emphasize the big ideas of healthy lifestyles and wellness. These advocates say that the best way for people to live happy, productive, healthy lives is to stop disease before it starts. The Hygiene Tree service learning project encourages students to identify the daily routines and other home health practices that can help them maintain good general health and prevent the spread of some diseases. In talking with their parents about the results of health care routines, students learn that dental hygiene is much less expensive (and more comfortable) than repair of cavities at the dentist. As students study the effects of home health routines, they discover that bathing, hand washing, and shampooing can help them avoid colds, flu, and other respiratory diseases and wash away fleas, ticks, and microscopic soil worms that can produce skin irritations and even cause Lyme disease or damage the gastrointestinal system.

As students research, they learn that cleaning cuts and scratches and treating them with antibiotic ointments prevent infection and that covering cuts can reduce the spread of blood-borne pathogens. Students learn that healthy lifestyles result in good job attendance and therefore enhance job success. As students compare their "illness feelings" with their "wellness feelings," they find that they are happier and have more fun when they are well. The Hygiene Tree service learning project helps students share the opportunity for good personal hygiene with others in the community as they learn about the personal benefits that they gain by using wellness habits. See Figure 4.2 for the alignment model for service and educational goals.

Reciprocity: The Community of Learners

As students learn language arts and mathematics skills and review or learn the importance of personal hygiene practices, they pass this information along to recipients of the hygiene kits in various ways. Students produce posters advertising the availability of the kits as soon as they have a community partner and a production deadline, and these posters include slogans promoting the importance of health-enhancing hygiene. They include information in each kit, much like the information that comes in packages of over-the-counter pharmaceuticals, with suggestions for use of products, benefits to personal and community wellness of good personal hygiene, and suggestions about other sources of these materials. If students do not make personal contact with the recipients of the hygiene kits, they still give homeless or needy community residents good information about improving their overall wellness.

Many needy or homeless people learned, at one time, the information that students give them. The material that the students produce reinforces and reviews

Figure 4.2 The Hygiene Tree: Aligning Service and Educational Goals				
Major Subject	**Learning Goals**	**Life Skills**	**Big Ideas**	**Service Actions**
Consumer Education	Wellness issues Hygiene routines that promote wellness	Maintaining wellness through personal hygiene and first-aid routines Being an informed consumer	Wellness Healthy lifestyles	Brainstorming the product list Purchasing products Obtaining funds
Health	Health-promoting products Preventing the spread of disease	Awareness of health-promoting and first-aid products	Healthy choices Informed consumerism	Personal hygiene Becoming aware of the problems of the homeless and poor
Language Arts	Clear writing Precise use of language	Clear, precise communication	Wellness Empathy	Writing essays and journals Discussing issues with community service liaisons
Mathematics	Precise calculation Using percentages, fractions, and decimals	Predicting amounts Precision in calculating	Estimating Proportionality	Calculating amounts/sizes of products to use in kits Calculating cost of kits

that prior learning. The recipients of the hygiene kits and the community partner learn to see the students in new ways, to see them as kind, caring people who want to reach out to all segments of the community. Seeing students with these new understandings is one of the most important learnings that hygiene kit recipients and community partners gain from this service learning project.

Some comments from community partners express these insights into students who participate in service learning projects:

- A trick is to provide a balance between giving youth a voice in planning and implementing service learning projects and giving students the focus and guidance that they need to have a successful experience.
- A goal is for students to be involved in doing such important and significant work that adults "sit up and take notice." Community partners who are committed to the service learning ideal want students to be more than token members of advisory boards.
- Focus on leadership development and team building empowers students and results in improved abilities to guide the service learning project.

(Johnson, M., 2001, p. 14)

MANAGING THE SERVICE PROJECT: THE HYGIENE TREE

Because this project requires the coordination of several different elements—doing the fund-obtaining to buy the hygiene products, buying the products, making the tree, making the kits, and delivering the finished hygiene tree to the service agency—the teacher will want to have a detailed management plan for the project. The teacher needs to review and revise the plan as the project moves along. This project can be carried over from year to year, so ongoing revision of the management plan really helps the teacher in the future. The grid shown in Figure 4.3 is a model management plan for the project.

FOSTERING REFLECTIVE LEARNING

Every student does a reflective log entry after the initial hygiene product list brainstorming, the discussion focusing on the need for the project (based on information obtained from parents and news media sources), the visit to the store to get price information, making the hygiene kits, and delivering the hygiene tree to the community partner for distribution of the kits. The vocabulary that the teacher uses to focus the reflections is age appropriate for the grade level of the students, and older students may be encouraged to consider a greater variety of ideas than younger ones. The basic elements of all of the reflective logs focus on the same ideas: What is the need for the service? What did the student do well? What did the student learn about academic content and skills, life skills, and service skills by doing the community service?

See the reflective logs for elementary, middle school, and high school levels at the end of this chapter for strategies to prompt reflections. These models consist of sentence stems or starters and open-ended questions about the service learning project.

The use of the reflective log reinforces content learning and helps the students understand how they are helpful to their community, as well as understand their personal strengths and areas for personal goal setting and improvement. It is one of the tools that make service learning particularly valuable to students.

Figure 4.3 Management Plan: The Hygiene Tree

Phase	Planning	Monitoring	Evaluating
1	Contact social service organization to arrange partnership. Discuss project with students. Write a letter asking for parent helpers. Write project description for parents and students, plans for reflective logs, assignments, and assessments. Send home letters to parents, including written permission slips and project calendars.	Maintain contact with service organization liaison. Have students and families evaluate the need for hygiene tree. Collect signed parent permission slips. Make a list of parent helpers with phone numbers.	Discuss student and family evaluations of project. Confirm project selection.
2	Brainstorm list of hygiene products for kit. Discuss "My Personal Hygiene Routine and Practices" writing assignment and reflection logs. Assign base teams. Assign collecting information from news media about homeless/low-income families in this town. Begin The Hygiene Tree unit.	Read and score "hygiene" essays. Discuss need for hygiene kits based on homeless/low-income family information collected from new sources.	Revise calendar as needed. Do content learning assessment: quizzes, tests, class discussion.
3	Visit store with parent chaperones to get price information. Decide on plans for the tree box, artificial tree, or one made of wood. Arrange for parent volunteer(s) to help with tree. Focus on impact of personal hygiene on community wellness (preventing spread of infection/contagion, for example). Arrange fundraising. Write kit inserts.	Do most calculations. Raise funds for purchase of hygiene products and tree materials. Spot-check reflective logs.	Students self-evaluate progress and discuss in base teams. More content learning assessment—math skills and impact of hygiene on community wellness. Share reflective log insights in base teams.
4	Buy hygiene products. Make hygiene kits. Put everything together to deliver to the social services organization.	Check hygiene kits for completeness. Arrange for delivery of hygiene tree. Check with parent chaperones. Deliver the tree. Spot-check reflective logs.	Final hygiene content test. Share reflective log insights in base teams.
5	Celebrate project completion by writing a "will" asking future classes to continue the project. Share portfolios in base teams. Write whole-class letter to the service organization liaison saying, "Thank you for your help." Students and teacher each write one goal for future personal service work.	"Eavesdrop" on portfolio sharing. Ask students to tell each other their greatest learning AHA!, their most burning unanswered question, what they liked most about the project, what they found least comfortable, what they felt they did best, and what they would do differently (and better) next time.	Students and teacher discuss project strengths and areas for improvement. Each person shares with whole class his or her greatest AHA! and personal goal for future service work.

Students always want to know how their project has affected others. We have received letters from the recipients of our foster care boxes and from the community partner. A 16-year-old recipient wrote: "I just wanted to thank you for the Christmas gift. It was amazing. I loved everything you put in it." Our community partner wrote:

> We cannot thank you and your students enough. Your great generosity is appreciated more than I can possibly express in words. I have received so many thank-yous from foster parents and can imagine all of the smiles and happy faces there will be on Christmas. You and your students have demonstrated the true spirit of this holiday season.

Another teacher who was involved in this project met a foster parent on the golf course last summer. The foster parent expressed how the foster care boxes were such a true gift last Christmas. She expressed her appreciation for such age-appropriate gifts. This parent had an older foster care child, whereas many gifts in the past have been geared toward younger children.

—Stephanie Smith, AmeriCorps Volunteer, Ionia, MI

ASSESSMENT AND EVALUATION

The teacher does some assessment of content learning using traditional tools such as class discussions, question-and-answer sessions, and paper-and-pencil quizzes and tests. Before students begin the writing assignments, the teacher gives them a rubric that is used to score the final draft of each assignment and shows them how the rubric is used to score written work. The teacher can do this by explaining how several sample writing pieces were scored using the rubric. Students can then use the rubric to self-evaluate the quality of their rough drafts and improve their own written work. A sample rubric for scoring student writing is included in the Reproducible Masters section at the end of this book.

Each student also assembles a project portfolio that includes written work, the reflective log, quiz or test scores, and other evidences of learning that complete the picture of the student's learning that resulted from the project.

Each student will have the following specific portfolio pieces:

- Reflective log
- Essay: "My Personal Hygiene Routine and Practices"
- "Need for the Service" notes: information collected from parents and the news media
- Brainstormed list of personal hygiene products for the kit
- Store prices of products list
- Total cost calculations

- Draft and final copies of information insert for hygiene kits
- Greatest AHA! and personal service goal
- Quiz and test scores
- Three other evidences of learning chosen by the student

Each student is required to select these final three pieces for the portfolio. They could include photos of the student doing some work involved in making the hygiene kits, videos, audiotaped interviews with community service people or personal reflections, or related extension projects brainstormed by the student or the whole class.

Each student shares his or her portfolio with base teammates during the project celebration. This final feedback helps students realize how much they have learned about course content and themselves as service-givers by doing The Hygiene Tree service learning project.

Elementary Reflective Log

Today's hygiene kit job was to . . .	This helps to get the kits made because . . .
This is what I learned about • hygiene/wellness/calculating/ communicating • how my feelings about the homeless and needy are changing	What I did well was . . .
Today's big idea is wellness/empathy/ sharing because . . .	What I can do better next time is . . .

Middle School Reflective Log

My hygiene kit job today was to . . .

This job helps get the kits made by . . .

Here are my most important learnings about

- hygiene and personal wellness/individual hygiene and community wellness

- the homeless or needy in the community, community service agencies, myself, and my attitudes toward community service:

- doing community service:

The learning I most want to remember is . . .

I want to remember this because . . .

My best actions and thoughts as I worked were . . .

Next time I want to improve . . .

Improvement is important to me because . . .

High School Reflective Log

My thoughts about

- hygiene and wellness or disease/empathy/sharing/service:

- some specific personal hygiene ideas, skills, or disease facts that I learned:

What I learned about the impact of social problems on the community is . . .

The life skill learning that I most want to remember is . . .

I can use this life skill again when I . . .

My greatest insight about the importance of doing community service is . . .

My thoughts and feelings about my role as a member of this community are . . .

My thoughts and feelings about community needs are . . .

The personal strengths I brought to the project today are . . .

Next time I want to strengthen . . .

PART II

Intermediate Service Learning Projects

5

Reading Pals

A Language Arts and
Life Skills Service Learning Project

DESCRIPTION OF THE PROJECT

Throughout much of history and in practically every culture, people have treasured the art of storytelling and have enjoyed listening to stories. The storyteller has always been a respected, valuable contributor to society. Students who do this service learning project become storytellers as they read to young children in day care centers or to senior citizens who live in elder care facilities. Each student partners with a young child or a senior, spends at least two hours a week reading aloud to that partner and discussing what has been read with the partner, and keeps a record of the reading that the student and partner have done.

While the student is doing the reading as part of this project, he or she also focuses on improving personal reading skills. Each student takes a reading comprehension test, as determined by the teacher, before the start of the project. The teacher scores the tests, and each student receives a copy of his or her test results to file in the project portfolio.

The student also answers questions in a reading strategies survey:

- Do you read all printed matter (fiction, newspapers, magazines, advertisements, nonfiction, and textbooks—such as math or science) at the same speed?
- If you vary your reading speed, which kinds of material do you read more slowly and why?
- Do you ever stop during reading and ask yourself, "Do I know what I just read?"

- Do you ever go back and reread? If so, why do you do this?
- Do you ever take notes as you read?
- If you take notes, what kind of reading are you doing, and why do you take the notes?
- Do you ever have questions as you read—questions that are not answered in what you are reading?
- If you ask questions, do you write them down and look for answers or just forget about them?
- As you read, are you ever aware of connections with prior knowledge? Do you make notes about these connections?
- When you read, do you ever make inferences about the author's personal politics, religious or cultural background, or personal circumstances?
- Do you think that knowing more about the author of a particular work might help you understand that selection better? When might that be the case?
- On a scale of 1–5, with 1 being your first choice and 5 your last choice, how likely are you to choose to read for pleasure?
- If reading were a color, what color would it be and why?
- If reading were a type of music, what type would it be and why?
- Draw a face that shows how you feel about reading—smiley, frowney, or neutral.

The teacher reads each student's answers to these survey questions and discusses the answers with the student. The teacher asks questions to clarify a student's answers or suggest areas for future focus. The student files the completed survey with the teacher's notes and his or her answers to the questions in the project portfolio.

As soon as the student has a reading partner and the student and partner have met, they discuss the partner's interests and use them as the basis for selecting a book to be read together. A young child may say, for example, that he or she "likes" animals, and the student can then look for stories about animals, farms, circuses, zoos, or animal care to read to the child. A senior citizen may have fond memories of traveling for pleasure and ask the student to find a book that describes a real or fictional sightseeing trip, voyage of discovery, mountain climbing expedition, or guided tour.

Keeping Records and Building a Portfolio

To find just the right book, the students begin by exploring what is available at the day care or elder care center library—whatever the case may be. If further searching is necessary, students visit the school and/or local public libraries. Community service resale shops often have a wide variety of books. These books are priced low, and resale shops, with their commitment to community service, often loan books to students who are involved in reading projects. Minigrant money, when available, covers the cost of buying books from these resale shops. Each student makes a list of sources of books and puts a copy of the list in his or her project portfolio.

When students decide to do this project, they have a variety of reasons. Some students remember their parents reading to them when they were preschoolers and the effect their parents' reading had on their desires to learn to read and on their enjoyment of reading. Other students have had experience with a visually impaired friend or relative and can tell the rest of the class how important a reading service is to someone who does not see well. One or two students may have participated in a storytelling camp or workshop, experienced renewed appreciation for hearing stories told aloud, and learned the power that accompanies the storyteller role. Students can find cultural connections to the project. For instance, a student may bring a Pueblo storyteller figurine to class and tell his or her classmates about the storyteller tradition among this group of southwestern Native Americans.

As students explore doing the Reading Pals project, they also discuss cultural insights that reading can give to people and the connections to other topics or interests that people discover as they read. A rich fabric of interrelated experiences underlies this project.

Finding the reading partners is discussed later in this chapter. Students need to plan how to get to and from the reading sites. The teacher and students can brainstorm solutions to transportation problems. Parents can offer "taxi service" if that is permitted by school and state law. Minigrant funds cover transportation when all of the students have partners in one or two destinations. If the day care or elder care centers that provide reading partners are near the school, students can walk to the sites, school codes permitting. Otherwise, with parental permission, students can use public transportation to get to their reading sessions. In many cities and towns, large or small, public transportation is used in place of traditional yellow school buses.

Each student and his or her partner spend their first meeting discussing the reading partnership. They talk about the partner's interests, and the student makes a list of these ideas to use in searching for a book. The student and partner set up a reading and discussion schedule with the understanding that the schedule is somewhat flexible and that a session will be moved to a different time or day if one of the partners is ill or has another pressing or emergency obligation to tend to. The student makes three copies of the reading calendar: one to keep in his or her project log, one to give to the reading partner, and one for the project liaison person from the site.

Each student keeps a two-part project log. The first entry for each meeting with the partner is a reading log in which the student notes the highlights of the reading, the ideas that surfaced during the follow-up discussion, questions that the student or reading partner had that the reading did not answer, where to begin reading next time, the setting of the book, the author, the cultural or societal background of the book, and any other concerns. The second part of the log entry for each session is the reflective log for the day, which is discussed in detail later in the chapter.

After the first meeting with their partners, students locate at least two books to bring to the next session. If the reading partner is a child, a student wants to ask someone from the day care center or library to check the selected books for age-appropriate vocabulary before checking them out, keeping in mind that a young child's comprehension vocabulary is much more advanced than his or her reading vocabulary.

Students may want to do a whole-class brainstorm to develop a list of places where they may be able to find books for the project. Sources include the following:

- The school or community library
- A regional lending library service (the school or town librarian would have more information about this option)

- Local day care or elder care facilities
- Resale shops that might be willing to donate books to the project
- Home libraries

Each student has the books selected and in his or her possession in time for the next appointment with the reading partner.

At the next meeting with the partner, the student tells the partner the titles of the books that he or she brought to the meeting and a little bit about each book. The student and partner discuss the books and pick one to start reading. The student needs to stop reading at a good "break off" point in the book and leave enough time in the session to discuss the reading with the partner and brainstorm a list of questions that the student or the partner wants to have answered before the next session. Ideas for possible questions or issues are suggested by the reading survey questions found earlier in this chapter.

The student and partner also do some affective processing before the end of the session. Each student ensures that they do the following:

- Discuss what they enjoyed about the session.
- Identify what they feel they could each do to make the next session better.
- Thank each other for the enjoyment of sharing the story together.
- Confirm the date and time of the next session before leaving.

Each of the next several reading sessions follows the same general format. The student and partner exchange greetings, and the student reads his or her notes reviewing the reading from the former session using a "last time in this book or program" format. The partner adds to or comments on this review. Discussing the answers to the questions from the last session, the student tells the partner any additional information about those questions that he or she learned from online research or print sources in the school or town library. The student then reads another section from the book, leaving time to review the reading, brainstorm the questions, and do the affective processing. The student confirms the time and date of the next session; the partner and student thank each other for the shared reading experience; and the session is finished.

When the student and partner finish reading their first book together, they have a celebration. Some possible celebrations include sharing one or more of the following with each other:

- The greatest AHA! gained by reading the book
- An overall impression of the book
- Inferred impression of the author
- A personal goal for the next shared reading

Celebrations can include singing, acting out favorite scenes from the book, mimicking favorite or less liked characters, and feasting. The reading partner and the student discuss and plan the celebration before the final reading session.

Student and partner also express special thanks for the sharing that occurred as they were reading the book together, identifying one key benefit that they received from the experience.

Each student schedules a minimum of 20 reading hours with his or her partner. During this time, a student and child partner are able to complete several books, while a student and adult partner may complete only one. The discussions and questioning make the learning from the reading more contextual and therefore more likely to be remembered. A reading partnership is often the basis of a friendship that continues long after the formal service learning project has ended. The student experiences the pleasure of helping someone who wants to learn from stories and has trouble doing the act of reading for himself or herself; the student also experiences the feelings of value, importance, and appreciation that attach themselves to the storyteller role.

After students and reading partners have worked together for a minimum of 10 weeks, each student takes another reading comprehension test and compares this score with the preproject test score to look for improvement. The new test score is entered in the project portfolio, along with a short note from the student explaining how he or she believes the project has helped improve reading skills. The student takes the reading strategies survey again and compares his or her answers with those from the first survey. The student writes a short note identifying which strategies have changed, explaining how these changes have helped foster better reading comprehension.

ASSESSING RISKS: ESTABLISHING PROTOCOLS FOR HEALTH AND SAFETY

Schools are notorious breeding grounds for infectious and contagious diseases. Day care and senior care facilities also experience outbreaks of colds, flu, and digestive upsets. To protect each other's health, the student and the reading buddy agree that if one of them is ill, he or she contacts the other, and the reading session is rescheduled. This contact must be made at least one day before the scheduled session so that the message has ample time to reach the partner. If one of the partners is injured or experiences a serious illness and has doctor's orders to suspend normal daily activities for a prescribed length of time, he or she is certain that the partner has that information. Reading sessions resume when both partners have regained their good health and full strength.

Transportation to the reading site must be safe and secure. Reading sessions are often scheduled for afterschool hours, and this means that special attention must be paid to the means that students use to get to and from the day care or senior care facility. If several students have partners from the same facility, they schedule reading sessions for the same days and times. They then travel to the reading site together. Parents will, school code permitting, meet their students at the facility to escort them home. If several students have partners at a facility that is within walking distance of the school, the teacher or other adults may accompany them to the site. However it is arranged, students must agree to use only approved transportation. Students who walk must review safe routes to their reading sites, paying particular attention to placement of pedestrian walkways and crossings. Students who use motorized transportation, whether school buses or public transportation, review bus numbers and routes and safe comportment while riding. Parents receive letters that explain the service learning project, and they are asked to sign forms permitting their children to travel from the school to the senior care or day care facility.

Some adult literature contains material that students and/or their parents may find objectionable. For this reason, each student who pairs with a senior partner submits to the teacher a "permission to read" form signed by the student's adult guardian or parent prior to the first session between the student and the senior reading buddy. The form states that the parent/guardian has reviewed the book and that he or she gives consent for the student to share the book with the reading buddy. Students, teachers, parents, or reading buddies can find helpful resources including book reviews by critics and readers at many Web sites, and this material helps students screen books and determine their suitability for use in this service learning project.

SELECTING THE SERVICE LEARNING FOCUS: READING PARTNERSHIPS WITH THE COMMUNITY

A language arts teacher can begin a brainstorm for project ideas by saying to his or her class,

Part of our focus this year is going to be on reading skills—understanding the reading content, developing questions about the material we're reading, following the thread of a story, seeing connections with prior learning, adjusting our reading strategies for what we're reading, and becoming better, more capable readers. We also are going to be doing a service learning project. What community service projects could connect to our reading goals?

Teachers in other content areas can also find ways to do service learning projects that tap into some of the elements of Reading Pals.

Exemplary Project: Writing and Sharing Science Books

When I asked my high school chemistry students how they might make a difference in the community, some of them suggested reading to elementary school children. Shared reading is a well-established form of community service. Well, when the students asked me, "What about reading to little kids?" I answered, "Yes, if you partner with an elementary school teacher who can guide you in using grade-level-appropriate vocabulary, you read one or more books about chemistry, and *you write and illustrate the books.*"

I assigned students to base teams that included one member who had demonstrated visualization strengths, one whose strengths were verbal expression, and one whose organizational skills were excellent. The students produced wonderful books, the elementary school teachers appreciated the "expert" help in teaching science, and the young students loved having the older ones read to them.

Here's a bit more about how it worked. While the students and I were working outside of class time finding elementary teacher-partners, in class we brainstormed the attributes of an engaging children's book. A requirement was that their book be written for students no older than fourth grade. Students and I brought in award-winning books for students in those younger grades and analyzed them: How were they illustrated? How much text per page? What about cover design? From the analysis of the books, we developed a rubric that we agreed we would use to score the student-produced books.

Student teams decided on topics for their books. As soon as we had teacher-partners on board, students started writing. The elementary teacher-partner checked books for age-appropriate language; I evaluated them for science accuracy. Student teams revised, illustrated, and bound their books, and each team set a date for sharing its book with its elementary partner class.

It almost goes without saying that the high school students treasured the time that they spent sharing the books with their elementary partners, and many of them continued the partnership for the rest of the school year. The elementary students reveled in the attention of the high schoolers. One young student wrote, "It was fun having *them* teach us science." Another student commented, "I learned a lot about Adam Atom from the book, and I really liked that they wrote the book just for us."

I treasure those memories, and I still have some of the books in my archives. Every once in a while, I pull them out and read through them, always with a warm glow in my heart and a silly grin on my face. My "kids" reviewed learnings from earlier in the year and learned the value of being able to communicate what they knew accurately and simply enough that the little ones could understand them. The elementary teacher-partners received much appreciated help in teaching science, and everyone basked in the glow of enjoying each other's company. Brilliant!

Making Connections With the Community

To further explore the project idea, the class brainstorms a list of service ideas, reflecting on community needs.

The teacher primes the pump by suggesting that students consider the following:

- Helping the school librarian reshelve returned books or repair damaged books
- Helping the town librarian catalog new books
- Collecting books for a used-book sale or "Friends of the Library" book sale
- Cleaning out bookshelves at home and donating some older books to the classroom or school library
- Establishing a reading partnership project with a senior citizen who has difficulty reading (or who would like some companionship) or a child who is just learning to read

The teacher then asks the class, "Which of these projects do you think would help you become better readers? If one of our goals is to improve reading comprehension, which project helps us reach that goal?" After looking over the list, students probably decide that actually reading out loud to a partner and discussing the reading with that partner would result in the greatest gains in reading comprehension. Some gentle steering by the teacher often helps students reach this conclusion.

Students then discuss the ideas with their families. The teacher suggests that students talk with their parents about the value of shared reading and reading out loud to a partner. Students and parents discuss the importance of reading to a preschool child to help that child develop an interest in learning to read. Also, they

Figure 5.1 Sample Project Evaluation Rubric: Reading Pals

Ranking / Criteria	1 (high)	2 (medium)	3 (low)	Comments
Interest	X			We would like to take on the role of storytellers, improve our reading, and help the community.
Need	X			Libraries need assistance. Seniors and young children need reading pals.
Accessibility	X			A day care center and an elder care center are near our school.
Appropriateness	X			We can work to improve reading skills and perform a service, make a difference.
Time Frame	X			We can schedule sessions every week during the school term.

examine changes in eyesight that occur when people age and what that often means about the value of a reading partnership to a senior citizen. If students live near older family members or if students know senior citizens who live in their neighborhoods or go to their places of worship, they will want to talk with these people about how changing eyesight has changed their reading habits.

The students and teacher evaluate the need for and interest in the service project using a rubric such as the one shown in Figure 5.1. Strategies for using this rubric have been discussed in Chapter 1 of this book.

The teacher and students select a target date for the start of the project. The students prepare for the project by practicing their oral reading skills. The teacher and students spend some time on the telephone connecting with community service partners and finding reading partners.

WORKING WITH A COMMUNITY PARTNER

Each student needs a reading partner, either a child or a senior citizen. The teacher will want to survey the class before contact is made with community agencies to find out how many students would like to read to younger children and how many want a senior partner. Some students may have strong preferences, and the teacher will want to be able to match each student with a partner in the desired age category. The teacher makes a list of which students want children as partners and which students want seniors.

Once the teacher has done this survey, he or she contacts day care centers and elder care facilities in town to set up the partnerships. When the teacher and students talk with the day care or elder care facility, they explain the service project and the learning goals and ask if the agency is interested in becoming a service learning partner. They tell the agency how many reading partners are needed. They ask the agencies to match students with reading partners and to provide some services from a staff person. In many cases, the staff liaison does the initial introducing of each student to his or her partner and provides the teacher with a list of partner names. Each student, to ensure safe arrival at the reading site, checks in with the liaison at the beginning of each reading visit so that the agency knows that the student has arrived safely. Because of this checkin requirement, the agency liaison asks each student for a copy of the reading sessions calendar so that staff of the agency know when to expect the readers.

Each reader knows that he or she is responsible for informing the agency contact if he or she has to miss or reschedule a reading session. The reader tells the agency contact the reason for changing the session and asks the agency contact to inform the partner of the change. Readers need to understand that sessions are to be canceled or changed very infrequently. Of course, the agency liaison also contacts the school to let the reader know if the partner needs to miss a session. These protocols ensure that if either member of the reading team is ill or has a personal emergency, the other has been notified accordingly.

"I loved reading to the little kids, and I especially loved reading a book that we had written and illustrated. Writing the book was harder than I thought it would be. We found out fast what we didn't know and what we knew really well. We also found out what we were clear on and what was fuzzy."

"Getting the chemistry right and using little kid language was tough. The grade school teacher helped a lot."

"I want to do this again. It's a great way to really review a chemistry topic."

—High school students, Palatine, IL

Some students ask permission to find their own reading partners, and they often have special partners in mind. For example, a student who is a member of a religious congregation that has a senior or child care program may want to work with someone from the congregation. The coordinator of the program can pair the student with a reading pal. If a student arranges for his or her own reading partner, the student tells the teacher the name of the sponsoring agency and the name of the partner. Once again, an adult who works for the program is the site liaison for the student and is available for the site contact work described above.

As teacher and students find community partners and reading partners and as the project develops, students will want to learn more about service learning projects that focus on reading. There are many online resources from which the student, with adult supervision, can obtain information.

ALIGNING SERVICE AND EDUCATIONAL GOALS

Students who participate in the Reading Pals service learning project demonstrate their improved reading skills as they use information from the reading to activate prior knowledge, show how they can adjust reading rate, demonstrate comprehension strategies to suit the type and difficulty of the text, and enrich the reading experience by identifying the author's point of view (language arts).

Tapping Into Multiple Intelligences: Storytelling in Nature

Naturalist, Kinesthetic, and Spatial Multiple Intelligences

Help students connect to nature by asking them, "How is birdsong like storytelling?" Tell them that they have a few days to brainstorm answers to the question and suggest that they can look for and listen to birds in their environment. Even in the middle of an immense city, students can find groups of pigeons and observe their interactions with each other, interactions that are quite definitely influenced by their vocalizations. In more rural or wooded settings, students can observe a variety of bird species, listen to their songs, and find connections between actions and songs.

Why is the nature connection important? A number of studies show that there are profound links between a natural environment and cognitive functioning (White, n.d.). And not only do children who spend time with nature think better, those with symptoms of ADHD appear to focus better after spending time in a natural setting, and all children who appreciate nature and spend time out-of-doors have higher scores on tests of concentration and self-discipline.

Strong links exist between human storytelling and vocal communications of many different species of animals. Once students have taken the time to investigate birdsong, ask them to find more examples to share during class discussions.

Student Responsibilities and Curricular Areas

The teacher encourages each student to keep a personal record of the reading that the student does to fulfill course requirements, for assignments for other teachers, or for personal pleasure. After each student has kept such a reading/reflective log for 10–12 weeks, the teacher asks the students to look through the entries and reflect on how this experience is helping them to use literature to better understand themselves and others by interpreting literary texts accordingly (language arts).

Through their work with young children or senior citizens, students learn to identify and appreciate the benefits of cross-generational relationships (life skills). The success that each student experiences in discussing the readings with his or her partner, brainstorming unanswered questions, looking for cultural influences, or reviewing prior readings helps each student improve communication skills and strengthen skills in interpersonal relationships (life skills). As they work with their reading partners, students often find that they want to learn more about that age group. They find themselves developing an interest in the growth and development of young children, the changes in physiology and function that accompany aging, and the development of the brain in people of all ages. Throughout this project, students and reading partners discuss and analyze the function and importance of the storyteller and oral traditions in world cultures (social studies), comparing the oral reading that they are doing with the storytelling/storyteller tradition that developed in cultures that did not have a system of writing or producing printed materials.

A brainstorming session to select this project shows that students can identify service needs of the community and actively participate in service to address those needs (service learning). The pre- and posttests, as well as the reading strategies surveys, give students a chance to demonstrate an increase in curricular skills through participation in the project (service learning).

In addition, students reflect on the significance of their service learning experience and how it has helped the community and their own learning (service learning) when they look back over their reading and reflective logs and realize how much they and their reading partners did together.

A celebration that is shared at the end of each project reinforces this last learning, giving students some additional feedback about the value of this partnered reading to the development of personal skills and to the quality of life of another member of the community.

The Reading Pals service learning project links the big ideas of literacy, early childhood development, and aging. Literacy is the basic skill most associated with success in life. Successful people communicate well, both orally and in writing, are good at getting new ideas and information by reading, and are attentive listeners. Students who do the Reading Pals project are asked to focus on their own reading comprehension skills, practice oral communication skills as they discuss what they are reading with their partners, and enhance their writing skills as they keep their reading and reflective logs.

Students whose reading partners are young children learn that frequent early stimulation, such as being read to, helps the brain grow, and that the positive feelings that are associated with the reading partnership are "wired" into the growing brain, helping the child learn to read more easily. Students who choose senior citizens as partners learn about the changes in vision and processing of information that occur with aging. The teacher may have these students try to read using a pair of magnifying glasses that blurs their vision and ask, "How did you feel about that reading experience? What does that tell you about how your senior partner might feel about trying to read without glasses?"

These students learn that continued stimulation, like the reading partnership, can help their senior partners maintain the dendrite connections that already exist in their brains and grow new dendrites. The students who are reading pals know that their service learning project is helping them gain an important life skill while it gives their young partners a springboard for future growth or helps their older partners maintain active, alert minds. See Figure 5.2 for a model alignment of curricular goals and service learning covered in this section.

Figure 5.2   Reading Pals: Aligning Service and Educational Goals

Major Subject	Learning Goals	Life Skills	Big Ideas	Service Actions
Social Studies	Appreciation of the role of storyteller Oral traditions in world cultures	Role awareness Comfort in taking on different roles Appreciation of literature and storytelling	Cultural awareness and literacy appreciation	Discussing storyteller and oral traditions with partner
Family Studies	Physiological changes with age Stages of brain development Interpersonal skills	Cross-generational relationships Communication and interpersonal skills	Child development Aging	Finding a partner Establishing a working relationship with the partner
Language Arts	Fitting reading rate to content Understanding self and others through literature Activating prior knowledge	Reading for information and effect Cross-generational and cross-cultural understanding	Literacy World community	Selecting readings Reading and discussing books Keeping a reading log or journal

Reciprocity: The Community of Learners

Because the students who are providing the service are focusing on developing the skills that improve reading comprehension and communication, they will, implicitly or explicitly, be helping their reading pals develop those skills. If the teacher models metacognitive monitoring of reading, he or she stops and asks students, "Did you notice that I just went back to reread the last few lines?" or "Now what does that sentence tell us about the author's mind-set?" or "I wonder what that word means? I want to remember to look it up; I'd better write it down." Students often find that they do the same kinds of "thinking out loud" when they read to their pals. This passes the skills along to the reading pals and helps them find deeper meaning in reading that they do on their own.

The reading sessions also teach the reading pals the importance of storytelling to maintaining personal memories (Sylwester, 1995). Storytelling partners help each other hold on to their memories by giving each other the opportunity to review and refresh those memories. Stories that are shared are remembered better and longer, understood more deeply, and tied more meaningfully to personal experiences and stories. That is quite probably a reason why close friendships often develop between reading buddies.

MANAGING THE SERVICE PROJECT: READING PALS

Because students who do this project set up individual service schedules, work with individual partners, and work at a variety of sites, the teacher needs to make a management plan that helps him or her keep track of the curricular goals and the service learning goals during the course of the project. An overall plan for this project is shown in the management grid in Figure 5.3.

Many students find that they want to continue the reading partnership after the end of the service learning project. To extend this project, the teacher can offer help by making suggestions about new reading strategies to provide additional development of reading comprehension. Students who continue the partnership are demonstrating their appreciation of intergenerational relationships and the empowerment and love that accompany the storyteller, service provider, and listener roles.

FOSTERING REFLECTIVE LEARNING

Students use a double-entry reading/reflective log for this project. One section of the log for each date contains the reading log in which the student notes the highlights of the reading and the ideas that surfaced during the follow-up discussion. Also, this section includes questions that the student or reading partner had that the reading did not answer, where to begin reading next time, the setting of the book, the author, the cultural or societal background of the book, and any other concerns. Finally, the reading log section contains the affective notes detailing what the student and partner enjoyed about the session and what each one feels he or she wants to do better next time.

The other section is the reflective log in which the student records his or her thoughts about the big idea learning; the meaning and value of the community service; and ideas about personal strengths, areas for improvement, and changing roles and self-perceptions that result from the Reading Pals service learning experience. (Note: This project may not be appropriate for some primary-level students whose reading skills need more traditional development prior to the student becoming a storyteller.)

The use of the reading/reflective log reinforces curricular learning, helping the students to understand how they are helpful to their community, assess their personal strengths, and find areas for personal goal setting and improvement. Reflection is one of the tools that make service learning particularly valuable to students.

Figure 5.3   Management Plan: Reading Pals

Phase	Planning	Monitoring	Evaluating
1	Select the project from the student brainstorm. Write letters telling parents about service project and asking for volunteers to help students get to sites. Give preproject reading comprehension test. Hand out reading strategies survey forms.	Score comprehension tests. Check completion of surveys. Discuss portfolios with students.	Return comprehension test scores. Repeat curricular goals—how can we use test scores to evaluate progress toward goal? Confirm project selection.
2	Set up reading partnerships. Arrange for first meeting between students and partners. Brainstorm sources of reading materials. Discuss service log and personal reading log.	Check on results of first meetings. Check on student acquisition of books to discuss with partners. Confirm parent volunteers, and pair students who need transportation with parent provider, confirming parental permission grants. Students go through a first meeting with partners.	Spot-check project reading/reflective logs/ personal reading logs. Did students remember affective processing with partners? Do students have list of questions from the readings? Who needs help?
3	Continue student/partner reading sessions. Help students find new books as needed. Fine-tune transportation arrangements as needed.	Spot-check reading/reflective logs. Contact site liaisons to ask for information: Are there any problems? How are the partnerships going? What can I do to help? How about celebrations? What is being identified as significant learning?	Students self-evaluate progress and discuss in small groups in class. Look back at curricular goals—this will focus self-evaluation. Remind students that a posttest and a new reading strategies survey are coming soon.
4	Complete the 10-week (20-hour) reading service project. Give the postproject reading comprehension test. Ask students to retake the reading strategies survey.	Score postproject comprehension tests and return results to students. Spot-check surveys. Students begin organizing their portfolios.	Students self-evaluate progress by comparing pre- and postproject test scores and survey answers, writing short analyses of project results in reaching curricular goals. Co-verify evaluations. Students and teacher decide whether or not to continue the reading partnerships.
5	Celebrate project completion by writing a "will" asking future classes to continue the project. Share portfolios in base teams. Write individual letters to liaisons of child care and elder care facilities liaisons saying, "Thank you for your help." Students and teacher each write one goal for future personal service work.	"Eavesdrop" on portfolio sharing. Ask students to tell each other their greatest learning AHA!, their most burning unanswered question, what they liked most about the project, what they found least comfortable, what they felt they did best, and what they would do differently (and better) next time.	Students and teacher discuss project strengths and areas of improvement. Each person shares with whole class his or her greatest AHA! and a personal goal for future service work.

See the reflective logs for elementary, middle school, and high school levels at the end of this chapter for strategies to prompt reflections. These models consist of sentence stems and open-ended questions about the service learning project.

ASSESSMENT AND EVALUATION

The teacher will want to assess reading comprehension improvement by using varied standardized reading comprehension tools as well as discussing understandings and insights with students. The teacher also expects each student to keep a personal record of reading done for schoolwork and/or for pleasure with notes about how well the student understood the reading and how enjoyable it was. Furthermore, the teacher may have students do the affective processing by drawing smiley or frowning faces or describing the reading experience as a color and giving the reasons for picking that color. The comprehension tests results will be examined for evidence of improvement in reading skills over time, and of course, the teacher hopes that the personal reading log reflects an increase in reading enjoyment. Following is a sample personal reading log:

Date: _____

Title of reading selection: _____

Reason for reading: _____   Comprehension: _____
(assignment/pleasure)   (scale of 1 to 5: 1 = low; 5 = high)

Synopsis: Enjoyment: _____
                                     (scale of 1 to 5: 1 = low; 5 = high)

Reading "face":   Reading "color" and reason:

Each student also assembles a project portfolio that includes the reading and reflective log, reading comprehension test scores, the reading strategies surveys, and other evidences of service and learning that the student can use to complete the picture of his or her reading partnership.

Each student will have the following specific portfolio pieces:

- The reading and reflective log
- Notes on the end-of-book celebrations (may be in the log)
- Preproject reading comprehension test score
- Postproject reading comprehension test score
- Preproject reading strategies survey
- Postproject reading strategies survey

- List of book sources
- Written comparisons of pre- and posttests and surveys (two written notes)
- Personal reading log
- Greatest AHA! and personal service goal
- Three other evidences of learning chosen by the student

Each student is required to include three evidences of learning of his or her own choice. These could include personal lists of books for future reading, rough drafts of the student's own "first book" (creative writing), a list of books on tape to listen to, or ideas for extension service learning projects.

Each student shares his or her portfolio with a small group of classmates during the project celebration. This final feedback helps students realize how much they have learned about course content and themselves as service-givers by doing this project and recognize how good their reading comprehension skills can become if they practice a variety of strategies and become more frequent readers.

Elementary Reflective Log

The story we read was about . . .	The service I provided was . . .
Here's what I learned about • reading: • myself: • helping my reading pal:	What I did well was . . .
I "picked up" this big community service data . . . I like this idea because . . .	What I can do better next time is . . .

Middle School Reflective Log

Summary of reading:

Through this project I learned . . .

Here are my most important learnings about

- other cultures and the role of storyteller:

- myself:

- doing community service:

My best actions and thoughts were . . .

Next time I want to improve . . .

High School Reflective Log

Synopsis of reading:

Insights about the selection and the author:

Ways I helped my reading pal:

Ways my reading pal helped me:

My feelings about my role as a member of the reading community are . . .

The personal strengths I brought to this service project today are . . .

Next time I want to strengthen . . .

6

The Soup Troop

A Health and Family
Education Service Learning Project

DESCRIPTION OF THE PROJECT

Students involved in The Soup Troop project learn about nutrition and serving needy members of the community by working in community facilities such as soup kitchens, local food pantries, or in-school kitchens or cafeterias. To begin the project, the teacher and students discuss the various opportunities for such community service and determine where and how often to offer their services, such as working twice a month in a local community kitchen or food pantry or the school cafeteria.

As they prepare for the project, the teacher and students contact local agencies ahead of time to survey needs, connect with an adult liaison, define student duties, and explore the best way to schedule student service. If the project involves working in the local township's food pantry, for instance, student teams can help with unpacking, sorting, and taking inventory of food donations, and they often make up food baskets for homeless, disadvantaged, and needy community residents.

As this service project is a cooperative venture between the class and a food provider, the teacher and students discuss both the variety of possible community partners and the different activities that each venue requires. The teacher has the students brainstorm the nature of The Soup Troop service project, participating in the decision as to which of the project venues to explore: working in an established community soup kitchen; working in a food pantry; having an in-school soup kitchen; or working in the school cafeteria to prepare lunches, with students serving as cooks, servers, dishwashers, or in other roles as assigned. At this point, the teacher assigns students to cooperative teams.

Knowing how to plan a nutritionally balanced and complete diet and prepare foods safely are skills that help students live healthier, more successful lives. Doing this project gives students an opportunity to learn those skills in a meaningful context, serving community needs at the same time. Lengths of The Soup Troop projects vary; a typical project involves students working in three-hour shifts, twice a month, for a minimum of three months. The exact scheduling, of course, depends on arrangements made with the community kitchen or food pantry, with school administration in the case of an in-school "soup kitchen," or with the cafeteria staff if students are helping with lunch preparation.

One option that some teachers explore as they plan The Soup Troop project is working cooperatively with a colleague in the special education department within the school district, arranging for each student to be assigned to a partner who is physically or mentally disabled or challenged. Such an arrangement, as in a peer-mentoring approach, adds a special learning opportunity and benefit for both students.

If the school administration has established partnerships with community services for the homeless, the needy, or seniors, which is the case in some areas, a viable option is sponsoring monthly meals for homeless or needy families or senior citizens, preparing and serving the meal in the school cafeteria. Local grocery stores, community organizations, or community food pantries are often willing to donate the food for such meals, with volunteer students doing the preparation, cooking, serving, and cleanup as the focus of this service learning experience. The teacher and students need to ask the administration about the school district policy regarding using school facilities for this kind of function. In some districts, visitors to schools must clear background checks before entering the building.

Whatever the context of The Soup Troop project, if food and facilities are not provided through donations, teachers, students, and project sponsors need to explore sources of funding and possible sites ahead of time. A tour of such potential sites needs to be arranged with a liaison at the community kitchen or food pantry. When service learning is part of the school curriculum, funding is sometimes available through the school or through parent-teacher organizations. Money is also available in most states through grants. If a service project is to be done at a remote site, teachers work cooperatively with the school administration and seek out parent or adult volunteers as necessary for transporting students to and supervising students at community sites.

The teacher will want students to learn the following information and have food-preparation experience before they begin work at the community kitchen or food pantry:

- Menu-planning basics
- The food pyramid
- Plans for healthy, nutritionally balanced meals that include items from the different food groups
- Actual meal preparation in a school kitchen to learn proper food storage, refrigeration, preparation, cooking, serving, and cleanup techniques

If the school kitchen or food lab has a pantry for storing nonperishable items, the students practice sorting, storing, and taking inventory of the items on hand. If the food lab (kitchen) in school does not have its own pantry, teachers need to organize an "in-school field trip" to visit the storeroom of the school cafeteria. Students who work in a community food pantry find it helpful to see how large quantities of food are inventoried and arranged.

Once students have been assigned to working teams and work sites and duties have been arranged for The Soup Troop project, work schedules are set and students begin their volunteer service. If publicity of a meal event for the community or a food pantry is in order, the teacher assigns some students to prepare posters with appropriate information and arrange to have them placed in community centers and businesses.

To get the community service off to a smooth start, before the volunteer duty is scheduled to begin, the teachers, students, and adult volunteers involved in the project tour the kitchen, cafeteria, or food pantry in which students will be working so that they are prepared and know the procedures that need to be followed.

Keeping Records and Building a Portfolio

As part of this service learning project, students study the food pyramid. Each student makes up sample menus for breakfast, lunch, and dinner for two days. The meals for the two days may not be identical; the student is required to plan two distinct menus for each type of meal.

For each day's menus, the student includes a chart showing that the diet of a person eating those meals fits the recommendations of the FDA's food pyramid (available in health or nutritional science publications as well as on the Web). The student writes the names of the foods from the menus in the appropriate spots using a chart format, indicating the basic food group and the meal at which that food is eaten.

As students explore nutrition, they learn that the brain likes a serving of protein early in the day, along with other foods, and that too many carbohydrates at lunch may produce an attention-disrupting energy surge early in the afternoon—followed by an energy crash later on. The teacher, mentor, or a partner/peer check the menu plans with the food pyramid analysis prepared by each student, and that material becomes part of each student's project portfolio.

Students take basic recipes and scale them up to decide how much of each ingredient is needed to make enough food to serve the anticipated number of clients. Each student keeps a copy of the original recipes, the scaling calculations, and the scaled-up versions of the recipes to file in his or her project portfolio.

ASSESSING RISKS: ESTABLISHING PROTOCOLS FOR HEALTH AND SAFETY

Whether they are working in kitchens or food pantries, students need to rehearse techniques for managing objects that are stored on high or low shelves. Some cooking pots are very heavy, and commercial-size containers of foods are bulky, so students will need to practice using step stools or ladders to retrieve or store these objects if they are placed on high shelves; and they need to learn to lift with the legs, not the back, when handling objects that are stored near the floor. Students also need to hear that all items must be placed a few inches back from the leading edge of a shelf. Items that are placed too close to the edge may accidentally fall, and cans, bottles, bags, or boxes of food that topple onto unwary students can cause injuries.

Students who are preparing food must wash hands thoroughly before handling any unpackaged materials. Hands need a good minute of washing with soap and hot water and rubbing in order to be clean enough for safe food handling; and frequent washing, especially if students are handling raw meat, poultry, or fish, is essential to prevent accidental spread of infectious organisms. Any utensils or containers used in food preparation also need washing with hot soapy water, and countertops need frequent cleaning.

Sharp objects such as knives or scissors can cause cuts even in the hands of experienced cooks. Students must be told that any cuts are to be reported to the teacher or adult supervisor immediately. Often cuts do not begin bleeding for several seconds, and students do not want to contaminate food with blood. Broken glass or crockery must be cleaned up and discarded safely, and any items that are chipped or cracked must be turned over to an adult for proper disposal.

Hot pots and pans look just like cold ones; students need to be reminded that if an item is on the stovetop or in the oven, it must be handled with hot pads or kitchen mitts. Any cookware that is sitting near a sink, waiting to be washed, could be hot, and students need frequent reminders to approach these items with care.

Adhesive bandages, antiseptic creams and ointments, and gels or lotions containing aloe are handy items to have in a first-aid kit. Adults need to know about any food allergies that students have, and they need to warn students who are cooking to read food labels carefully before taste-testing. Food products may not be as safe as they seem; for example, many packaged prepared foods contain peanut oil, and many people are allergic to peanuts.

A list of telephone numbers for physicians, emergency services, and poison control centers must be posted near the telephone where any adult or student can find them quickly and easily. If emergency help is required, it needs to be summoned as fast as possible.

As student members of the soup troop sort and store food or work on its preparation, they are learning lifelong kitchen skills. These are skills that they will use on a daily basis for the rest of their lives, and The Soup Troop project experience gives them a good foundation of safety practices on which they can build.

SELECTING THE SERVICE LEARNING FOCUS: A COMMUNITY NUTRITION PROJECT

At this time during the project, teachers get service commitments from the adult volunteers they have identified, confirming schedules and arrangements for transportation to and supervision at the work site. Having a backup plan in case of emergencies or illnesses is imperative to ensure the success of The Soup Troop project. Students, teacher, and the liaison from the project partner finalize the work schedule. The teacher makes copies of the schedule and gives one to each student or adult involved with The Soup Troop project. To establish a mental picture of what the service will look like, each student makes a mind map, diagramming the activities at the community kitchen, food pantry, or school facility.

Making Connections With the Community

The teacher asks students to discuss the need for the service project with their families and neighbors. Students are often not aware of the extent to which hunger is a problem for low-income, homeless, or disabled members of the

	Figure 6.1	Sample Project Evaluation Rubric: The Soup Troop			
Ranking / **Criteria**	**1** (high)	**2** (medium)	**3** (low)		**Comments**
Interest	X				This really applies to our in-class learning.
Need	X				Community kitchens, local food pantries, senior meals, and canned food drives tell us this service is needed.
Accessibility	X				It is possible to have our own community soup kitchen right here at school.
Appropriateness	X				We'll be learning about nutrition, helping people from the community, and working as a team.
Time Frame	X				Cooking six dinners in the next three months is "just right," and we may decide to extend the project and "will" it to next year's class.

community other than through their experience with the food drives in which schools often participate. Many community residents often do not know about elderly residents who, as a result of developing dementia or inattention, do not eat a balanced, nutritious diet. As students and parents discuss the service learning project, they can learn what services already exist in the community. As students get involved with dialogues about community services, they build a list of the community agencies that deal with the hunger and needs of the elderly, homeless, or disadvantaged in the community. This list is placed in their service learning project portfolios.

Teachers and students evaluate the service learning idea for this project using a rubric. If the final project format is the in-school soup kitchen, the rubric looks like the one shown in Figure 6.1.

Tapping Into Multiple Intelligences: Who's Got Rhythm?

Musical, Kinesthetic, and Intrapersonal Multiple Intelligences

Music is a form of communication that speaks powerfully to our minds (Sylwester, 2000). Not only is music embedded in our culture, it seems to be one of the oldest communication forms, and it involves the whole brain (Lazear, 1999). Enhancing the musical intelligence maximizes our power for dealing creatively with a variety of situations and for remembering information.

To test this last statement, do some personal processing: Think of a song or jingle that you first heard years ago that advertises a product or service. Ask yourself, "How long has it been since I actually heard this jingle? How perfectly do I remember it?" Ask yourself, "When I need to alphabetize information, and I'm not using a computer—just my brainpower—how do I do that? Do I hear anything musical in my head?" Songs and jingles can be very powerful memory aids. Have students use them to remember all kinds of information. Here are a few examples:

- A restaurant chain has notices above the sinks in their bathrooms stating that you've washed your hands long enough if you've had time to sing through one verse and chorus of "Old McDonald Had a Farm."
- Jingles help students remember procedures. Some of the author's students, to remember how to mix water and concentrated acids, composed this:

    You really, really oughta

    Put acid into watta (water).

- Jingles help students remember information. Another composition from the author's students:

    Red in acid,

    Blue in base,

    Litmus's color,

    In either case.

- Jingles state rules in a fun-to-remember way. To remember the importance of setting food away from the front edges of shelves, students wrote this:

    The edges of ledges

    Say "Danger" to strangers.

- Students can advertise their soup troop service using songs and jingles. Familiar tunes from children's songs provide good platforms for creative lyrics. Often students prefer using a hip-hop or rap format. Advertising jingles are hugely memorable and effective ways to sell a product.

Some critics say that having students put information in jingle form is "hokey" or that kids won't buy into this kind of activity. In 30 years of teaching high school chemistry, the author's experience was the opposite. Students not only used rhythm and rhyme to remember, they did so spontaneously as time went by.

WORKING WITH A COMMUNITY PARTNER

The teachers whose classes are forming the project teams contact community agencies to find a partner for the service learning project. Community kitchens or food pantries are listed in the yellow pages of the telephone book under "Social Service Agencies" or a similar title. Teachers who want to set up an in-school community soup kitchen need to brainstorm sources of funding and discuss the idea with the principal to find out if the school cafeteria and kitchens are available for use after school or, as an alternative, whether students might help with lunch preparation two or three times a month. Using the school as the community partner for this project does strengthen the school's connections with the community and help the community see the school as a service provider in nontraditional ways.

> At our local high school, senior citizens were invited to come for a weekly lunch that was prepared in large part by students doing service learning. The senior citizens, many of whom lived alone, said those were their best meals of the week.
>
> —Author

To find out what other communities and schools do to feed the hungry, the disabled, or seniors, students will want to search the Internet for information about "senior citizen meals," "meals on wheels," "soup kitchens," and "food pantries."

They need to find Web sites featuring information about "nutrition," "food pyramid," or "healthy eating." Students often find Web sites that include interactive features, such as quizzes, that evaluate their base knowledge about these topics. Teachers, parents, and other adults need to monitor student use of the Internet.

Teachers who are exploring the possibility of having their students work with students with special needs can find much information online about inclusion and differentiating instruction. The special education teachers are in-house sources of valuable information about effective strategies for working and communicating with their students.

ALIGNING SERVICE AND EDUCATIONAL GOALS

As students learn about the food pyramid, they learn about food groups and about applying food pyramid principles in making daily food choices (family education). Students in foods and cooking classes also study different ethnic cuisines, learning to recognize and appreciate cultural influences on individual and family food choices (family education).

Also in this project, students learn about the effect of diet on health, are able to discuss some physiological effects of healthy diets and unhealthy diets, and identify responsible diet behaviors that contribute to overall wellness (health education). They explain how behavior can impact wellness and disease prevention and demonstrate these behaviors (health education). For instance, students learn about careful cleaning of food preparation, service, and storage areas and disposing of kitchen waste to prevent contamination of those areas.

Figure 6.2 The Soup Troop: Aligning Service and Educational Goals

Major Subject	Learning Goals	Life Skills	Big Ideas	Service Actions
Family Education	Food pyramid Menu planning Influence of culture on foods chosen by families	Planning balanced menus Food preparation (cooking) Kitchen cleanup and food storage	Combating hunger in the community is everyone's job. Proper nutrition helps the brain and body work.	Planning menus Buying food Cleaning up the kitchen and storing leftovers
Mathematics	Ratio and proportion Percentages	Comparing Computational skills	Proportionality	Scaling up recipes
Health Education	Diet and wellness Diet and brain function Diseases related to improper food preparation or storage	Making healthy food choices Identifying homeopathic value of foods	"We are what we eat." "A sound mind in a healthy body" starts with good nutrition. Epidemics	Explaining "healthiness" of planned menus Cooking and cleaning up; using disease-preventing food-handling procedures
Visual Arts	Producing effective advertising	Illustrating Describing Explaining "Selling"	"A picture is worth a thousand words."	Making posters to advertise the service

Students develop and demonstrate enhanced skills in interpersonal relationships (life skills) by working pleasantly, politely, and respectfully with their project partners as well as with members of the community for and with whom they serve during this project.

As students decide on the venue for this project, they identify a nutritional need of the community and actively participate in a thoughtfully designed service learning project that addresses that need (service learning). Through their menu planning and recipe scaling, as necessary, students show that they are acquiring curricular knowledge and skills through participation in an integrated service learning project (service learning). If the teachers, students, and school principal decide to use the in-school soup kitchen format for this project, they are demonstrating the value of school-community partnerships (service learning). See Figure 6.2 for a model alignment of service and educational goals, such as those discussed above.

Student Responsibilities and Curricular Areas

All students who participate in this project keep a reflective log that demonstrates their thinking about the significance of the service learning experience (service learning). Teachers give students time to reflect with their partners or teams so that the students can develop their reflective log entries together, benefiting from each other's thoughts and insights. The reflective log is an artifact in each student's project portfolio.

The Soup Troop service learning project focuses students' attention on the big idea of hunger. Depending on the nature of the class, to prompt reflection and empathy, the teacher may ask students the following questions: "Can you imagine going to bed hungry? Really hungry? With gnawing, cramping hunger pangs in your stomach and a light-headed, weak feeling? Can you imagine having no food in the house to eat? Can you remember complaining that there was "nothing to eat" in your house? Have you read or heard stories about people who have been stranded during a disaster and have really run out of food? Have you ever wondered what those people did as they tried to find food to eat?"

As students research nutrition and the effects of an improper diet and malnutrition on the body, they may discover that poor nutrition can and does affect brain function and learning.

The Soup Troop project is about developing empathy and a community service ethic. As students become immersed in this service learning project, they are encouraged to demonstrate their concern and empathy for those who are indeed truly hungry in their community. The volunteer service that is the focus of The Soup Troop project is one that students can continue doing after they have completed this specific learning experience.

During the early stages of a community service project, one of the students on the team expressed concern about not fitting in with the other kids. She was thinking about dropping out of the project, and I suggested that she "hang in there." Our kids are pretty accepting of others, especially when they see that they are willing to work hard. At the end of the project, the student said to me, "I'm surprised you kept encouraging me, but I'm glad you did. Doing this project has made a real difference for me."

—Tammy Lancioni, Teacher, Ontonagon, MI

Reciprocity: The Community of Learners

Almost all communities include residents who are disadvantaged in some way. Whether the individual has a physical disability, is elderly, or is needy or homeless, he or she appreciates receiving a good-tasting, nutritious meal. Many elderly citizens enjoy the companionship they receive by attending a community meal. As students meet these residents and share soup troop stories with them, community members develop deep appreciation for the service providers and their knowledge and skills. Because students do much of the food preparation and serving, residents develop a picture of them as caring, capable young people. Menus and recipes that include nutritional analyses give community members information that they can use to make healthy eating choices in the future. As students and service recipients share stories about using diet to manage chronic diseases such as diabetes, they help each other learn about the food pyramid, food exchanges, or the glycemic index. Because they are learning new techniques of preparing and seasoning food, the students inform community residents about ways to make nutritious food taste good. For centuries, sharing food has been a way in which people celebrate community. The Soup Troop service learning project gives students and residents a way in which they can celebrate a sense of community and form friendships that last beyond the end of the project.

MANAGING THE SERVICE PROJECT: THE SOUP TROOP

The management plan for this service learning project looks different for each of the different project formats. Careful planning and monitoring by the teacher is the key to success, regardless of project format. A model management plan geared for the in-school soup kitchen project format is provided in Figure 6.3. The careful planning indicated in this model plan is needed no matter what project format is followed. With either the soup kitchen or food pantry project format, management plans need periodic reviews and may need revising as the project moves through its phases. Such a management plan devised by the teacher and students can also serve as a guide for the future.

FOSTERING REFLECTIVE LEARNING

Every student writes a reflective log entry after working with his or her partners during the project, keeping a record of trust building and communicating with classmates and community agency liaisons. They also write log entries after participating in the cafeteria tour, planning and scaling up recipes for the dinners, serving the dinners, working in the food pantry, and so on. Teachers schedule time for members of the student teams to share their soup troop reflective log entries after individuals have gathered their thoughts.

Some students who are less verbal than others appreciate help in phrasing their thoughts and reflections. These students find mind maps or other graphic organizers to be helpful prewriting tools. In any case, all students benefit from hearing others' ideas and insights.

The reflective logs for The Soup Troop project focus on the following ideas:

- What is the need for the service?
- What did the students do well?
- What did the students learn about academic content and skills, life skills, and service skills by doing the community service?
- How have the students' perceptions of themselves and others changed after their work with people who are needy, homeless, hungry, and living in poverty?

Figure 6.3 Management Plan: The Soup Troop

Phase	Planning	Monitoring	Evaluating
1	Teachers plan together and with the principal. Set up student partners or teams, write letter to parents, put out call for adult volunteers, discuss project with principal. Discuss project with students. Students consider different formats. Focus on the nutrition unit of the course. Give students assignment descriptions: two-day menu plans, reflective logs, etc.	Do partner/team trust building and communication skill exercises. Students reach consensus on project format (in-school community kitchen). Set up calendar with dinner dates. Inform potential volunteers about calendar. Quiz: food pyramid.	Student and partner evaluation of teamwork. Confirm food and funding sources. Grade and return quizzes.
2	Assign two-day menu plans. Arrange for kitchen tour. Practice cooking and cleanup skills in food lab. Contact community agencies for information about number of people to feed. Plan first dinner menu as a model for students. Give students recipes and numbers to feed information. Students scale up recipes and do "interpersonal skills" essay.	Collect two-day menu plans. Do kitchen tour. Collect scaled-up recipes and interpersonal skills essays. Observe student pair/team communication skills during tour. Have student pairs/teams work on reflective logs.	Check menu plans and recipe calculations. Return to students. Spot-check reflective logs. Give feedback on communication skills observations. Score and return essays. Have students self-evaluate curricular, teamwork, and intrapersonal skills.
3	Confirm adult volunteers. Cook, serve, and clean up first meal. Plan for next dinner. Scale up recipes as needed. Continue nutrition unit. Practice skills in the school's kitchen or food lab.	Watch/help students as they prepare the meal. Ensure that adult volunteers help with work and monitoring. Check new recipe scale-up calculations. Recheck food and funding sources. Continue reflective log partnerships.	Have students reflect on and self-evaluate meal preparation, serving, cleanup skills, and teamwork, as well as address more content-learning assessment. Spot-check reflective logs.
4	Work through service meals calendar. Do meal plans and recipe calculations as needed. Continue food lab and nutrition studies and reflection partnerships.	Continue service work and curricular skills monitoring. Do curricular quizzes and tests as appropriate. Spot-check reflection logs. Begin portfolio assembly.	Evaluate math skills by giving students new recipe scaling to do. Ask students to do a scale-down and check answers for sense. Grade and return quizzes or tests. Ensure that students and teacher concurrently evaluate content learning.
5	Celebrate project completion by writing a "will" asking future classes to continue the project. Share portfolios in base teams. Write whole-class letter to principal or other source of food or funding sources saying, "Thank you for your help." Students and teacher each write one goal for future personal service work.	"Eavesdrop" on portfolio sharing. Ask students to tell each other their greatest learning AHA!, their most burning unanswered question, what they liked most about the project, what they found least comfortable, what they felt they did best, and what they would do differently (and better) next time.	Discuss project strengths and areas for improvement with students. Have each person share with the whole class his or her greatest AHA! and personal goals for future service work.

111

As teachers are sensitive to the needs of their students, the vocabulary that the teacher uses to focus the reflections is appropriate for the grade level of the students. Older students may be encouraged to consider a greater variety of ideas than younger ones in their reflections.

See the reflective logs for the elementary, middle school, and high school levels at the end of this chapter for strategies to prompt reflections. These models consist of sentence stems and open-ended questions about the service learning project.

The use of the reflective log reinforces content learning, helps the students understand how they are helpful to their community, asks them to analyze their personal strengths, and emphasizes areas for personal goal setting and improvement. Reflection is one of the tools that make service learning particularly valuable to students (Billig, 2005).

ASSESSMENT AND EVALUATION

The teacher does some assessment of content learning using traditional tools such as class discussions, question-and-answer sessions, and paper-and-pencil quizzes and tests. Before students begin the writing assignments, the teacher gives them a rubric that is used to score the final draft of each assignment and shows them how the rubric is used to score written work. A sample rubric for scoring student writing is included in the Reproducible Masters section at the end of this book.

To demonstrate this rubric, the teacher discusses evaluations and explains the scoring of several sample writing pieces. Students can then use the rubric to self-evaluate the quality of their rough drafts and improve their own written work.

The teachers also assess students' food-preparation, cooking, and cleanup skills. Teachers do this by observing students as they work in the kitchen or food pantry, making notes about what the students are doing well and what they may need to improve. Teachers may choose to use a checklist such as those found in the Reproducible Masters section at the end of this book to create a paper record of their impressions of each student's work habits. Students may also use these checklists to self-evaluate their contributions to their service learning teams.

Each student also assembles a project portfolio that includes written work, the reflective log, quiz and test scores, and other evidences of learning that complete the picture of the student's learning that resulted from the project.

Each student will have the following specific portfolio pieces for this project:

- The reflective log
- Essay: "Interpersonal Skills That I Strengthen by Doing This Project" (with prewriting organizer)
- List of community agencies with ties to this project
- Menu plans for two days with food pyramid nutritional analyses
- Recipes for service project dinners: original recipes, scale-up calculations, and scaled-up versions of recipes
- Greatest AHA! and personal service goal
- Quiz and test scores
- Three other evidences of learning chosen by the student

Each student must include the three final portfolio pieces. They could include interviews with people who run soup kitchens or food pantries in the community, videotapes showing the student working in the soup kitchen, audiotaped conversations between the student and soup kitchen managers or customers, reflections on hunger and homelessness, or ideas for extension projects.

Each student shares his or her portfolio with base-group teammates during the project celebration. This final feedback helps students realize how much they have learned about nutrition, community needs, and themselves as service-givers through The Soup Troop project.

Elementary Reflective Log

What we did was . . .	Our service is needed because . . .
Here's what I learned about • menu planning and cooking: • myself: • helping my community:	What I did well was . . .
Today's big idea was . . .	What I can do better next time is . . .

Middle School Reflective Log

My service-connected actions were . . .

This service is important to the town because . . .

Here are my most important learnings about

- nutrition, cooking, and hunger:

- myself:

- doing community service:

- working with my teammate(s):

My best actions and thoughts were . . .

Next time I want to improve . . .

High School Reflective Log

My learning about hunger today is . . .

Some specific nutrition and cooking ideas or skills I learned are . . .

The life skill learning that I most want to remember is . . .

Working with my teammate(s) helped me learn that because . . .

I can use this life skill again when I . . .

My greatest insight about the importance of The Soup Troop project is . . .

My thoughts and feelings about my role as a member of this community are . . .

The personal strengths I brought to the service project today are . . .

Next time I want to improve . . .

7

Computer Tutors

An Instructional Technology and Language Arts Service Learning Project

DESCRIPTION OF THE PROJECT

Capitalizing on the fact that today's students from pre-kindergarten through college have far better computer skills than many middle-aged or senior adults do, this service learning project sets up students as mentors—computer tutors. These students have grown up with computers in their classrooms or their homes and have played computer games or used applications for as long as they can remember. Few young people today are uncomfortable with computers, so students tend to develop computer skills quickly and remember them well.

On the other hand, many older adults are "computer illiterate," and they may even be "computer phobic" or "technophobic"—terms for an attitude best expressed by, "I've gotten this far in life without using a computer, and I'm too old to learn that new technology." As use of computers in the workplace increases, some adults are finding that they need to acquire some basic word-processing, spreadsheet, database, or graphics skills. Others need to learn specialized applications for their employers. They are often reluctant or afraid to tackle learning these skills on their own, so they look for a place to take a basic computer skills course. Retirees who are computer illiterate often want to learn e-mail and Internet search skills. Through conversations with friends, they have heard that online shopping offers convenience, that Internet auction sites proffer a wide variety of goods, and that e-mailing family and friends is a fast, reliable way to stay in touch.

Typically, older adults want to find someplace where they can learn applications that they use on the job or at home and where they can receive some personal attention and tutoring as needed. Community adult education programs often include at least one course focusing on computer use. Because community education courses are easily accessible and affordable, they often fill to capacity quickly, shutting out significant numbers of adults who want to enroll. If the courses are offered at inconvenient times, they fail to attract the minimum number of students and are cancelled. The adults find themselves caught between the need or desire to become computer literate and the lack of available training.

Computer skills courses usually have maximum class size limits. The number of machines available in the computer lab is one factor that determines class size. The instructors for these courses want one student per computer to give each person maximum practice time. Another factor that limits class size is the number of students that the instructor feels he or she can effectively manage at one time. One instructor often has a hard time giving several computer-anxious students the individual attention that each one wants and needs. Because of these concerns, class enrollment cannot be expanded to include everyone who wants to take the course. Computer-literate school-age students have the skills required to help fill the need for computer tutoring as a community service, and that is where this service learning project finds its purpose.

Students often receive formal instruction in using computer application software when they are in elementary or middle school. The teacher monitors his or her students' computer skills to decide when the students are ready to start this service learning project. After students have become skillful in using appropriate applications, the computer teacher asks them, "Do any of you know an adult, perhaps one of your parents' friends, who is having trouble learning how to use a computer?" When some of the students volunteer that, yes, they do know at least one adult who has poor computer skills, the teacher asks, "How much of a problem do you think this is in the community? How can we find out?" As students brainstorm, they suggest that members of the class could interview their parents, neighbors, or friends' parents to get more information about the problem. Students prepare to do the survey by writing a questionnaire such as the following:

Do you use a computer for work, personal business, or pleasure?

- If yes: What kinds of applications do you use?

  How did you learn your computer skills?

  How comfortable do you feel using the computer?

  What do you do when you have a computer use problem?

- If no: Do you want (or need) to learn some computer skills?

  Would you feel comfortable teaching yourself how to use a computer?

  Would you describe yourself as being uncomfortable with computers?

  Would you be willing to learn a computer application if you could take a community education course and get personal attention with problems?

Keeping Records and Building a Portfolio

Each student agrees to interview at least five adults and have information ready to share with the rest of the class a few days after the brainstorming session.

Students interview adults and record their answers on survey forms. Each student keeps his or her survey results to file in the service learning project portfolio. The students quite probably discover that many adults in the community, particularly older adults, do not have any skill in using computers. Often, these older adults believe the computer is a tool that is so complicated they would never be able to figure out how to use it. In some cases, the belief that their employers want them to learn some computer skills fairly soon leads to anxiety about job performance and security.

When they reflected on connecting students with middle-aged or senior adults, community partners and volunteers said that these connections

- often break down intergenerational barriers,
- bond two groups, youth and older adults, who are often not taken seriously or respected in our society,
- encourage two-way communication between members of the two groups, with the adults often contacting students before a scheduled service day to ask about upcoming activities or remind students of service details that are easy to overlook,
- give members of both groups a chance to mix and mingle with each other, a process that leads to enhanced cooperation and learning for members of both groups.

—(Johnson, M., 2001, p. 18)

After the class discusses the survey results, the teacher asks, "How can we do something to help adults in our community learn how to use computers? Think about an answer. What can we do?" Students brainstorm a variety of answers to this question: inviting adults to join the regular school class, teaching adults how to use the computer in their own homes, teaching adults how to use the computer in the students' homes, or helping out with a community education computer course.

In a typical scenario, students and teacher agree that the last option is the most realistic and practical. Many adults work during school hours and cannot attend regularly scheduled school classes. School policy probably requires visitors such as senior "computer students" to obtain security clearance before they are allowed to participate in in-school activities. Adults who are computer illiterate probably do not own computers, and the computers in students' homes are for use by the whole family, not just the student. A generally acknowledged fact is that the community education program has introductory courses scheduled and has the computers available.

In this scenario, the next issue that students and the computer teacher address is how students can help with the community education computer course. Younger students still need to develop the communication skills that they need to actually be the teacher of an adult course. Older students need to develop facilitation skills and a comfort with leadership skills to be effective as the person in charge of a room full of adults.

Before proceeding with the service learning project, the teacher and students contact a community education computer instructor to determine interest in their services. If they learn that there is interest in and need for their help in adult education courses, the students and teacher begin preparation for the project. They brainstorm and design a one-page flyer describing their qualifications and services and distribute it to the administrators and computer instructor of the community education school. Here is a sample flyer for this scenario:

Computer Tutors Available

The fifth-grade Computer Skills class at Northern Lakes School is now making the following special offer: We will tutor adult students who are taking the community schools course, Introduction to the Computer.

- We know how to use the software.
- We know about and like using computers.
- We will help students in this course by serving as assistants to instructors; we will be computer tutors.

No matter how the teacher introduces the computer tutors concept, the teacher and students need to make contact with the adult education instructor or representative to arrange a partnership between the students and the community education program. To be the most helpful and effective, students sit in on the computer class sessions, observing and listening to the instruction and directions, and then they tutor individual members of the class during practice time. Sometimes the instructor identifies class members who need help. At other times, each student is assigned to be available to help one or two specific adults. The ideal tutoring team consists of one student and one adult.

During such tutoring, the student sits or stands near his or her assigned adult learner, watching the adult use the computer during practice time. If the student sees the adult having trouble or doing something incorrectly, the student facilitates immediate correcting of mistakes. This student-adult pairing results in improved learning *and* improved intergenerational communication and respect. The community education instructor and the students can also arrange for extended tutoring hours, time of day and availability of facilities permitting. If the computer lab can be open and supervised during the hour prior to class, students can be available to help adult members of the class who want to have individual problems solved or who want to get some extra practice using the computers.

As students become more comfortable with their leadership role and become more proficient tutors, their adult partners may want them to spend their tutoring time at the adults' workplaces. Students and adults can work together to solve specific hardware or software problems and help the adults become more comfortable and confident in working with computers. Students, teacher, and adult work together with the adult's employer to determine the feasibility of this kind of tutoring and to work out a schedule. In these situations, the teacher must insist that two students work together, accompanied by an approved adult volunteer, to promote safe working conditions for the students.

Often, students have family members who want to learn how to improve their use of personal home equipment. These students and the teacher can design a service plan for the students to teach their family members how to use computer hardware and software. The student and family member need to use a log sheet to keep track of the tutoring service. Here is a typical log sheet:

Name of Student:

Date: Time Spent:

Person Tutored:

Application/Task:

I verify that the information in this log is correct.

Signed:

Each log sheet is signed by a family adult who is present when the tutoring occurs.

If all of the students are not needed as tutors for night school students or family members, the teacher and students brainstorm other community sites where adults often need help with computer use. For example, computer users at the community library often need assistance as they search databases for information or do Internet research. The teacher, students, and librarians can discuss how the students can help, how many are needed to work in the library at any one time, and what training the students need with the library computer (i.e., the online catalog) system. Students possibly need some instruction in using the library system before they are ready to help adults. The students and librarian use a log, similar to the home log, to verify the students' community service.

The teacher will want to be sure that students have transportation and an escort to and from tutoring sites. Many community education programs use K–12 school facilities to run their classes, and this allows student tutors to walk to their regularly attended school to do the tutoring. If this is not the case, community volunteers need to be scheduled to serve as escorts or to provide tutors with transportation to and from the school for the adult education classes. The teacher must ensure that adult volunteers are available to escort or transport students to and from all tutoring sites, including adult partner job sites. This usually means that the teacher builds a large pool of adult volunteers who have flexible hours for escorting students before discussing the project with students. Older student tutors can often use public transportation to get to and from the tutoring sites, and they sometimes drive themselves. The goal is to provide maximum flexibility in the tutoring program while ensuring the safety of the student tutors.

Each student keeps a reflective log that includes a record of the dates and times that the student did tutoring, the adults with whom the student worked, the work site, the computer-related tasks that the adults were doing, problems encountered in doing the task, and solutions to the problems. The reflective portion of each entry features the student's thoughts about being in the teacher-leader role. Sample log formats are included later in this chapter.

As students do their tutoring service learning project, they are improving their own computer skills. In the project portfolio, each student keeps at least one sample of word-processing, spreadsheet, database, and graphics work from the beginning of the student's own computer class and one sample of each kind of work from near the end of the tutoring project so that the student can demonstrate how his or her skills have improved over time.

ASSESSING RISKS: ESTABLISHING PROTOCOLS FOR HEALTH AND SAFETY

The classroom computer teacher needs to be sure that at least two students and two adults are present at all times when students are working at the community school's computer lab or at the adult student's job site. At least one of the adults must have appropriate background clearance. This practice not only ensures the appearance of propriety, it also promotes safe working relationships between students and adults. Students and adults need to be comfortable with each other, and they also need to act respectfully and appropriately when they work with each other.

Transportation to and from tutoring sites needs to be safe and secure as well. For younger students, this means that adult chaperones accompany the students whether they are using public transportation, walking, or using the adult's vehicle. The teacher needs to talk with the school administration about all transportation possibilities, and teacher, students, and administrators must develop protocols to be rigorously observed regarding student transportation. Whenever possible, at least two students travel together to and from a tutoring site.

Because students often do their tutoring away from the school building, they telephone their community partner when they are leaving for a tutoring session, and they contact the teacher or their parents when they arrive at work. If a student does not arrive at work within a reasonable amount of time, the adult supervisor at the tutoring site contacts the teacher or the student's parents. These communication links must be established before the tutoring begins.

SELECTING THE SERVICE LEARNING FOCUS: COMPUTER EDUCATION PARTNERSHIPS

The process of choosing the Computer Tutor project often follows the scenario described earlier in this chapter. When a teacher skips the survey and brainstorming activities and simply presents the idea to the class, he or she runs the risk of students not buying into the project. A class discussion focusing on the need for the project and the value of the service to the community education instructor does encourage student buy-in. As stakeholders in this service learning project, students feel more "invested" if the teacher uses the first approach to selecting the project. Students

Figure 7.1 Sample Project Evaluation Rubric: Computer Tutors

Ranking / Criteria	1 (high)	2 (medium)	3 (low)	Comments
Interest	X			We feel comfortable with computers and we like using them.
Need	X			Survey results show many community adults are computer phobic.
Accessibility	X			The adult class meets in our school computer lab.
Appropriateness	X			We are the most computer-comfortable group in the community, and we have the skills and training we need to be good tutors.
Time Frame	X			We'll do tutoring during the term when we're taking our own computer class.

who believe that they had some say in determining the service learning project work harder to ensure its success.

The students and teacher will want to use a rubric such as the one in Figure 7.1 to summarize their thinking about the project.

Tapping Into Multiple Intelligences: Analyze, Prioritize

Logical, Verbal, Interpersonal, and Intrapersonal Multiple Intelligences

Early in the school year, explain service learning to students. Check for understanding to be sure that they are clear about the difference between community service and service learning.

Next, give students copies of charts showing the alignment between service and curriculum goals for four to five different service learning project possibilities. Be sure that each possible project shows alignment with goals from two to three content areas.

Say, "If you want to come to class in two days prepared to participate in a class discussion, examine the charts and rank the projects from 1 to 5, with 1 being the project that you'd like to do the most and 5 being your last choice."

On the designated day, have students discuss the rankings in their base teams before engaging in a whole-class discussion. Tell teams that they need to reach consensus on the project they most want to do. Explain that consensus does not mean unanimity; it means that everyone has had a chance to present his or her thinking, the team has voted, and everyone agrees to live with the majority.

Insist that during the team discussions, students give the reasons for their rankings. Stress the importance of aligning the reasons with the goals of the projects.

Moderate a whole-class discussion, asking each team to tell the class which service learning project it has selected as its favorite and its reasons for wanting to do that project. Again, emphasize the importance of connecting reasons to the goals met by the project.

When all teams have presented their ideas, reach consensus with the whole class on the service learning project that the class will be doing.

Students welcome the opportunity to express their opinions about the projects, and they appreciate the respect they are shown during this selection process. By using this process to choose the service learning project, the teacher signals that he or she believes the students are capable of making reasoned, well-thought-out decisions based on data or documentation, in this case, the goal alignment charts.

Making Connections With the Community

Working cooperatively with the school administration, the project sponsor—usually the teacher but perhaps the school principal—telephones the community education computer instructor to ask about forming the tutoring partnership. The teacher, students, and the community partner discuss possibilities for placing student computer tutors in the community education classroom and at job sites around the community.

To ensure the greatest cooperation among all parties, the computer teacher, student representatives, principal, and community education director meet together to work out this service learning project. If the work site option is viable and supported by all parties involved—and the teacher has a pool of escort/transportation volunteers (e.g., parents and other security-cleared adults) who would be available for transportation—the idea of work site tutoring is considered at this time.

WORKING WITH A COMMUNITY PARTNER

The teacher needs to ask the community education instructor how many computer tutors can work in the adult education class at one time. If the room is too small to accommodate the adult students, the equipment, and all of the younger students who want to tutor, student tutors are assigned to work in shifts. For example, if the community education class is two hours long, some students can work for the first hour while others take their place for the second hour. The computer teacher and community education instructor ask how many of the adults would like an in-class tutor and how many would like a work site tutor.

At this point in the project, the computer teacher then finds out which students are interested in each tutoring option and makes arrangements according to these preferences. Each tutor sets up a tentative tutoring schedule during the first work session. This schedule, with any adjustments or changes noted, becomes part of the project portfolio. Each student works a minimum of 15 hours as a tutor during the course of the project.

Teachers and students can go online to find additional information about computer or other tutoring programs. Each student tutor develops a personal list of Web site addresses where he or she has found information about teaching or tutoring others who are learning computer skills. Using Google or Yahoo! and key words such as "tutoring," "volunteer tutoring," or "teaching computer skills," each student makes a list of at least 10 useful Web sites that he or she finds. Each student makes a list of the URLs for the Web sites and the key words and phrases, and this list is placed in the student's project portfolio. The teacher, a parent, or another authorized adult must supervise student Internet searches.

Teachers say that identifying the real needs of a community requires surveying community adults because the issues that make the headlines are not always reflective of community needs.

Teachers also say that we need to expand our definition of "community." They stress that "community" could be as small as the person sitting next to you or as large as the population of the planet, and it includes all possibilities in between.

(Johnson, M., 2001, p. 24)

ALIGNING SERVICE AND EDUCATIONAL GOALS

To qualify as a computer tutor, a student needs to demonstrate correct use of computer hardware and software and perform proper computer maintenance such as cleaning of the mouse, keyboard, and screen (instructional technology). Each computer tutor also must be able to use graphics software to illustrate and highlight work, use word-processing software to produce a written document, create a database with a minimum of five fields and twelve records, and create and use a spreadsheet (instructional technology).

Student Responsibilities and Curricular Areas

To ensure understanding of and agreement about individual skill level, each prospective computer tutor and the teacher concurrently evaluate the student's computer expertise. When the teacher and student agree that the student has the computer skills that are needed to tutor and can explain those skills clearly, the student is ready to help other classmates reach this level of proficiency and, eventually, become a computer tutor who works with adults. Working with his or her classmates helps the prospective tutor develop needed facilitation and leadership skills. See Figure 7.2 for a model alignment of service and educational goals.

Figure 7.2 Computer Tutors: Aligning Service and Educational Goals				
Major Subject	**Learning Goals**	**Life Skills**	**Big Ideas**	**Service Actions**
Instructional Technology	Hardware use Software use Graphics Internet	Ability to use hardware and applications at home and at work	Computer literacy	Tutoring adults in hardware and applications use and Internet
Family Living	Teaching techniques Cross-generational communication	Teaching skills	Cross-generational relationships Empathy	Finding partners Helping an adult at home Tutoring
Language Arts	Clear communication Precise use of language Interpreting nonverbal cues	Clear, precise communication Teaching skills	Effective communication	Troubleshooting Problem solving Writing poster advertising service Tutoring
Other				

This face-to-face concurrent evaluation strategy means that each tutor can communicate clearly and effectively in a teaching situation, evaluate nonverbal feedback from others, and use language that is appropriate to the audience and the purpose (language arts). The teacher discusses the importance of clear communication with students at the beginning of their preparation to become tutors. Teacher and students analyze the role of effective communication skills in the art of teaching and tutoring. Students agree that knowledge of computer skills must be linked with good communication skills in order for their tutoring to be effective.

Next, each student analyzes the needs of the community (service learning) as he or she does the computer use survey with adults, as described previously. The Computer Tutor service learning project helps students work in partnership with members of the community (service learning). Ensuring that the student develops and demonstrates curricular knowledge and skill (service learning), the student does self-evaluation concurrently with the teacher's evaluation.

One of the big ideas in this service learning project is computer literacy. Today, employers generally look for computer literacy coupled with computer comfort. Job applicants do not necessarily need to know specific computer applications. Employers know that these specific applications have very limited lifetimes. What employers are looking for is a comfort level around computers, as well as a feeling that applications and hardware can be handled competently. Applicants who are computer phobic or computer illiterate will not be hired to do jobs that pay much more than the minimum wage. Computer literacy, along with willingness to learn new applications and hardware systems, is an important skill for all job applicants. Even minimum-wage jobs require some level of computer comfort and skills. Counter people in fast-food restaurants, servers in restaurants, checkers in discount stores—all of these individuals must be able to work with job-specific computer skills, and the list is expanding.

By helping community adults develop these skills, the computer tutors in this project provide true service, improving both the adult students' employability and their own. The learning partnership between the adults and the computer tutors addresses another big idea associated with this service learning project: the development of cross-generational links that promote respect, trust, and cooperation among community residents of all ages.

Reciprocity: The Community of Learners

Students are ideally positioned to learn new computer applications and technology. As they receive instruction in using the hardware and software in the school, they are often meeting computers and programs that are newer than those their parents have at home. Because instruction in using this technology is part of most school programs, students receive information in the course of their school years that adults must make an effort to seek out. When students become computer tutors, they pass this information along to the adults in the community, whether those adults are learners in a continuing education course or parents at home. Everyone benefits when students pass their expertise along to adults.

During the tutoring sessions, community adults learn to see the students in a new role. Traditional roles are reversed: The young become the teachers, and the elders are the learners. This switching of roles leads to powerful intergenerational insights, understandings, and appreciations. Participants in this service learning project develop an understanding that they are all truly teachers and learners together, that they are all members of one team in which roles can and do change as circumstances demand.

MANAGING THE SERVICE PROJECT: COMPUTER TUTORS

Because computer tutors are doing their work at different times, at different sites, and even on different days, the teacher will want to have the big picture of this project mapped out well in advance. A model service project management plan for the Computer Tutors project is shown in Figure 7.3.

In addition to this kind of management plan, the computer teacher keeps a master calendar on which he or she records each tutor's schedule and transportation or escort arrangements. The master calendar helps the teacher know where students are working and how many escorts are needed on any given day, and it includes telephone numbers for each work site, escort, and adult supervisor. All of the information that the teacher needs to track the movement of student tutors is readily available on the calendar.

Figure 7.3 Management Plan: Computer Tutors

Phase	Planning	Monitoring	Evaluating
1	Begin computer course. Ask students about adult computer phobia. Plan survey. Start looking for adult escort/transport volunteers. Discuss tutoring and reflective logs.	Students complete survey and discuss results. Brainstorm computer tutor service project. Find out who wants to tutor in adult class, who wants to go to adult job site. Watch students use equipment in school computer lab.	Score use of equipment in computer lab. Students self-evaluate word-processing skills.
2	Contact community schools. Continue teaching students how to use computers. Confirm adult volunteers. Plan flyer.	Collect samples of student word-processing work. Look at graphics use in illustrating work. Duplicate and distribute flyer.	Concurrent evaluation of word-processing and hardware use and care skills. Co-verify readiness for tutoring.
3	Work with community education instructor and adults in class to set up computer tutor schedules. Each student needs 15 hours. Match students with adult escorts as needed. Develop database and spreadsheet skills. Students begin Internet searches for Web sites contributing to the project.	Watch in-class use and development of database and spreadsheet documents. Check with community education instructor for effectiveness and helpfulness of tutoring. Spot-check progress on Internet searches.	Concurrent evaluation of spreadsheet and database use. Check tutoring schedules—are they complete? Does everyone have one?
4	Students do tutoring and keep their reflective logs. Continue to polish computer skills in school.	Spot-check Internet search results. Continue to review and score student work on documents that they produce using the computer. Begin portfolio assembly.	Score student-produced work. Does it show growth over time? Get feedback from continuing education instructor and adult students. Does the tutoring really help? Spot-check reflective logs.
5	Final course and tutoring work. Celebrate project completion by writing a "will" asking future classes to continue the project. Share portfolios in base teams. Write whole-class letter to community education instructor saying, "Thank you for your help." Students and teacher each write one goal for future personal service work.	"Eavesdrop" on portfolio sharing. Ask students to tell each other their greatest learning AHA!, their most burning unanswered question, what they liked most about the project, what they found least comfortable, what they felt they did best, and what they would do differently (and better) next time.	Students and teacher discuss project strengths and areas for improvement. Each person shares with whole class his or her greatest AHA! and personal goal for future service work.

FOSTERING REFLECTIVE LEARNING

Every student does a reflective log entry after planning the tutoring needs survey, collecting survey answers from adults, completing the concurrent evaluation session verifying the student's tutoring readiness, and after each tutoring session. The vocabulary that the teacher uses to focus the reflections is appropriate for the grade level of the students, and older students are encouraged to consider a greater variety of ideas than younger ones.

The basic elements of all the reflective logs for the Computer Tutors project focus on the following:

- What is the need for the service?
- What did the student do well?
- What did the student learn about academic content and skills, life skills, and service skills by doing the community service?

See the reflective logs for elementary/middle school and high school levels at the end of this chapter for strategies to prompt reflections. These models consist of sentence stems and open-ended questions about the service learning project.

The use of the reflective log or journal reinforces content learning. Keeping a log helps the students understand how they are helpful and connected to their community. Reflection also helps them identify their personal strengths and set personal goals for further learning and improvement. It is one of the tools that make service learning particularly valuable to students. Students may include reflections that are recorded in the form of sketches, poems, song lyrics, or graphic organizers, in addition to those written in conventional paragraph form.

ASSESSMENT AND EVALUATION

The teacher does some assessment of content learning by observing students as they work in the school computer lab. Teachers of computer technology often have checklists that they use to chart each student's skill development. Each student meets with the teacher to discuss work that the student has produced during the computer class. During these meetings, the teacher asks the student to explain specifically how he or she used the computer hardware and applications to produce the work, what problems were encountered, how these problems were solved, and what the student did to take proper care of the computer equipment. The teacher and student use these discussions to concurrently evaluate the student's computer and communication skills and to decide when the student has gained the proficiency that he or she needs to become a tutor.

Each student also assembles a project portfolio that include samples of personal work, the reflective log, and other evidences of learning that the student selects to complete the picture of his or her learning that resulted from the project.

Each student will have the following specific portfolio pieces for this project:

- The reflective and tutoring log
- Survey: "Need for Computer Education for Adults"
- Flyer advertising tutoring service
- Personal tutoring calendar: schedule, escort/transportation help, "tutoree," site
- Early course work samples: word processing, spreadsheet, database, graphics
- End-of-course work samples: word processing, spreadsheet, database, graphics
- List of computer tutor Web site addresses with search phrases or key words
- Greatest AHA! and personal service goal
- Three other evidences of learning chosen by the student

The student-selected items are required to complete the portfolio; they give insight into the most important actions and learnings experienced by a student who is a computer tutor.

At the end of the service learning project, students meet in small teams to share portfolios and celebrate success. During these celebrations, students share with each other their insights into the skills and personal qualities needed for effective teaching, their greatest AHAs, and favorite stories about working with the adults whom they tutored. These celebrations help make Computer Tutor learning permanent.

Elementary/Middle School Reflective Log

Dates/hours worked on project:	Name of tutoree:
Tutoring site:	Description of job or assignment:
What went well:	Problems/solutions:
Importance of this service to the community:	

Here are my most important learnings about

- the computer application:

- myself as tutor/leader:

- doing community service:

My best actions and thoughts were . . .

Next time I want to improve . . .

Improving is important to me because . . .

High School Reflective Log

Date/hours worked:	Name of tutoree:
Tutoring site:	Description of job or assignment:
What went well:	Problems/solutions:

Some specific computer application or hardware skills I learned are . . .

What I learned about being a leader is . . .

My greatest insight about the importance of doing community service is . . .

My thoughts and feelings about my role as a member of this community are . . .

My connections to the community have been strengthened because . . .

The personal strengths I brought to the service project today are . . .

Next time I want to strengthen . . .

PART III

Advanced Service Learning Projects

8

The Voice
of the People

A Social Studies and Library
Technology Service Learning Project

DESCRIPTION OF THE PROJECT

Students and the adults around them frequently feel very connected to their town or neighborhood government, somewhat distanced from the state government, and completely detached from and ignored by the federal government. Students in a social studies or humanities class can learn about public issues and the workings of representative democracy while they learn about the structure of the United States government and the functions of each branch. With help from their social studies teacher, students can form a communications organization that gathers information about pending federal legislation; gives that information to adults in the community; collects voter questions, concerns, and opinions; sends that information to the legislators and administration in Washington; and reports back to the community adults about the progress a bill is making through Congress and the ultimate fate of that piece of legislation. As students do this service learning project, they learn about current events and the workings of the U.S. government, and they discover ways in which private individuals can affect public policy.

The first step in this project is for students to get descriptions of federal legislation—bills that are pending before Congress in Washington, DC—to collect information about the history of and the perceived need for those bills. Students predict whether those bills will ultimately die in committee or on the floor of the Senate or House of Representatives, fail to pass both houses of Congress, or pass both houses, receive the president's signature, and become law.

In a typical scenario for The Voice of the People project, the social studies teacher and students begin the service learning information search by contacting the federal legislators' offices to ask for lists of pending legislation for the upcoming term. The teacher may contact these offices in late July or early August, or the teacher may decide to wait until school starts and ask students to make the initial request for information, which is explained in detail on the next page. Students and teacher ask the offices to send a summary of each pending bill directly impacting the school's legislative district and a description of the actions that would be mandated by each bill.

If students don't already know the names of their legislators, they can obtain that information from a number of sources. How to obtain such information on the Web is described below. Students can, of course, obtain the names and office addresses of their legislators from their local public library, the office of their local municipality, or from a voters' service organization. During the course of the project, students will want to send hard copies of information to their U.S. senators or representatives. Because senators and representatives have offices in several different buildings in Washington, DC, students need to get specific addresses for their legislators. They can use a local government information source or visit www.congress.org. As students navigate the Web site and type in their zip codes in the appropriate box, they receive names of their U.S. representative and senators, the Washington, DC, postal addresses for their representative and senators, home district postal addresses, and access to e-mail links for these individuals.

The mailing address for the president is 1600 Pennsylvania Avenue, The White House, Washington, DC 20505.

Summaries of pending legislation can be found at http://thomas.loc.gov.

Students can obtain information about floor activities for the Senate by accessing www.senate.gov/index.htm and clicking on "Information & Records." Similar information for the House of Representatives can be found at http://house.gov. Click on "Clerk of the House" and then "Bill Summary and Status." The *Congressional Record* is at www.gpoaccess.gov/crecord/. Links to many other political and voter organizations can be found at www.yahoo.com/government/politics/. Because of the nature of this service learning project, students need to develop a list of Web sites that can provide them with up-to-date information about the status and progress of legislation.

Once students have a list and description of the legislation that Congress will be considering during the upcoming session, they collect information about the background of at least eight bills as well as implications and public issues or concerns associated with their home district. The teacher assigns the students to small groups. Each group researches one bill, using the collected information to produce a pamphlet that includes a summary of the bill, a list of its mandated actions or policies, and arguments for and against its passage.

At this point, the teacher assigns "buddy groups" who check each other's pamphlets for accuracy, completeness, and clarity of writing. Each group revises its own pamphlet, and the teacher arranges to make at least 100 copies of each pamphlet with each student receiving a copy of each piece to place in his or her project portfolio.

To cover the costs of pamphlet duplication, teacher and students need to establish sources of funding before beginning the pamphlet production. Grant monies are available to fund a variety of service learning projects, and the teacher needs to be aware of funding sources and their application deadlines. If the project does not receive grant funding, and if the school or parent-teacher organization cannot help, teachers and students need to consider a student fundraising project, or they may approach a civic organization for donations.

Students distribute the completed brochures to adults in the community. The students need to ask legislators, through e-mail links, which bills are most likely to reach the floor of the legislature first and begin by handing out information about one of those bills. Each student in the class takes a few brochures, one for his or her parents and a few more for adult neighbors. The student asks the adults to read the information and be ready—in a few days—to ask questions about, give their opinions of, or voice concerns about proposed legislation.

Students write questions like the following that they can use to survey the adults about the pending bill:

- Do you have questions about the need for the bill or its mandated results or actions?
- What are your concerns about the results of the bill?
- What changes would you like Congress to make in this bill?
- As the bill stands now, are you in favor of it or against it?

Exemplary Project: Passing the Referendum

Gerard O'Brien, along with students, parents, and other school personnel and community volunteers, carried out a service learning project to educate voters about the need for the district in which he teaches to pass a school-funding referendum. After years of running budget surpluses, the district was now having difficulty balancing the budget. Without an infusion of funds, the administration was facing the need to make some tough decisions to cut programs, reduce staff, and increase class size.

This service learning project aligned with social studies, language arts, computer technology, and citizenship standards. The students learned about the process required to propose a referendum and schedule an election; they wrote pamphlets that informed community residents about the problems that would result from a funding shortfall; students desktop-published the pamphlets and with school personnel, parents, and adult volunteers, went door to door, talking with community residents about the issues and the need to vote "yes" in the special election. Making connections with state and federal legislative processes, students compared the referendum process with that needed to sponsor funding bills.

A steering committee composed of O'Brien, students, school personnel, and adults from the community met several times a week, often early in the morning, so that "block" or precinct leaders could report on their progress in contacting community members. O'Brien described the teams:

Our teams consisted of teachers, teaching assistants (TAs), students, and some parents. "Parents" was probably our smallest percentage of workers, but having a few really made a difference.

This process was time-consuming and carried out by many who had to be "coached up" to leave their comfort zones and sell the importance and necessity of this issue. By the time the vote came around, I am confident that we hit every registered voter.

When the referendum passed, everyone breathed a huge sigh of relief. Reflecting on the project's impact, O'Brien said that not often do students have the opportunity to be in such a vital sponsorship role, perform such a crucial service for their schools, and learn lessons that will stick with them for the rest of their lives.

Keeping Records and Building a Portfolio

Each student surveys the adults who received the information about the bill from them. Discussing the highlights of the bill with each adult, they take time to draw out the adult's questions or concerns. Each student records all answers to the survey questions and reports these results to his or her team. Teams develop composite answers to report to the rest of the class, being careful to honestly and accurately reflect the adults' opinions and concerns. Students scrupulously follow general guidelines for effective interviewing and ethical reporting. The students remember that they are serving as a conduit between the community and the legislature. Each student files the survey records he or she made during the interviews in his or her project portfolio.

When all of the adults have answered the survey, the whole class compiles the results. The group that wrote the brochure for a given bill composes a message to the legislators and the president.

To inform the president and legislators about the voice of the people, students include the following information they obtained as they researched the bill and conducted the survey:

- The final public opinion tally on the bill
- Any questions that voters had about the need for the bill
- Any concerns about the results of the bill
- Any changes that voters think would make the bill better
- A summary of the learnings about the issue, the legislative process, and how the federal government works

The group sends the message by e-mail to both senators from their state, the representative from their district, and the president. Also, the group sends a hard copy of the message to each of these individuals.

The teacher makes copies of the message for students to give to the adults who participated in the survey. Each student returns to his or her adult community members, gives each adult a copy of the message that the class sent to the president and the legislators, thanks the adult for participating in the survey, and asks if the adult would like to be an ongoing partner in the project. Each student keeps a copy of the message to place in his or her project portfolio.

As the project continues, students return to the community adults with brochures about other pending legislation. Each time that students hand out information, they return in several days to conduct the survey and report the survey results to the class. Before the end of this service project, each team writes a message to the legislators and president about the survey and brochure.

The teacher and students also will want to set up communication lines with the adults in the community for collecting opinions and concerns about other government business. Students will want to place a "Questions/Comments/Opinions for Washington" mailbox in the main office of their school, and they need to discuss the positioning and display of this mailbox with the school administration. Adults are invited to put notes containing their written ideas in the mailbox at any time. If they use this system, students pick up the "mail" once a day and send the ideas to senators, members of Congress, and the president as new e-mail.

At this point, the teacher assigns a different student to pick up the mail and send the e-mail each day. That student asks members of his or her team to help with reading the mail and checking the e-mail for accuracy before sending it.

Students include the following essential information about themselves as constituents with each e-mail message:

- The name of their school
- Their grade level
- The teacher's name
- The name of the school and city, town, or village

At the end of the project, students give the community adults a pamphlet that contains the e-mail and postal addresses for their legislators as well as telephone numbers that students used to contact Congress or the White House while doing The Voice of the People project.

While students are involved with this service learning project, they are studying the structure of the U.S. government and the duties of each of the legislative houses. This communications project gives them a citizen/government interactive context in which to learn. Students learn about the workings of their government, the role that citizens can play in a representative democracy, and the concerns and issues that are addressed in the legislation while they communicate with the senators and representatives from their state and the president.

Through The Voice of the People project, students develop the understanding that their community is made up of many interrelated groups with intertwining concerns and that the actions of any one group affect all other groups. They learn that events are linked in feedback cycles and that no legislation can predict and control everything that it targets. Finally, students learn that citizens' voices can be heard by those in the federal government, that much can be gained by listening to others in their community, and that concerned citizens can speak for others in their communities by asking elected officials to act in their best interests.

ASSESSING RISKS: ESTABLISHING PROTOCOLS FOR HEALTH AND SAFETY

Any time that students do door-to-door canvassing in the community, the teacher and administration need to educate them about safety. An ideal solution to this pressing safety concern is to ask that each student be accompanied by a parent or adult who has guardianship authority whenever the student is contacting neighbors. If this is not possible, adult volunteers from the community can often be found to step in and chaperone the students. Each student must submit a waiver, signed by a parent, giving the student permission to participate in the community interviews. In established neighborhoods, parents often feel comfortable giving students permission to visit a few neighbors without their supervision. With younger students or in less stable neighborhoods, the teacher and a student team may canvass as a small group. A key is to stress the safety that is found in numbers, especially when those numbers include someone well known to and trusted by the student.

Access to many schools is tightly controlled. Visitors need to be admitted by adult supervisors, and once inside the building, they are to be accompanied to a central office to receive permission to visit other areas of the building. Students need to inform community members about restricted access to the school and about procedures for delivering messages to the mailbox.

Messages that are left in the mailbox or e-mailed to students may contain offensive language, or a correspondent may be a child predator. The teacher needs to screen all mail, whether it arrives through the school mailbox or e-mail, before passing it along to students. If parents or other adult volunteers are helping with this project, these adults may take turns screening the mail. The key is to protect students from offensive content or overtures.

Students make extensive use of the Internet to do this service learning project. Because they need to know the current state of pieces of legislation and because they communicate frequently with senators and representative from their district, they are online daily. Adults must supervise student use of the Internet to ensure the appropriateness of accessed Web sites. Schools and families often have firewalls in place, but they never replace adult oversight.

SELECTING THE SERVICE LEARNING FOCUS: A COMMUNITY-GOVERNMENT COMMUNICATION PIPELINE

To set up this project with students early in the school year, the teacher asks his or her class,

> How many of you have ever heard an adult say, "I wish I could get those people in Washington to listen to me," or "Those people in Washington don't care about little people like us." Raise your hand if you have ever heard an adult say something along those lines.

Typically, many students indicate that they have heard at least one adult make such a statement. Next the teacher asks,

How many of you know an adult who has communicated with a member of the House of Representatives or the Senate, or with the president about his or her concerns? Or an adult who has written a letter to Washington, DC, sent a fax, called a comment line telephone number, or sent an e-mail message expressing concern or strong feelings, pro or con, about a national policy, proposed legislation, or a pending appointment? Raise your hand if you know an adult who has sent at least one message to Washington.

Often few if any hands go up. In such a scenario, the teacher then says,

I think that communicating with our elected representatives is a very important step we can take to help ourselves and the other members of our community. I want to teach you how to do that. I also want us to help some of the adults in the community get their opinions to Washington. I think we can act as a "voice of the people" to get that job done. Let's discuss such a service learning project for our social studies class.

The teacher then facilitates a class discussion to examine The Voice of the People project and how it fits the goals (content learning) of the class.

Making Connections With the Community

A preliminary discussion such as the one described above brings out some of the things that students do in the project: researching the issues behind the bills, designing the brochures, conducting the surveys, and composing letters and e-mail messages. The teacher explains that the students are learning about the branches of government, the process by which a bill becomes a law, election laws and cycles, and other features of representative democracy—using the resources in the school media center, the Internet, and the local public library to research the issues and concerns behind the proposed legislation. The teacher also explains that this service learning project puts the curricular learning into the context of a participatory democracy so that students are learning about their form of government while they communicate with their elected representatives.

The teacher and students evaluate the service idea using a rubric such as the one shown in Figure 8.1. As students become immersed in this service learning project, they experience the feelings of belonging and empowerment that grow from making a positive contribution to the community. The teacher helps them remember the curricular focus that accompanies the service goals.

WORKING WITH A COMMUNITY PARTNER

The social studies teacher and his or her students are able to do most if not all of the work for this project on their own or with help from the school principal. Students can obtain input for the messages to legislators and the president from their parents and neighborhood adults. The school can provide Internet access. If the school is not online, the community library probably is. The community librarian and social studies teacher can schedule times for students to use the library's computers.

Figure 8.1 Sample Project Evaluation Rubric: The Voice of the People

Criteria / Ranking	1 (high)	2 (medium)	3 (low)	Comments
Interest	X			We'll learn about using the Internet and e-mail to access elected officials, and we'll learn about our form of government.
Need	X			It seems everyone complains about the government. We'll do something about it.
Accessibility	X			We'll inform and survey our parents and neighbors. The "Mailbox," computers, library research tools, and media are right here in school.
Appropriateness	X			We'll soon be voting citizens ourselves.
Time Frame	X			Ongoing—as we study the structure of our government.

Organizations that can advise the teacher on ways to coordinate the curricular objectives with the service learning project are the most helpful partners. One such organization is the League of Women Voters. They are strictly nonpartisan and are dedicated to helping all U.S. residents become better informed about the structure and functions of the branches of government and the contribution that a voter makes to the success of the nation.

If they do not have grant money for the project, the students and teacher can ask some local organizations for help with funding for printing brochures and survey forms and postage. Groups that often sponsor service learning projects include the American Legion and VFW or service clubs such as the Lions, Rotary, Eagles, or Junior Women's League, as well as local political party offices.

ALIGNING SERVICE AND EDUCATIONAL GOALS

The curricular studies that accompany this service learning project focus students' attention on the basic features and functions of the branches of the federal government (social studies).

Student Responsibilities and Curricular Areas

Students who are involved in the service learning project model an example of the rights and responsibilities of citizens while they organize, analyze, and explain information about selected public issues (social studies). As they distribute the brochures to members of the community and conduct the surveys, students practice forms of civic discussion and participation that are consistent with the ideals of citizenship in a republic (social studies). See Figure 8.2 for a model alignment of service and educational goals.

To write the brochures about pending bills, students use the school and community library to search for materials by subject and key word (library skills). They demonstrate that they can use electronic databases to find information in periodicals and use search engines to find information on the Internet (library skills). As students select what material to include in the brochure and what to discard, they demonstrate their ability to evaluate sources of information for accuracy and bias and synthesize information from various sources (library skills).

Students produce text for the brochures that shows that they can write using precise vocabulary and standard English construction (language arts). Students who participate in this service learning project develop an understanding of the value of the school-community relationship (service learning). By acting as a communications link between the community and the federal government, students demonstrate their understanding of civic responsibility through service learning (service learning). They keep reflective logs to examine the changes that occur in their thinking and skills during the life of the service learning project, and they plan new ways to use their skills to help the community after the project has ended.

One of the big ideas for this service learning project is connectedness. Students see as their focus moves from one piece of legislation to the next that all actions of government are interrelated and interconnected. No action or decision of any government occurs in a vacuum, and every action can have unanticipated consequences with both pluses and minuses. Good legislators and executives try to predict these consequences by looking for historical parallels to present situations. They may be able to minimize the unexpected. They are never able to completely avoid it.

As students work with each other and adults, they begin to appreciate the interconnectedness of their community. As students survey adults and seek to understand their points of view, they begin to appreciate the variety of experiences and knowledge that play a part in shaping opinion. Later, in the reflective log entries, each student is asked to focus on his or her role in the project as messenger. The messenger seeks to understand the opinion of another person well enough to speak for that person. This deeper understanding of communication strengthens the connections between the student and the community, helping the student appreciate the belonging and trust that can grow from such interaction.

Figure 8.2	The Voice of the People: Aligning Service and Educational Goals			
Major Subject	**Learning Goals**	**Life Skills**	**Big Ideas**	**Service Actions**
Social Studies	Branches of government Rights and responsibilities of citizens Civic discussion and participation	Involved citizenship	Civic responsibility	Obtaining the congressional calendar Summarizing bills Surveying community adults Communicating with legislators and the White House Maintaining the community mailbox Reporting to the community
Library Skills	Using electronic databases Accessing and using the Internet	Library research skills Going online to use the Internet and e-mail	Connectedness	Researching bills Surfing the Internet Sending and receiving e-mail
Language Arts	Evaluating for bias Synthesizing Using precise language	Explaining Analyzing Writing/communicating	Connectedness Honoring the speaker	Writing brochures and questionnaires Reporting e-mail answers

Reciprocity: The Community of Learners

As evidenced by the low percentage of voters who participate in national elections, U.S. citizens often feel disconnected from and powerless to influence the national government. People who do not take time from their schedules to vote seldom explore ways in which they can communicate with elected national officials. When these community members make contact with students who are involved in The Voice of the People service learning project, they learn that it is relatively easy to write to representatives and senators in Washington, DC. Anyone who knows his or her zip code and has Internet access can reach elected officials through the congress.org

Web site. During the course of this service learning project, students teach community adults how to use communication links to write to senators, representatives, and the president. Students show adults how to track legislation through committees, onto the floors of the legislative chambers, and into the Oval Office.

When adults read the e-mail answers that students receive from legislators, they learn that their elected officials do care about local issues and interests. Answers from representatives and senators often address the specific issue targeted in e-mail correspondence sent by the students.

Community members also receive valuable information about legislation that could impact their city, town, or village, and they learn how they can act on that information—how they can communicate personal concerns and wishes to their elected legislators. Adults in the community learn to see students as participatory, responsible community citizens who are quite likely to vote in elections and be active in the political process as adults. Students and adults together can celebrate finding a voice in the national government.

Our tiny village on Lake Superior had its existence threatened by Corps of Engineers budget cuts. If our harbor mouth is not dredged, the silt that collects prevents Great Lakes ships from entering the harbor and delivering coal to local industries. A Voice of the People writing campaign resulted in restoration of the funds needed to maintain the harbor. Projects like this one do make a difference.

—Author

MANAGING THE SERVICE PROJECT: THE VOICE OF THE PEOPLE

The management plan for The Voice of the People project shown in Figure 8.3 demonstrates how the initial process of gathering information about pending legislation may begin before school starts in the fall. A plus associated with the early information gathering is that it shortens the start-up time for the service learning project, giving the students more time to do the library or online research and brochure planning. A minus is that it reduces the opportunity for student voice in planning the project, and it reduces the role that students have in collecting the initial information. The management grid shown in Figure 8.3 includes the preschool information gathering; if a teacher has time, more student involvement is always better.

Flexible in nature, the structure of this management plan is based on the assumption that the service learning project is integrated into a full-semester or one-year course focusing on a study of U.S. government. While involved in this service learning project, students read, write, produce graphics, role-play, write songs or chants, and do other assignments to learn the course content. They participate in class discussions as well as take quizzes and tests to demonstrate their content learning. Students often spend very little time doing community service on some days. Over the course of a semester or entire school year, they see that serving for small amounts of time on many days over several months results in a very significant service contribution to the community.

Figure 8.3 Management Plan: The Voice of the People

Phase	Planning	Monitoring	Evaluating
1	Contact senators and members of Congress to get legislation information. Write a letter explaining the project to students and parents, seeking parental involvement. Ask local voters' and political or service organizations for help with funding. Contact political and voters' groups listed on the Web for information about advice, speakers, etc. Plan curriculum.	Select 12–14 pieces of proposed legislation to present to students—they can refine the list down to 8–10. Set up hints and guidelines for library research. Check curriculum plans for connections among branches of government. Plan specific assignments, tests, quizzes, etc.	Finalize curriculum/service project syllabus. Check for alignment of goals. Revise plans as needed.
2	Discuss curriculum and project with students. Hand out assignment sheet and reflective log instructions. Send home letter to parents. Assign base teams. Begin curriculum study. Confirm funding sources. With students, decide on "final" list of bills for brochures and surveys. Assign one bill to each team. Have teams do library research and write brochures.	Buddy teams check over each other's brochures. Revise brochures and get them duplicated. Check curricular progress with discussions, student graphics, quizzes, tests.	Score content learning assessment: quizzes, tests, class discussion, graphics. Students self-evaluate library skills and plan for improvement.
3	First round: Distribute brochures, explain project to community adults, do survey, compile results, send e-mail, and mail hard copy to legislators and president. Have students explain "mailbox" to community adults; invite their questions. Pass comments to legislators and president using e-mail.	Discuss survey results in class. Discuss any feedback from e-mail messages. Analyze brochure/survey process; refine it. Continue curricular study/assessment. Assign students for mailbox check. Handle mailbox pickup and e-mail concerns. Spot-check reflective logs.	Score content learning assessments. Students self-evaluate progress and discuss progress in base teams. Students discuss reflections on their roles as messengers.
4	Continue content study and brochure/survey/e-mail/feedback/self-evaluation cycle. Students maintain reflective logs and collect evidence of content learning. Teacher and students generate a list of portfolio pieces.	Last month of course: Assemble and check portfolios. Students do last assignments, take final exam, revise/improve portfolio pieces. Spot-check reflective logs.	Score curricular assignments. Students and teacher concurrently evaluate learning. Check portfolios—are they ready for sharing? End of course: Score final exams. Determine final grades.
5	Celebrate project completion by writing a "will" asking future classes to continue the project. Share portfolios in base teams. Write whole-class letter to e-mail to legislators and president, saying, "Thank you for listening." Students and teacher each write one goal for future personal service work.	"Eavesdrop" on portfolio sharing. Ask students to tell each other their greatest learning AHA!, their most burning unanswered question, what they liked most about the project, what they found least comfortable, what they felt they did best, and what they would do differently (and better) next time.	Students and teacher discuss project strengths and areas for improvement. Each person shares with whole class his or her greatest AHA! and personal goal for future service work. Note: This may be done before final exam.

Tapping Into Multiple Intelligences: Storyboarding the Project

Visual, Kinesthetic, and Interpersonal Multiple Intelligences

While the management plan grid does an excellent job of organizing "to-do's" for the service learning project, it does not bring the project alive. Many students need to see a more visual representation of the step-by-step progress of the project in order to understand what actions they need to take and how they will sequence those actions. Students and teacher can borrow a page from advertising, television, and film production and storyboard the upcoming phase of the service learning project. Here's how it works:

1. First, students and teacher brainstorm the activities that they need to do in the next phase of the service learning project and sort those ideas into the three categories: planning, monitoring, and evaluating.

2. Next, student teams take the sticky-notes for each category and sequence them. What planning activity do they need to do first? What comes second?

3. Teams do the same sorting and sequencing with the planning and evaluating sticky-notes.

4. Then teams integrate the sticky-notes from all three categories to obtain a single sequenced list of activities for the phase of the service learning project. Some of the activities from different categories may occur more or less simultaneously. Students lay out the sticky-notes along a time line, with simultaneous activity sticky-notes placed in a vertical column hanging down from the horizontal time line.

5. Next, students use the sticky-notes to create images, much like the images in a comic strip, with separate frames in the strip representing different activities. Students decide whether they want a frame for each step along the time line or whether they prefer to combine some steps. A more detailed "comic strip" gives a more complete picture of the project's activities.

6. Students use color and images as they create the storyboard. The final product shows a team's mind's-eye "movie" of how doing the service learning project will look.

7. Members of a team sign the finished product before hanging it on a classroom wall.

8. Teams do a "gallery walk" to view each other's storyboards. As they rotate from one storyboard to another, the team correspondent jots down notes about similarities and differences between another team's sequence and their own.

9. After the gallery walk, the teacher leads a class discussion focusing on similarities and differences in the sequencing. The whole class reaches consensus on the sequence of activities for the upcoming phase of the project.

Doing the storyboard does take time away from other in-class activities. The payoff is the improved understanding that students develop about what they will be doing, when they will be doing it, and how the tasks will be done. The teacher can save some in-class time by asking each student to make a personal set of sticky-notes and saying, "If you want to come to class tomorrow prepared to help your team and the class, you will use the sticky-notes to develop a time line of activities and tasks for the next phase of the service learning project." He or she spends some time checking for understanding about what a time line is and how to use the sticky-notes to accomplish the task. Students who do this advance preparation need less in-class time to develop the sequence, so they can spend more time creating the storyboard.

FOSTERING REFLECTIVE LEARNING

Every student maintains a reflective log or journal for this project.

Students construct journal entries after each of the following steps:

- The initial class discussion of the project
- Each session of library research about the legislation
- Each small-group session spent writing and revising the brochure
- Each distribution of brochures to selected community residents
- Each survey of the adults and discussion of survey results
- Each message transmission/mailing to legislators and the president
- The receipt of each communication (feedback) from the legislators and the office of the president
- Each checking of the mail and the relaying of those messages to Washington, DC
- Each opportunity for reflection on the messenger role

The reflective log entries show how the student's understanding of connectedness and being a messenger has grown and developed over the course of the service learning project. The vocabulary that the teacher uses to focus the reflections is appropriate for the grade level of the students.

The basic elements of all of the reflective logs focus on the following:

- What is the need for the service?
- What did the student do well?
- What did the student learn about academic content and skills, connections, and being a messenger by doing the community service?

See the reflective logs for the elementary/middle school and high school levels at the end of this chapter for strategies to prompt reflection. These models consist of sentence stems or starters and open-ended questions about the service learning project.

The reflective log makes service learning particularly valuable to students by helping them focus on their intellectual, social, and ethical growth. As students write and share their reflections, they explore the meaning of the service role, the contributions of the service to the community, and their personal growth as service providers and learners.

ASSESSMENT AND EVALUATION

The teacher assesses content learning using class discussions, writing samples, student-produced graphics, songs and chants, role-plays, question-and-answer sessions, paper-and-pencil quizzes and tests, and portfolios. Students and teacher work together to develop rubrics to score writing, graphics, songs, and participation in discussions. Because this service learning project is seen as complementing a semester or full-year course, the teacher will want to use a full range of strategies to assess curricular learning.

The teacher also asks each student to assemble a project portfolio that includes the following:

- One copy of each of the brochures highlighting pending legislation
- Results from face-to-face survey interviews about each bill
- The whole-class summary of survey interviews for each pending bill
- Copies of the messages to Washington, DC, about each pending bill
- Copies of any correspondence received from Washington, DC
- "Mailbox" e-mail messages and copies of feedback from Washington, DC
- The reflective log
- Greatest AHA! and personal service goal
- Quiz and test scores
- Five other evidences of learning chosen by the student (at least two writings, at least one graphic, at least one song or rap, and one more artifact of any type)

At this point, the class brainstorms a list of extensions to The Voice of the People project. Each student shares his or her portfolio with base teammates during the project celebration. This final feedback helps students realize how much they have learned about course content and themselves as service-givers by doing this project.

Because this project involves a one-semester or full-year course, school policy may also require students to take a paper-and-pencil final examination at the end of the course. Because this final exam will probably be scheduled for the last class meeting, its results are not included in the project portfolio. The teacher and students will want to have plenty of time to focus on portfolio conferences, goal sharing, and interconnected review and assessment of personal and whole-group growth.

Elementary/Middle School Reflective Log

My job during The Voice of the People project was to . . .

This service is important to the community because . . .

Here are my most important learnings about

- the structure and function of the United States government:

- the connections among the branches of government:

- the connections among community, government, and me:

- me as service-giver and messenger:

I believe that the following are the most important ways a messenger interacts with others:

My best actions and thoughts were . . .

Next time I want to improve . . .

Improving is important to me because . . .

High School Reflective Log

My job during The Voice of People project was to . . .

My service is needed by my community because . . .

Here are my most important learnings about

- the structure and function of the United States government:
- the connections among the branches of government:
- the connections among community, government, and me:
- some implications of those connections/feedback spirals:
- me as service-giver and messenger:

I believe that the following are the most important ways a messenger interacts with others:

My best actions and thoughts were . . .

Next time I want to improve . . .

Improving is important to me because . . .

9

Community Vision

A Visual Arts and Library Technology Service Learning Project

DESCRIPTION OF THE PROJECT

Large blank outdoor surfaces such as the walls of buildings or bridge structures in communities or rural areas often become covered with graffiti. Not only is graffiti unsightly, it often signals danger to many community residents and visitors from out of town. Students participating in the Community Vision service learning project perform a significant service to communities faced with a graffiti problem—or to those communities that simply wish to beautify existing areas with public art.

This project not only engages students in cleanup (graffiti removal) activities, it engages them as visual arts students, planning and producing a mural that covers one of these surfaces. Also, students engaged in this project research on the Web and in print media for information on community art. The mural that is the final product is of greatest value if it offers a vision of the community as a place that respects its culture and the contributions made by individual community members. Because this mural project is designed to celebrate the best that the community has to offer, the community at large cares about and respects this public work of art. If the mural succeeds in achieving a vision of the community, graffiti painters in the community are deterred from "tagging" these large outdoor surfaces.

Visual arts students do this service learning project in conjunction with their study of works of art and the cultures that produced them. As they explore the culture-art connection, students find examples of contemporary murals that other students or artists have produced to beautify their community as they discourage graffiti. The students gather information about the cultures of these communities so that they can analyze the ways in which the murals reflect and celebrate their communities. Students use the Internet for Web sites containing useful ideas, and they search local libraries' electronic databases to find newspaper and magazine features about the production of neighborhood murals.

Just three of the many books on public art and murals are *Street Gallery: Guide to 1000 Los Angeles Murals* (Dunitz, 1992), *Chicano Graffiti and Murals: The Neighborhood Art of Peter Quezada* (Quezada & Kim, 1996), and *The Virgin and the Dynamo: Public Murals in American Architecture, 1893–1917* (van Hook, 2003).

The increasing use of public art to clean up and discourage graffiti has resulted in an explosion in the number of Web sites relating to the topic. Students can find hundreds of informative sites by using a search engine such as Yahoo! or Google and key words such as "community murals," "outdoor murals," "neighborhood art," and "graffiti cleanup."

After students have researched the topic of contemporary community murals, each student writes a short essay highlighting what he or she has learned about the connections between neighborhood culture and public works of art. This essay becomes a piece of the project portfolio.

While students are doing this background learning, they and the teacher will

- locate an available community site for the mural
- set up project funding
- arrange a schedule and transportation for students to and from the mural site
- identify community partners for the project

The teacher and students will want to identify an available site, a large surface of at least 20 by 40 feet (or two to three smaller surfaces whose combined areas result in the same total), which students can use for the mural. The merchants' association or department of public works can help with the selection of a mural site, and a fine arts association, an individual artist, or an art museum or art school can provide some expert tips on mural design and execution. If the students, teacher, or administration have concerns about the risks involved in working on an outside wall, one option is to locate an available wall on school property and work in conjunction with the visual arts teachers to design a mural to fill that space.

The best mural sites are highly visible to the rest of the community. The surface to be painted may be a side or end wall of a building, a freeway noise barrier, or a large retaining wall for a highway or railroad overpass.

After clearing permission for this project with the school administration—as well as with proper local authorities if the area is on public property, or with the property owner or manager if the area is on privately owned property—the teacher and student assistants survey the site, confirm the measurements, and take photographs of the wall that is to hold the mural. The class can then study the overall shape, proportions, and location of the proposed mural site. Students will find it helpful to sketch the shape of the surface, especially if it is irregular. They also need to note any special features of the mural site, such as small doorways, windows, or other structural elements that will intrude into the finished product. At this point, the teacher and students need to estimate the number of visits that will be needed to complete the mural project and arrange transportation for students to the site. Many schools do provide bus transportation if, as with any field trip, arrangements are requested in advance. If the school cannot provide a bus, the teacher needs to arrange for adult volunteers or parents to drive students to and from the mural site if this is permitted by local and state school codes. If the teacher has received a grant to do the project, funding for transportation is provided by the grant.

Next, the teacher assigns students to small working groups and asks each group to brainstorm a list of the aspects of the local community or neighborhood culture that they want to feature in the mural.

The teacher asks students to begin their discussions with a focus on the fine arts: visual art, literature, music, and dance. Students also list other components of the local culture that they believe are unique or important.

In the mural, students may want to feature, for example,

- the nuclear or extended family structure within the traditional culture
- an easily pictured ethnic food or local specialty
- a local cultural attraction
- a portrayal of local history
- traditional clothing

After the small groups have some time to do the brainstorming, the teacher facilitates a class discussion to generate a master list of cultural components that could be pictured in the mural. The teacher or a student writes the list on chart paper and displays it on the wall of the classroom. Each student makes an individual copy for his or her project portfolio. The teacher and class continue to study the public art–culture connection, and students begin to study the elements of effective mural design.

As course work and mural planning continue, students analyze contemporary and historic public murals to identify the aspects of the culture that each includes. The class can use this information to refine the list of cultural features that students want to include in their mural.

When the class as a whole has agreed on 8 to 12 components for the mural, each student designs an individual mural prototype that contains all of the agreed-upon cultural elements plus two more of the student's choosing. This prototype is a rough sketch indicating placement, arrangement, and interrelationship of the elements in the mural, showing how the mural fits the site and makes allowances for any existing architectural features of the site. Each student includes a copy of his or her prototype sketch in the project portfolio.

The working groups meet so that teammates can show and explain their prototypes to each other. After each group has discussed the individual sketches, the group designs a composite prototype that members agree combines the best design features from the individual versions. The member of the group who is the quickest at sketching does a pencil draft of the group prototype mural. The teacher—or students if scanners or other copying equipment is available to them—makes a copy for each member of the group to place in his or her project portfolio.

As soon as the working-group prototypes are complete, each prototype is mounted on a large sheet of chart paper. These are taped to the classroom wall, and small groups do a "gallery walk" in which each group studies the prototypes produced by all of the other groups.

Keeping Records and Building a Portfolio

As each group visits a sketch, the teammate with the most legible handwriting (the correspondent) writes comments about the elements of the sketch that the group really likes and questions that the group has about the overall composition of the mural sketch. The teacher then tells the students that they are almost at the point of creating a single draft sketch for the community mural. The teacher suggests that each student jot a few notes in his or her reflective journal, focusing on any unifying elements that the student noticed in the working-group sketches.

The whole class discusses the students' ideas about unifying elements and decides on a focus or theme for the public mural. For instance, in many existing community murals, the unifying theme has been music—either popular music of local musicians or music of a specific ethnic group. This concept furthers the vision of music as a cultural voice that reflects the identity of the community and celebrates the human spirit.

No matter what the subject of the mural, a class will want to choose a focus or unifying theme that creates a powerful connection between the public art and the community. Using the scenario above, a group may decide to feature or portray actual performers from the community. In the case of portraying any actual people in the community or outside of the community, the students first ask permission of those individuals to include their images in the public mural. The teacher keeps signed "Permission to Portray" letters on file in the classroom.

Maintaining a clear vision of this unifying theme, the students and teacher next brainstorm a prototype for the mural. The teacher or a student who sketches quickly produces this prototype on a large sheet of newsprint or chart paper. The main concern is the overall design of the mural.

Students and teacher evaluate the placement of the different elements in the mural, the relationship of these elements to each other, visual flow within the mural, and clear expression of the unifying theme. Students and teacher generate three or four sketch versions so that they can try different compositions before deciding on the one that they like best.

At this point, each group will

- be responsible for two versions of its mural section
- render a detailed pencil drawing of the mural section
- render a painting in watercolor

The teacher or students make copies of the pencil drawings for students to place in their project portfolios.

If the school has Internet access, the teacher and students will want to ask the principal about developing a Web site that features this service learning project. Included on the Web site are student-written explanations of the project and its curricular connections, before-and-after photos of the mural site, comments from community members about the completed mural, photos of students working in the classroom and at the project site, and other elements documenting the history of the mural project and its connection to the community. Construction of the Web site is one way for students and teacher to celebrate successful completion of the Community Vision service learning project.

Student groups use watercolor paint to assemble a completed color prototype of the mural, fitting the separate pieces together like parts of a jigsaw puzzle. The students and teacher analyze and discuss the color prototype and suggest changes in colors, arrangement of individual elements, or sizes of separate drawings. Each group makes a final drawing of its mural section that incorporates these changes. Next, students make these final drawings on graph or grid paper. Each student places a copy of the revised drawing in his or her project portfolio.

Students must next produce full-scale drawings of the mural sections. They can do this using a full-scale grid. Students translate each small line from a square in the small grid into a full-scale line in the corresponding square in the full-scale grid.

Bit by bit, students enlarge the mural drawings. Students can also produce the full-scale drawings by making transparencies of the small drawings, projecting the images onto the full-scale grid paper to make sure that the final image is the desired size, and tracing the projected image onto the larger grid paper. The teacher or colleagues in the school's visual arts department may have other suggestions about producing the full-scale drawings. These drawings are used as mural blueprints at the outdoor site.

The teacher and students draw a grid on the outdoor mural surface, reproduce the drawings on the surface, and do the final painting. The actual production of the mural takes some time to complete. During this time, students distribute small drawings of the mural to members of the community, explaining what they are doing and how they believe the mural contributes to community pride and safety. Copies of the mural with student comments are available at the community offices and welcome center. As word of the project and its purpose spreads, community members become better informed about public art and its impact on community perceptions.

Also, students suggest that care and maintenance of the mural are everybody's business and ask friends, neighbors, and local businesspeople to help them protect the mural and prolong its life. Each student and the teacher sign the completed mural. They arrange an official unveiling ceremony, complete with a short dedication speech presenting the work to the community and music performed by local residents. Arrangements are made to photograph the mural so that each student has a copy of the photograph for his or her project portfolio.

Exemplary Project: Northern Latitude Visions

Several years ago, an inspiration struck a nonprofit community agency in Ontonagon, MI. There were several old weathered fishing shanties on an island in the Ontonagon River whose sides, in the opinion of the agency, were simply begging to be decorated with murals. The Ontonagon schools have a strong K–12 art program, and the agency asked the art teacher if children might be interested in participating in the design and execution of the mural. The teacher, seizing a golden opportunity to do a service learning project that she *knew* the community wanted, asked her students if they wanted to be part of the mural project, and many of them did. Because Ontonagon is in the northern latitudes, most of the mural painting was scheduled for the following summer.

During the school year, the teacher, community volunteers, students, and agency members met to brainstorm the themes and designs of the murals. One volunteer, Carol Huntoon, took charge of one of the murals. Carol says that the committee decided to do most of the painting in the village recreation building, which is large enough to provide a work space that is sheltered from the weather. Carol knew that the best mural design would permit many children to all be painting at the same time. Carol explained,

> We decided on an underwater scene for the mural, which would make it possible for any child to have his or her own fish on it. Because of its size and ultimate location (at the island on an historic fish shack), the mural was painted on several large sheets of commercial-quality billboard material and then mounted after the sheets were completely dry.
>
> Logistically, then, the best way to involve the children and encourage their artistic expression was by hosting several "Paint-a-Fish" sessions. These were held at the mural-painting site at the community center.

The children each painted an individual fish so that each child could select a design and colors. Once the mural background was mounted on the fish shanty, each individual fish was mounted on that background. The mural can grow over time; if anyone wants to add more fish at a future date, they are welcome to do so.

The children who participated take great pride in their work. One child said, "I like to bring people to the island to show them the mural. I like to show them *my* fish."

Another child said, "I showed my grandma the mural, and I told her, 'That's *my* fish and it's going to be there for a *long* time.'"

ASSESSING RISKS: ESTABLISHING PROTOCOLS FOR HEALTH AND SAFETY

When students work with materials such as paints and solvents, they need to take adequate measures to protect themselves from exposure to those agents. Wearing an apron or a smock helps protect clothing from being smeared with paint or drenched with water or mineral spirits. Skin may be irritated by strong solvents like mineral spirits or by harsh detergents, so students need to wear rubber gloves when they are cleaning up their paintbrushes. Those same solvents or detergents irritate and possibly damage delicate eye tissue, so students need to wear protective safety glasses with side shields when handling those materials.

Although lead pigments are less common in paints that are available to the general public than they were in the past, the students and teacher will want to determine what substances produce the colors in the paints that are used, and they will want to be sure to clean up spills and spatters so that animals do not become ill from accidentally ingesting paints or other materials.

Students who are working on murals on out-of-doors walls or surfaces need to be safe from harassment or physical injury resulting from encounters with individuals from the community at large. Adult supervision is absolutely vital when students are working out-of-doors in the community. The presence of adults is a deterrent to harmful acts directed at the students, and adults who are observing the students as they work have the freedom and flexibility of action to be able to notify authorities if problems do arise.

Unless the mural is produced on one or more large sheets of billboard-quality wood and then attached to an outside surface, students are doing much of the actual mural production from scaffolding or ladders. Before they begin the production, the students and teacher need to rehearse and review safe techniques of working from these supports. Students can work from a "scaffolding simulator" that they and the teacher can set up in the classroom using long planks that are supported on either end by low step stools or other supports. By working from this simulator, students develop a feel for how far and how high they can reach with less risk than working on actual scaffolds. To rehearse working from a tall ladder, students can use short ladders or step stools in the classroom. Once again, they discover how far or how high they can reach without losing their balance. Students who are not rehearsing work from the ladder or scaffold act as spotters who can support classmates if they do start to fall.

As is the case with all service learning projects, students need to be told to report any and all accidents, however minor they may seem, to the teacher or another adult supervisor immediately. The adult can then draw on his or her experience to recommend any actions that need to be taken to safeguard the health and safety of the student.

SELECTING THE SERVICE LEARNING FOCUS: A COMMUNITY ART PROGRAM

At the beginning of the course of which this project is a part, perhaps a visual arts course, students study public art and its cultural connections. One scenario of an ensuing class discussion follows:

> The teacher asks the students, "What contemporary public art is the most noticeable in our community?" (In many communities, the answer is graffiti, and much of the graffiti at least looks gang-related, even in small isolated communities.) The teacher then asks, "What feelings do many people have when they see graffiti? Do they feel safe? Do they believe that the graffiti painters are showing respect for others in the community and their property? Let's discuss some answers to these questions tomorrow. Tonight, please ask your parents these questions and find out what they think and what they have heard from other adults in the community."

In the follow-up to such a discussion, many students report that community members believe that graffiti communicates threat, disrespect, and a lack of community pride. The presence of graffiti heightens feelings of danger, including possible physical harm. Many people routinely precede the word *graffiti* with *gang*, and gangs mean drugs, weapons, and random violence. Feeling that marking someone else's building with graffiti is a way of forcibly taking ownership of that property, most adults say that the way to show respect for another person's property is either to leave it alone or help keep it clean and in good repair. Carrying the above scenario one step further, the teacher can then say to the class,

> In some communities, classes like ours have used what they learn about public art to design and paint murals that express respect for the community and celebrate a vision of the community as a safe, trusting place.
>
> As we study public art, we also will be learning about designing large pieces of community or neighborhood art. Do you want to use our learning

to create a vision of our community as a safe place? Will you become my partners in creating a mural that celebrates our culture and expresses our respect for each other?

As the teacher and students discuss the idea and work cooperatively, the students become committed to doing this service learning project. Students can begin to collect information about cities where murals have replaced graffiti and find procedures used by searching the Internet for information.

The teacher and students use a rubric such as the one shown in Figure 9.1 to evaluate the need for the Community Vision project.

Figure 9.1 Sample Project Evaluation Rubric: Community Vision

Ranking Criteria	1 (high)	2 (medium)	3 (low)	Comments
Interest	X			We learn by doing visual arts—that's why we're taking this class. We'll learn the public art–culture connection by doing it.
Need	X			Remarks from parents and other adults reflect their discomfort with "gang" graffiti.
Accessibility	X			We'll do the planning right here in the art lab. We'll have a bus or adult drivers when we need transportation to and from the mural site.
Appropriateness	X			We understand the public art–culture connection better than any other community group. We also have strong design and execution skills.
Time Frame	X			The mural project and course content will reinforce each other all year.

Tapping Into Multiple Intelligences: Here's What You Missed

Interpersonal, Logical, and Intrapersonal Multiple Intelligences

One of the most common beginning-of-class time-consumers is conferencing with students who have been absent to tell them what happened in class during their absences, what work or tests were assigned, what work was returned, what team decisions were made, and other important information. Here is a way to save that precious time.

Design a form on which an absent student's teammates keep a record of all of that information. Give it a title like "Here's What You Missed," and place a large supply of the forms in a location in the classroom that students can easily access.

Tell students, "If a teammate is absent, please do this:

- Pick up a Here's What You Missed form, and write the student's name and date in the spaces provided.
- Keep any of the student's work that I return and attach it to the form.
- Fill in the spaces during class.
- At the end of class, file the form and returned work in your team folder."

Continue: "If you are absent, please do this when you return to class:

- Pick up your Here's What You Missed information and returned work.
- Read through the form to be sure you understand new assignments.
- Ask questions about assignments if you need to.
- Get notes from a teammate.
- Ask me for clarification or help as needed."

The Here's What You Missed sheets are genuine sanity savers when there are large numbers of absentees. Students may have excellent attendance as a rule, but occasionally a flu epidemic or special event such as a PSAT test or an athletic playoff game results in a high absentee rate. When the absentees return to class, they have instant access to the information they need to get back "in the groove." Here's a sample form:

Here's What You Missed

Name:	Date:
New assignment:	Due on:
Test covering:	Date of test:

In-class activity:	Learnings:
Lecturette:	Learnings:

WORKING WITH A COMMUNITY PARTNER

The teacher and students will want to establish relationships with community partners who can each help with a specific project need. The PTO, an interested parent group, the school, or a service club such as Lions, Rotary, or the Jaycees may help with funding that is needed to purchase paint, brushes, cleanup supplies, small and large grid paper, and other materials. The community may have funding available for civic improvement and beautification, or the teacher may have applied for and received grant funds prior to the start of the school year.

Merchants' associations, the municipal police department, or the public works department may often be willing to donate some funding to the project. If permission has been secured to have a fundraiser for the Community Vision project, these types of organizations can provide assistance and advice. Any fundraising arrangements need to be made before beginning the project.

The students and teacher can find many ideas for community partnerships and mural design online. A Yahoo or Google search using the key words "community arts," "community murals," or "mural design" gives students many Web sites from which to choose. The teacher, a parent, or another adult will need to supervise student use of the Internet.

If scaffolding is needed for the actual production of the mural, the teacher will need to find a community partner who can set it up and take it down. The public works department or a building contractor can help with this aspect of the project by providing this equipment. The teacher also needs to have adult volunteers who can help monitor student safety during mural production. After proper clearances and parental permission have been secured, students learn how to use scaffolds and ladders properly, observing all safety procedures while they work on the mural.

Northern Latitude Visions

Some of our local woodworkers volunteered their time and band saws to cut out several different sizes and shapes of fish (also from billboard material) to have at the "Paint-a-Fish" sessions. Each child chose one fish of his or her liking and had a wide range of latex paints to choose from. We worked on tables and on the floor. That was nice because these horizontal surfaces eliminated a lot of paint runs. Once the fish were dry, they were arranged and mounted on the mural with screws. The mural grew over time as more fish were added.

I like the fact that this is a dynamic mural. At any time, we can add another fish whenever a new young artist wants to contribute.

—Carol Huntoon, Volunteer, Ontonagon, MI

ALIGNING SERVICE AND EDUCATIONAL GOALS

At the beginning of the visual arts course and service learning project, students compare various purposes for creating works of art and differentiating among many historical and cultural contexts and their relationship to their works of public art (visual arts, social studies). See Figure 9.2 for a model alignment of service and educational goals.

Student Responsibilities and Curricular Areas

As students go from the general to the specific and look at examples of contemporary community murals that have been created in conjunction with neighborhood cleanup and/or community beautification programs, they analyze contemporary meaning and purposes for specific public art works (visual arts, social studies). Students and teacher move from one historical period to another and one culture to another throughout the course of the school year.

As creative artists, the students apply a plan to create a work of public art and use visual systems, and they are able to explain their importance in creating the work of public art (visual arts). Once the mural is designed, students execute the design by creating the work of art that expresses their ideas (visual arts). Because the mural has the dual purpose of celebrating the community and encouraging respect, students are creating a work of public art that has both functional and aesthetic qualities (visual arts).

Students use the library and the Internet to collect information about historical art and culture connections and contemporary works of public art. As they do their research, students use electronic databases to access magazines and newspapers and use search engines to find information on the Internet (library technology). As they write about the influence of culture on public art, students show that they can synthesize information and ideas from various sources and evaluate sources of information for accuracy and point of view (library technology).

As students do this service learning project, they actively participate in a service that addresses the needs of the community, and they acquire and demonstrate curricular knowledge and skills, developing school and community partnerships (service learning). Each student's reflective log shows how the service learning project has helped the student grow intellectually and ethically.

One of the big ideas associated with the Community Vision service learning project is respect. People feel safe when they feel respected. People are capable of being their most productive and of making their best contributions when they feel free from threats and fear.

Figure 9.2   Community Vision: Aligning Service and Educational Goals

Major Subject	Learning Goals	Life Skills	Big Ideas	Service Actions
Visual Arts	Purposes of public art Forms of public art Public art themes Effective use of visual systems	Planning a project Completing a project Recognizing elements of public visual arts	Art often reflects the culture of the artist.	Designing prototypes Producing the mural
Social Studies	Cultural context of public art Meaning of symbols used in art Cultural respect; respect for property	Understanding cultural diversity Respecting others	Art often reflects the culture of the artist.	Reaching consensus on the mural design Removing graffiti and replacing it with the mural
Library Technology	Clear communication Precise use of language Interpreting nonverbal cues	Researching answers to questions Surfing the Net Recognizing bias	"Seek first to understand . . ." (Covey, 1989)	Researching public art Finding public art Web sites
Instructional Technology	Creating an Internet home page	Understanding technology	Connectedness	Featuring the mural on the home page for the project or on other Web sites

As students clean up the graffiti or accumulated grime from the mural site and replace it with pictures and designs that celebrate the cultural gifts of the community, they learn how it feels to act in respectful ways and how they can communicate respect through their words and pictures. This in-context learning wires the concept of respect into their brains. Research shows that brains "grab" strong visual images faster than words and learn in context more effortlessly than any other way (Jensen, 2000). The Community Vision service learning project gives students lessons about respect that they remember for the rest of their lives.

Reciprocity: The Community of Learners

In their visual arts class, students learn about the community or cultural connection, especially as it pertains to public works of art. They explore the link between how a community looks and the attitudes and beliefs that people have about their community. As students design and produce the mural, they focus on creating a piece of public art that communicates respect for the community as an inviting safe place to live, study, and work.

Often, community members are not aware that the visual appearance of their town or neighborhood has a powerful influence on the behavior that occurs there. Gladwell (2002) talks about the "broken windows theory" first proposed by criminologists James Q. Wilson and George L. Kelling. The theory postulates that crime is a function of disorder. If a window breaks and it is not repaired, passersby come to believe that no one cares and no one is in charge of maintaining order. If more windows break, this attitude deepens until less respectful (or more criminal) elements of the community begin to intentionally break more windows, paint graffiti on buildings, and commit other more violent crimes.

The Community Vision service learning project gives students the opportunity to teach the community that appearances do matter. If there are fewer broken windows and less graffiti, people feel safer and more respected, and these feelings translate into people acting in more respectful ways toward each other. Community members are given an opportunity to continue building that sense of well-being by helping students maintain the mural and keep its colors bright.

MANAGING THE SERVICE PROJECT: COMMUNITY VISION

The Community Vision project moves fairly slowly through a number of different phases. This slow unfolding gives the teacher the opportunity to revise and fine-tune the management plan for the project throughout the school year. See Figure 9.3 for one possible management plan for the project.

FOSTERING REFLECTIVE LEARNING

Every student does a reflective log entry after writing the essay describing connections between the cultural background of a community and its public art. This reflection focuses on the use of community public art to discourage graffiti.

Each student also writes a reflective log entry after

- the completion of the individual mural prototype
- the completion of the working team's mural prototype
- the completion of the whole class's mural prototype
- each session of actually working on the outdoor community mural

Figure 9.3 Management Plan: Community Vision

Phase	Planning	Monitoring	Evaluating
1	Ask students to discuss graffiti and neighborhood beautification with parents. Discuss doing a mural to learn about the public art–culture connection and learn design and production techniques. Assign library research and "connections" essay. Discuss reflective log. Find community partners, funding sources, mural site. Begin study of public art.	Collect and score "connections" essays. Discuss historical/cultural studies. Brainstorm ideas for cultural connections in our mural. Students complete reflective logs.	Quiz/test to assess content learning/knowledge of specific examples of public art. Return essays. Spot-check reflective logs. Refine/hone list of cultural connections for mural.
2	Continue history of public art and cultural studies. Do art studio design and execution work. Explore different visualization styles. Do individual mural prototypes. Confirm community partners, mural site, funding, and transportation (if needed).	Continue history of public art discussions, focusing on cultural connections. Working teams discuss individual prototypes and do team prototype.	Quiz/test to assess content learning about history of public art–culture. Use individual mural prototypes to assess ability to design aesthetic artwork. Students self-evaluate design ability. Spot-check reflective logs.
3	More history of public art and cultural studies. Discuss comments/feedback attached to working-group mural prototypes. Continue design studies. Do whole-class mural prototype. Assign working-team sections for detailed planning. Schedule transportation and scaffolding assembly.	More discussions. Assemble colored version of mural. Brainstorm revisions, changes, improvements. Working teams do revisions and large-scale mural "blueprints."	More quizzing/testing as appropriate. Working teams evaluate effectiveness of design strategies. Spot-check reflective logs.
4	Continue studying art-culture connections. Paint the mural. Plan the dedication ceremony. Arrange for scaffolding takedown.	Discuss learnings. Retouch mural as needed. Hold the dedication ceremony. Assemble project portfolios.	Evaluate overall effectiveness of mural design—aesthetics, functionality, celebration of culture, teaching of respect for property, community pride, etc.
5	Celebrate mural completion by writing a "will" asking future classes to do another one. Share portfolios in base teams. Write whole-class letter to all community partners saying, "Thank you for your help." Students and teacher each write one goal for future personal service work.	"Eavesdrop" on portfolio sharing. Ask students to tell each other their greatest learning AHA!, their most burning unanswered question, what they liked most about the project, what they felt they found least comfortable, what they did best, and what they would do differently (and better) next time.	Students and teacher discuss project strengths and areas for improvement. Each person shares with whole class his or her greatest AHA! and personal goal for future service work.

166

The students reflect on their roles as service providers, as well as on *respect:* what respect means, how respect ties a community together in positive ways, and how respect can be communicated—both verbally and nonverbally.

The vocabulary that the teacher uses to focus the reflections is appropriate for the grade level of the students, at the teacher's discretion. Of course, older students are encouraged to consider a greater variety of ideas than younger ones. See the reflective logs for the elementary/middle school and high school levels at the end of this chapter for strategies to prompt reflection. These models consist of sentence stems or starters and open-ended questions about the service learning project.

The use of the reflective log reinforces content learning and the community service ethic. It is one of the tools that make service learning particularly valuable to students.

ASSESSMENT AND EVALUATION

The teacher does some assessment of content learning using traditional tools such as class discussions and paper-and-pencil quizzes or tests. Each student produces an individual mural prototype and other assigned drawings, sketches, and paintings throughout the school year. The teacher can use this body of work to assess how well the student is learning to design and produce artwork. During the project, teacher and students develop a rubric to use in assessing the aesthetics, functionality, and overall effectiveness of each piece of student-produced art.

Before students begin doing writing assignments, the teacher gives them a rubric that is used to score the final draft of each assignment and shows them how the rubric is used to assess written work. The teacher does this by explaining how several sample writing pieces were scored using the rubric. Students can then use the rubric to self-evaluate the quality of their rough drafts and improve their own written work. A sample rubric for scoring student writing is included in the Reproducible Masters section at the end of this book.

Each student also assembles a project portfolio that includes the following:

- Essay: "Connections Between Culture and Public Art"
- At least one other writing sample
- The list of community or cultural connections that could be included in the mural
- The revised list of mural components
- The individual mural prototype
- A copy of the working-team mural prototype
- A copy of the whole-class mural prototype
- Copies of the prototype and final designs for the working-team mural section
- A photo of the completed mural
- Greatest AHA! and personal service goal
- Quiz and test scores
- Three other evidences of learning chosen by the student

As each student chooses the final three portfolio pieces, he or she will want to look through photos showing the mural in production, before-and-after photos of the mural site, taped interviews with members of the community focusing on the increased sense of safety and pride that the mural has brought to the community, or ideas for extensions of the service learning project.

Each student shares his or her portfolio with base teammates during the project celebration. This final feedback helps students realize how much they have learned about the connections between culture and public art, art design and execution, themselves as service-givers, and the importance of respect in the course of doing this Community Vision service learning project.

Elementary/Middle School Reflective Log

Description of today's work on the Community Vision mural:
This work helped me help my community by . . .
This help is important to my community because . . .
These are my most important learnings about • how public art reflects a culture: • elements of mural/painting design: • what respect means: • how I can show respect to others:
My best actions and thoughts were . . .
Next time I want to improve . . .
Improving is important to me because . . .

High School Reflective Log

Description of today's project-related work:

My new (or rediscovered) learning about the culture of my community:

This mural helps the community celebrate our culture by . . .

These are some very significant learnings about

- how public art reflects a culture and is affected by a culture:

- elements of mural/painting design:

- techniques of mural painting/production:

- what respect for property means:

- what respect sounds like:

- what respect looks like:

- what respect feels like:

My best actions and thoughts were . . .

Next time I want to improve . . .

10

Main Street Gardens

A Science and Visual Arts Service Learning Project

DESCRIPTION OF THE PROJECT

In many business districts in big cities as well as small towns, the sidewalks, storefronts, and traffic islands present a flat, rather colorless face to residents and visitors. In recent years, a growing number of urban and community planning commissions have begun to use ornamental plantings to soften and brighten the appearance of commercial buildings and streets. The Main Street Gardens project provides a service to such communities with students and teacher planning and planting ornamental gardens—whether they are in-ground flower beds, sidewalk containers, or window boxes—to add a touch of nature to public streets and sidewalks.

The "natural" touch contributes to the local economy by encouraging residents and visitors to spend more time in local business districts and may even influence prospective new home buyers to settle in the community.

A class that is studying horticultural science and/or landscape design, or even social studies, can learn much of its curricular content by doing this service learning project. After clearing the project through school administration, the teacher and students establish the foundation for the project by finding a gardening site, arranging for community partnerships with the merchants' association and town council, and scheduling transportation to the gardening sites. Grant monies can fund transportation; the school district can provide information about licensed transportation companies. To provide students with the greatest learning opportunities, the teacher, students, and merchants' association agree on a Main Street Gardens project plan that combines in-ground and container plantings; in-ground gardens and container plantings require different care and maintenance. All plans often need to be approved by the city or town council.

Once the business owners, students, and teacher have agreed on a plan, the students and teacher prepare a site description and blueprint and a project description to give to the school administration and the community partners. Before any work takes place, the teacher and students need to have these materials and specific plans developed. To receive funding, the teacher may need to develop an overview of the project before the beginning of the school year.

When students return to school in the fall, the teacher explains the curricular goals for the year to them. The teacher tells the students that much of their understanding of horticulture and landscape design will result from learning by doing. The teacher then gives each student a copy of the Main Street Gardens general plan, laying out the service learning project. Students and teacher work together to fill in the details as the school year progresses.

Students need to investigate a number of horticulture topics before they can design plantings for the containers and beds.

To explore the project and determine their planting and garden maintenance schedule, students need to learn about the following:

- The planting (gardening) zone where they live, in terms of the length of the growing season
- Average annual rainfall
- Seasonal extremes of heat or cold—factors that students need to consider in choosing annuals, perennials, and shrubs for community gardens
- The characteristics of a variety of flowering annuals and perennials that thrive in the local growing zone

For each species, students need to learn flower color, plant height, water and light requirements, and when in the season the species produces its blooms. Many annuals bloom from late spring until autumn frost. Students can rely on these plants to give the gardens some color throughout the growing season. Most perennials bloom for only a part of the growing season, and students will want to design their perennial mixtures so that some plants are just coming into bloom as others are fading.

As the students proceed, they need detailed information about the species so that they can design plantings that contain visually appealing mixes of color and texture and use the heights of the species effectively. They will want to find out about growing and blooming times as determined by the biological "clocks" built into the plant species. These clocks are sensitive to length of daylight, strength of daylight, daytime high temperatures, nighttime low temperatures, amount of rainfall, and the time since the last hard frost.

To research the project, students may refer to the many landscaping and gardening books available, which often contain color photographs of professionally planned gardens that students can use as models for their own.

Students can also look for help on the Internet. Using key words and phrases such as "landscaping," "landscape design," and "garden planning" and search engines such as Google or Yahoo!, students can collect much helpful information about horticulture in general and garden design in particular. The teacher, parents, or volunteer adults need to supervise students whenever they are doing Internet searches.

Keeping Records and Building a Portfolio

Each student keeps a personal notebook containing detailed information about a variety of annual and perennial species that can thrive in the Main Street Gardens. These notebooks become part of the project portfolio.

After students have collected their species information, the teacher assigns them to small working teams. A visual arts teacher may help students learn about visual systems and teach them some basic principles of design. Each working team prepares prototype plans for both the in-ground beds and the containers that are part of the Main Street Gardens project. Students will need to observe the growth of the plants in each garden approximately 6 weeks after planting, approximately 12 weeks after planting, and at the end of the growing season. Each team completes a set of color sketches during the observations, illustrations that show how the plantings appear at the various stages.

When the prototype sketches are complete, the teacher assigns pairs of "buddy teams." Each working team gives its buddy team feedback about what works well in the prototype sketches and what needs explaining. Teams meet to discuss and clarify their plans, and during the discussion each team identifies some elements of the prototype that could be strengthened. Working teams then revise their prototype plans to improve their designs and strengthen their visual systems. Each member of a working team makes a personal copy of the revised set of plans to include in his or her project portfolio.

At this point, each working team attaches its revised prototype sketches for the in-ground beds to a large sheet of newsprint or chart paper, and all of the plans are posted on the classroom wall. The teams conduct a gallery walk, during which each team looks at all of the Main Street Gardens plans. Each team writes comments on the newsprint or chart paper sheets, telling what they like best about the prototype plans. The entire class then discusses these comments, agrees on the most popular in-ground planting features, and designs a prototype garden that incorporates these features.

Next the teacher facilitates further discussion, making sure a student who is adept at sketching quickly (and well) is prepared to do the master plan on newsprint or chart paper. The teacher and class may want to use the services of two or three sketch artists so that they can consider a few different plans before deciding on the final one.

When the class agrees on a final design for the in-ground beds, the teacher asks a volunteer artist to make a clean small sketch of the plan. The teacher makes a copy for each student to put in his or her project portfolio.

With the in-ground plans complete, the teacher assigns responsibility for filling one of the garden plant containers to each of the working teams. Each working team decides on a final planting design for its container, and each member of the team does a color sketch of the plan for his or her project portfolio.

As soon as the final planting designs have been made, students can determine the soil mixtures that provide the plants with the best growing conditions. The teacher and students need to manage the project so that students can place the soil in the in-ground beds in the late fall. This soil receives the benefits of any moisture that is available from winter precipitation. Students spend much of the winter propagating and raising baby plants from seeds or cuttings, ordering plants that they cannot propagate themselves, and making their potting mixes for the Main Street Gardens containers. Students keep records of their plant-growing activities. They note which plants were grown from seed and which from cuttings, when they started the growth of the seeds and cuttings, what growing medium they used for each species, how much and how often they watered, details of plant feeding, and overall success of the growing plan. Each student includes the seed and cutting propagation notebook in his or her project portfolio.

To fund the seed and cutting propagation supplies, the teacher initially explores what funds are available through the school. Sometimes these service learning costs are included in the budget for a horticulture class. If additional funds are necessary, the teacher approaches the local merchants' association; chamber of commerce; or city department of parks, public works, or community development. Because students will be doing the plantings in public spaces, these agencies can often supply the soil ingredients and the flowerpots or boxes. The PTO, another interested parents' group, or local gardening clubs are sometimes able to help with funds. A teacher who does his or her planning in advance of the school year can receive grant funding from service learning agencies. If a garden design and planting service learning project is part of the regular horticulture curriculum, students from one year can raise some funds for the next year's class by having a spring bedding plant sale during which they sell flower and vegetable plants that they have started from seeds or cuttings.

The teacher and students will want to take advantage of local horticultural expertise by contacting the county extension (county farm bureau) agent for information about advice on fine-tuning the Main Street Gardens project plans.

In early spring, students fill the containers with soil. As soon as possible, students transplant their young bedding plants into the containers and in-ground beds and water and mulch them. Students care for the plantings until at least the end of the school year, watering the plantings, feeding them, removing weeds, and keeping containers and beds free of litter. The teacher finds a way for each student to collect a photographic record of the gardens. He or she can, for example, use course or grant funds to buy a disposable camera for each working team. A relatively inexpensive digital camera often provides greater flexibility; several student teams can share one camera, and images can be saved on a classroom computer. Students can make as many prints as they want or need from these stored photos.

Students photograph the gardens during planting and four or five times thereafter. If teams are using disposable cameras, one teammate is responsible for having the film developed and getting prints for each member of the team. Each student may make his or her own prints of digital photos. These photos become part of the students' project portfolios.

Many students often want to continue caring for the plantings after the end of the formal course work. This service learning project can result in a long-term partnership between the school and the community: The students keep the Main Street Gardens healthy; residents and visitors spend more time patronizing local businesses; and the business owners provide the funding. The result is a vibrant connection with nature that strengthens the local economy as it enhances the look of the commercial areas.

Exemplary Project: School Gardens

The students in a horticulture class at my school decided to ask the principal if the school would like to be their community partner for the service learning gardens for the year. When we had moved into the new high school building, the planning committee had selected shrubs and trees and paid a professional landscaper to plant them, but we had no flowers to add splashes of color to the school grounds. The teacher and her students had discussed how tight funding was for the year's service learning project, and the students came up with the brilliant idea that doing the work on school grounds would eliminate the need for off-campus transportation and that the school would probably be happy to pay for materials such as soil, mulch, and fertilizer because the plantings would beautify the school grounds. An added bonus was that the school maintenance staff would water the plantings and cut back spent blooms. Nice partnership between kids and schoolhouse!

The horticulture teacher was very creative. She knew that field trip funds were difficult to obtain, and she wanted to give her horticulture students hands-on experience in planning and developing ornamental borders. Curriculum standards addressed plant selection, propagation using a variety of methods, plant care, rotation of species—in short, all of the things that professional landscape services do to maintain attractive ornamental borders for their clients. In a previous year, she approached the administration during the summer break, before students returned to classes, and proposed that the horticulture classes do the small-plant landscaping when we moved into the new building. She knew that former students were well established in local landscaping businesses. She contacted them about becoming mentoring partners to her high school students, and they jumped at the chance to help out their "old school."

Students and teacher followed much of the project plan described in this chapter. In fact, this project was the inspiration for this chapter, and it is an excellent example of using the school as the primary community partner when doing service learning.

ASSESSING RISKS: ESTABLISHING PROTOCOLS FOR HEALTH AND SAFETY

Plant propagation, the act of planting, and garden care are dirty jobs. As they work in the school or gardens, students must be aware of the need to keep soil outside of their bodies. Hands need thorough washing after they have been in dirt. Hands and arms need to be inspected for cuts or scrapes before students work with soil, and any open sores need protection of some sort. Paint-on liquid bandage forms a water- and dirt-tight bond with the skin and is excellent for this purpose.

Because bags of soil and mulch are heavy, students need a reminder to lift with their legs, not with their backs. The teacher or another adult volunteer needs to monitor students when they are handling heavy materials to be sure that students do not try to lift an excessive amount of weight. Before moving materials with wheelbarrows or garden carts, students need to learn how to balance and maneuver these items. The teacher and students can place lighter loads in these garden helpers, and students can practice manipulating them in hallways—if that is permitted—or outside on school grounds.

Students also need practice in using gardening tools safely. Planting tools often have sharp edges that require respect. Students need to know that all tools, large or small, must be returned to the proper place as soon as they are not actually being used. A garden rake dropped on the ground with its sharp tines pointing up is an invitation to puncture wounds or, if the handle is levered up when someone steps on the tines, a rap on the head.

Some students may be allergic to fertilizers, and all students need to learn that pollens are found in soils. The teacher and each student's team need to know about any and all allergies so that students receive gardening duties that minimize exposure to allergens. Students also must remember that some fertilizers and other gardening materials are not to be ingested, so thorough hand washing is needed after handling these items.

When students work-out-of doors, they need to protect exposed skin from sunburn. Supplies for the main street gardeners must include plenty of sun block, and the teacher needs to encourage each student to bring a jacket, brimmed cap, and sunglasses to the work site. If the teacher believes that a student is not wearing adequately protective clothing, including a cap, that student is assigned to record keeping or photographing on that day.

The teacher must arrange transportation to and from the gardening site and proper chaperoning or adult supervision in accordance with school policies regarding field trips. The teacher and administration often make these arrangements together.

The teacher emphasizes that any and all accidents, however small, must be reported to him or her immediately. Activities that bring students in touch with the natural environment are supposed to enhance overall health and stimulate brain function (White, n.d.), and the teacher will want to be sure that small injuries do not jeopardize the well-being of students who are planting or tending Main Street Gardens.

Tapping Into Multiple Intelligences: Give Your Body a Break

Kinesthetic, Spatial, Rhythmic, and Intrapersonal Multiple Intelligences

When students sit for long periods of time, they lose focus. They may become lethargic, or they may become tense. Movement, large muscle movement, wakes up the brain, enhancing its alertness and ability to learn, calming "the jitters" or chasing "the blahs," and improving motor movements (Smith, 2005).

When the energy in the classroom seems to dwindle, ask students to stand and stretch and then do a "diagonal" walk, borrowed from the motion of Nordic skiers. In place or in actual motion, as students walk, they swing the left arm forward when the right leg steps forward and vice versa. This cross-body motion helps to coordinate both sides of the brain (Ellyatt, 2003), and the increased oxygen flow to the brain enhances its ability to learn.

Smith, Ellyat, and others advocate the use of "brain breaks" to increase the effectiveness of the classroom as a learning place. Giving students the opportunity to move also decreases problems with students who just can't sit still, and it provides those with a kinesthetic comfort zone an opportunity to tap into that intelligence.

SELECTING THE SERVICE LEARNING FOCUS: PLANTING LOCAL COLOR IN THE COMMUNITY

The fit between this service learning project and a course focusing on horticulture and landscape design is a "natural." As students learn about different types of plants and garden or planter designs, the teacher quizzes or tests their curricular knowledge by having them do prototype garden plans. If the prototypes are for plantings that students will actually be doing, they invest extra energy and effort into learning the material and planning their plantings. As students learn about growing plants from seeds or cuttings, they propagate many of the plants that they use to create the Main Street Gardens. Students know that, beyond all of the paper-and-pencil tests, the appearance of the actual gardens and the health of the plants is the proof that students have learned the course content.

The teacher and students do their homework long before the planting begins by examining the buildings and vacant spaces in the business district, developing sketches that show how in-ground gardens and flower boxes or sidewalk containers could beautify the main street, meeting with the merchants' association to interest its members in becoming project funding partners, and meeting with the town or city council to ask for assistance from the department of parks or department of streets. The teacher then suggests to the merchants' group that investing in the plantings could attract more customers to their businesses, and that an attractive downtown business district influences prospective residents to settle in the town. When it is most effective, the Main Street Gardens project helps young people connect with their community and forge a permanent link between the community and the school.

As part of the process, the teacher, the students, and the merchants' association look at the Main Street Gardens sketches and select a plan that combines in-ground beds and window boxes or large sidewalk planters. The teacher makes a clear, well-labeled drawing of the plan and has a copy made for each student in the horticulture class.

Near the beginning of the horticulture class, the teacher and students discuss the service learning project, and the teacher gives each student a copy of a letter that explains the project to their parents, encouraging the students to talk over the project with them. A few days later, the teacher and students discuss the parents' comments and opinions about the need for the project. The teacher and students evaluate the project using a rubric such as the one shown in Figure 10.1.

WORKING WITH A COMMUNITY PARTNER

If Main Street Gardens truly are planted in the town's central business district, and if they are to succeed, the merchants' association and the town or city council must agree to be community partners. Also, as suggested previously, the county extension agent is a valuable source of information about planting, plant care, fertilizing, pest control, and overall garden health. The teacher and students' interactions with the merchants and town council have been discussed earlier in this chapter. At this point, the teacher and students want the partnership to be well established and the funding to be in place before making specific arrangements with the administration for transportation and student supervisors.

The students and teacher can get ideas about other sources of help in the community from the Internet. Many Web sites have good information about school-to-work programs and volunteer or service projects. If the teacher and administration explore the availability of grants prior to the start of the school year, many of the funding concerns may be resolved before students are involved. If this is the case, the teacher shares information about project monies and their sources with the students. Students who are informed participants often make wiser choices about how and where to spend funds.

Figure 10.1 Sample Project Evaluation Rubric:
Main Street Gardens

Criteria \ Ranking	1 (high)	2 (medium)	3 (low)	Comments
Interest	X			The project is a practical application of what we want to learn by taking this course.
Need	X			The main street downtown has no trees, flowers, or shrubs—nothing natural. The gardens will help give the street a brighter, softer look.
Accessibility	X			We'll be doing much of the early work in the science classroom—the plant lab. When we work on the Main Street Gardens project, the school will bus us to and from the site.
Appropriateness	X			We'll be like town gardeners, and we'll be learning about horticulture.
Time Frame	X			Work on the gardens can parallel curricular learning all year long. The community gardens can be our final exam.

To actually carry out the project from bed and container preparation to planting and nurturing, the municipal public works department and the teacher and students work together to schedule the necessary earthmoving equipment to help students install the soil system for in-ground beds and schedule installation of the plant containers. Merchants whose buildings are to be decorated with window boxes can help with their installation. With the community, merchants, teachers, and students all working together, the Main Street Gardens can become a reality.

<hr>

Tapping Into Multiple Intelligences: Visual Patterning

Spatial, Kinesthetic, Logical, and Intrapersonal Multiple Intelligences

Because this is a yearlong project, students and teacher need to organize lots of information and ideas. They make many important decisions, and this often involves debate and reaching consensus. Graphic organizers—tools for organizing thinking, or as Robin Fogarty (1997a) calls them, "tools for structuring interaction with thinking"—make thinking visible and provide a way for visual learners to tap into their personal comfort zones.

From Venn diagrams for comparing and contrasting, to right-angle diagrams for associating ideas, to mind maps for visualizing and brainstorming, to concept webs for showing relationships among concepts and information, to "fishbones" for gathering and organizing information (the list could go on and on), graphic organizers are wonderful tools that teacher and students can use as they brainstorm, discuss, and debate. Often, a student who has difficulty writing or doing a traditional outline finds that the right graphic organizer makes a wonderful prewriting tool. Among other sources, teachers can find examples of many different graphic organizers in *Brain-Compatible Classrooms* (Fogarty, 1997a) and *Designing Brain-Compatible Learning* (Parry & Gregory, 1998).

<hr>

ALIGNING SERVICE AND EDUCATIONAL GOALS

During the entire span of the Main Street Gardens service learning project, students demonstrate their knowledge of topics in a field of science, in this case, horticulture. As they take paper-and-pencil tests, students demonstrate what they have learned about plant species by using them appropriately in their garden plans. As the teacher evaluates the plan for a single flower bed or container, he or she looks for the use of plant species that have similar water and light requirements and interesting use of colors. The teacher checks plans to see that taller plants do not hide shorter ones and that plants are spaced far enough apart. See Figure 10.2 for a model alignment of service and educational goals covered in the Main Street Gardens project.

As students get actively involved with the project, they demonstrate their knowledge of plant propagation by growing many of the seedlings for the gardens from seed or from plant cuttings. They show that they can grow annuals from seed or grow perennials from stem or root cutting or by dividing roots or bulbs.

Students may find some plants that can be propagated by poking the stem end of a leaf into the soil, filling in around the poked-in leaf with soil, and watering this leaf. Rooting compounds, available in lawn and garden stores, increase the success that students have in starting plants from cuttings or leaves.

Student Responsibilities and Curricular Areas

Students also show that they know which soils provide the best growing media for their plants by being able to describe, in writing, the characteristics of different soils and mixtures and demonstrate in the plant laboratory or the field that they can formulate a soil mixture that works well with their plantings. Because the gardens are a living, blooming demonstration of what students know about horticulture, the teacher is able to assess authentic learning.

Figure 10.2   Main Street Gardens: Aligning Service and Educational Goals

Major Subject	Learning Goals	Life Skills	Big Ideas	Service Actions
Science	Plant propagation Biological clocks in plants Landscape design	Gardening Nature appreciation	Connecting with nature "To everything there is a season."	Keep plant notebooks Plan gardens; propagate bedding plants Maintain gardens
Visual Arts	Visual systems Creating visually pleasing works	Design of all sorts	Walking in beauty Beautification of surroundings	Doing prototype plans and sketches Revising and evaluating plans
Instructional Technology	Finding information on the Internet	Using technology effectively for research and project execution	Technoliteracy	Finding and using information from gardening Web sites
Language Arts	Using precise language Persuasive skills	Effective communication skills	Community ownership Community belonging	Presenting plans to local merchants Obtaining permission to develop garden sites

Students also want the gardens to be aesthetically pleasing, so they demonstrate their ability to recognize visual systems and use them in creating the artwork (visual arts). In this case, the artwork consists of the planted and blooming Main Street Gardens. The photos taken by the working teams record the visual appeal of the gardens and the beauty of their flowers.

The teacher is possibly the first school person associated with this project who identifies the need of the community (service learning) for the gardens. This is true if the teacher is doing the pre–school year work associated with writing a grant application. As the teacher examines the appearance of the business district and visualizes what it could be with flowerbeds and boxes of flowers blooming from one end of the street to the other, he or she translates that vision into the sketches that are used to convince the merchants and city or town council to become project partners.

Students need to develop and demonstrate curricular knowledge and skills (service learning) in order for those gardens to become a reality. The ongoing cooperation between the students and the merchants, as well as the city or town council, cements the school-community bond, with the Main Street Gardens project improving the quality of life in the community (service learning) by bringing a touch of nature and color to the business district.

One big idea embedded in the Main Street Gardens project is beautification of the community. Local residents and out-of-town visitors appreciate the color and beauty of the business district. Research shows that powerful visual images strongly influence behavior (Jensen, 1996) and that a beautiful image encourages considerate, kind, positive actions.

Another big idea associated with this service learning project is connecting with nature. The human brain seems to grow and learn better when it is exposed to some natural-world stimuli (White, n.d.). If the business district, especially in a large city, includes only manufactured materials, people feel disconnected from each other and themselves. Native Americans traditionally are concerned with the need for people to restore their balance or harmony by getting in touch with Mother Earth. Today, people in general are beginning to understand that connecting with nature does help them stay connected to their positive behaviors, maintaining more effective control of their lives.

Reciprocity: The Community of Learners

Community members may not realize—until horticulture students begin to develop and plant the Main Street Gardens—how important connecting with nature is to maintaining a feeling of internal balance and harmony. Student gardeners demonstrate skill and knowledge as they lay out and develop beds and planters, and merchants and town residents alike may learn a thing or two about gardening as they watch the students work and ask questions about what they are doing and their reasons for doing it "that way." The teacher needs to encourage students to use these opportunities to talk with community members about the importance to mental and physical health of connecting with the natural world.

Communities often include residents who are skilled, dedicated gardeners, and students can learn from these individuals. As work and planting progress, the teacher and students discuss the importance of listening to and respecting advice and suggestions that community members volunteer, and students may hear a large number of those comments. Students can engage these community gardening experts in conversation, and the exchange of information can benefit all parties.

Residents who see students working hard to install beds and containers and prepare them for planting gain a new appreciation of the amount of work, often hard physical labor, that students are willing to do in service to the community. Respect and connections grow as strong as the plants in the Main Street Gardens.

MANAGING THE SERVICE PROJECT: MAIN STREET GARDENS

The teacher integrates most of the Main Street Gardens service project into his or her course schedule for the year. To maximize student involvement and buy-in, the teacher will prefer doing the initial site selection and community partnership activities after the start of the school year. If these steps must be taken before the teacher can apply for grant monies, he or she may do the site selection and solicit a community partner before the school year starts. See Figure 10.3 for a model management plan that highlights the Main Street Gardens project. Note that it is an overview, so it does not necessarily reflect the detail of the teacher's careful day-to-day course plans.

FOSTERING REFLECTIVE LEARNING

Every student does a reflective log entry after the first work session at the garden site(s) when the in-ground soil is mixed and in place.

Students do other reflective log entries as follows:

- After the first session of plant propagation
- Each time the seedlings are moved to larger pots or a different growing medium
- After installing the soils in the planting containers on the main street
- After planting the gardens
- After each work session in the gardens

Log entries focus on beautification, connecting with nature, the nurturing role of the gardener, and what the student learns about academic content and skills, life skills, and service skills by doing the Main Street Gardens project.

See the reflective logs for elementary/middle school and high school levels at the end of this chapter for strategies to prompt reflection. These models consist of sentence stems or starters and open-ended questions about the Main Street Gardens service learning project.

The use of the reflective logs reinforces content learning, helping the students understand how much they are learning about themselves as they do the service learning project. As a tool that students can use to discover hidden personal strengths and unsuspected dimensions, the reflective log can help students make sense of learning through community service.

ASSESSMENT AND EVALUATION

The teacher does some assessment of content learning using class discussions, performance observations, quizzes, and tests. Observing each student working in the plant lab at school and at the garden site, the teacher spends some time talking with each student about what he or she is doing and why. The teacher documents each observation and may use the informal discussions as oral quizzes, making sure that students know what is happening before the quizzing begins.

Figure 10.3 Management Plan: Main Street Gardens

Phase	Planning	Monitoring	Evaluating
1	Examine business district. Do garden sketch. Meet with merchants and town council. Establish partnerships. Contact county extension agent for advice. Set up rough schedule. Arrange transportation with school. Do garden plan sketch, project description, and letter for parents. Plan and start the course.	Discuss project with students. Send information home to parents. Check on content learning with quizzes and with plant lab observations. Assign plant species notebooks.	Check notebooks. Are they complete? First test the prototype garden using at least three perennials and five annuals listed in the notebook. Look at light and water compatibility, as well as overall arrangement.
2	Line up visual arts teacher to help with design elements. Begin study of soils. Assign working teams. Assign prototype team plans. Assign buddy teams.	Have buddy teams check each other's plans and discuss. Working teams revise/improve prototypes. The whole class agrees on in-ground plan and designs soil mix for in-ground beds. Students make personal copies of team and class plans.	Score plans for visual design and compatibility of plants. Give and score soils quiz. Spot-check student copies of garden plans.
3	Mix and install in-ground soil. Assign final container plans to working teams. Teams make plans and design soils. Start propagating seedlings from seeds and cuttings. Start reflective logs as site work begins with installing soil.	Check team-planting container plans. Observe work in plant lab with seedlings. Assign propagation notebook. Facilitate discussion of landscape design to include larger areas, larger plants, more varied terrain.	Spot-check propagation notebooks. Quiz/test knowledge of soils and soil mixes. Test larger landscape design skills. Evaluate success of seedling growth: thriving? dying? Will the plants be ready in the spring?
4	Mix container soils and fill containers. Transplant when weather allows. Mulch, feed, water, maintain beds. Give each team a disposable camera on planting day, telling teams to keep a photo record of garden growth.	Observe work on planting and maintenance days. Watch flower beds and containers for growth, blooms, soil texture, etc. Continue course work. Begin portfolio assembly.	Evaluate growth and appearance of plantings. Ask for input from merchants, town council, and visual arts teacher. Check portfolio progress. Photos developed? Reflective journals maintained?
5	Celebrate the community garden completion by writing a "will" asking future classes to continue the project. Share portfolios in base-group teams. Write whole-class letter to merchants and town council saying, "Thank you for your help." Students and teacher each write one goal for future personal service work.	"Eavesdrop" on portfolio sharing. Ask students to tell each other their greatest learning AHA!, their most burning unanswered question, what they liked most about the project, what they found least comfortable, what they felt they did best, and what they would do differently (and better) next time.	Students and teacher discuss project strengths and areas for improvement. Each person shares with whole class his or her greatest AHA! and personal goal for future service work.

Well-designed teacher-made tests include landscape designs for other projects and explore a student's knowledge of the following:

- Compatibility of different plant species
- Key features such as height, bloom color, or leaf texture
- Components and compositions of soils
- Procedures and materials for feeding and pest control
- Propagation from seeds or cuttings

Each student assembles a project portfolio that includes the following:

- The annual/perennial species notebook
- Personal copies of the working-team prototypes for the in-ground and container garden plans
- A personal copy of the class in-ground garden plans
- A personal copy of the final working-team container garden plan
- The propagation (from seeds and cuttings) notebook
- Transplanting notes and photos
- Notes and photos from gardening sessions
- The student's reflective log
- Greatest AHA! and personal service goal
- Quiz and test scores
- Three other evidences of learning chosen by the student

In selecting these final portfolio pieces, students may want to include before-and-after photos of the garden site, additional reflections on the importance of touches of nature in a manufactured environment, plans for future gardens to plant, ideas about using plants indoors, or ideas for extension projects. Each student shares his or her portfolio with base teammates during the project celebration.

The final evaluation of Main Street Gardens must be the effectiveness of the plan. If the plants grow and thrive, the merchants and municipal government departments reflect their satisfaction with the plans as they answer the questions, "Did the gardens do their job? Did they beautify the business district? Did they help all of us feel more connected with the natural world? Has that changed the way we treat each other? Did the gardens work?" Many towns that have experimented with business district gardens have kept them, which is the bottom-line evaluation of any service learning project. If created and maintained by students on an ongoing basis, the gardens gain special value as a service learning project that links the school and the community.

Elementary/Middle School Reflective Log

My job today as part of the Main Street Gardens project was . . .
This helped beautify our streets by . . .
I felt my connections with nature when I . . .
Here is how I felt knowing that I was helping things grow:
These are my most important learnings about • landscaping skills • my strengths in horticulture • doing community service
My best actions and thoughts were . . .
Next time I want to improve . . .
I want to make this improvement because . . .

High School Reflective Log

Here's the horticulture for the Main Street Gardens project that I did today . . .

This helped beautify Main Street by . . .

I felt myself connect with nature when I . . .

Connecting with nature is like a kind of food because both . . .

Today's most important learning about

- landscape design

- plant-nurturing skills

- my strengths in horticulture

- doing community service

My best actions and thoughts were . . .

Next time I want to improve . . . because . . .

Reproducible
Masters

Project Evaluation Rubric

Tentative Project Title: _____

Ranking / Criteria	1 (high, our favorite)	2 (medium)	3 (low, last choice	Comments
Interest	High	Medium	Low	
Need	Great	Some	Little	
Accessibility	Easy	Okay	Difficult	
Appropriateness	Good	Fair	Poor	
Time Frame	Just right	A bit long or short	Much too long or short	

Checklist for Evaluating Service
Number 1

Student: _____

Date: _____   **"Good Worker" Actions**

Observable Indicators	You bet! 5	So-so 3	Not yet. 0
Comes to the job prepared.			
Focuses on the job.			
Is on the site at least 90% of the time.			
Listens to coworkers attentively and actively.			
Keeps detailed log/journal/notebook.			

Student: _____

Date: _____   **"Good Worker" Actions**

Observable Indicators	You bet! 5	So-so 3	Not yet. 0
Comes to the job prepared.			
Focuses on the job.			
Is on the site at least 90% of the time.			
Listens to coworkers attentively and actively.			
Keeps detailed log/journal/notebook.			

Checklist for Evaluating Service
Number 2

Student: _____

Date: _____   "Good Worker" Actions

Observable Indicators	You bet! 5	So-so 3	Not yet. 0
Stays on the job.			
Helps with the task; does his/her fair share.			
Encourages coworkers to persist.			
Invites coworkers to participate.			
Celebrates success with coworkers.			

Student: _____

Date: _____   "Good Worker" Actions

Observable Indicators	You bet! 5	So-so 3	Not yet. 0
Stays on the job.			
Helps with the task; does his/her fair share.			
Encourages coworkers to persist.			
Invites coworkers to participate.			
Celebrates success with coworkers.			

Writing Evaluation Rubric

Performance Criteria	Pulitzer Material 5	Summer Fiction 3	Pulp Fiction 1	Box Filler 0
Focus Clear point of view	Text clear, focused, well elaborated throughout	Text sometimes cloudy; reader may need to clarify position	Text confused, shifting, or disjointed	Minimal text or text missing
Support Elaboration or explanation of major points	Each major point "backed up" with 2–3 pieces of accurate evidence	At least 50% of major points "backed up"	Support inaccurate or missing more than 50% of the time	No support; "take this on faith"
Organization Logical flow of ideas; clear plan	All points connected and signaled with transitions or clear indicators; flow "flows"	At least 50% of points connected; transitions may be weak; some points seem out of order	Connections and transitions are unclear; many are missing; flow is muddled	No logic to flow and no transitions
Conventions Use of standard English	Few minor errors, if any; clear, precise vocabulary and sentence structure	Some minor errors; no more than 1–2 major errors	Major errors that confuse meaning; ineffective sentence structure	Jabberwocky! (no use of standard conventions)

Bibliography

Ammon, M. S., Furco, A., Chi, B., & Middaugh, E. (2002). *Chapter 3: Teachers and the practice of service-learning*. Retrieved June 21, 2005, from National Service Learning Web site: http://www.servicelearning.org/ . . . /ca_sl_97-00/chapter_3_teachers_and_the_practice_of_service-learning_682k_pdf

Anderson, C. S., & Witmer, J. T. (n.d.). *Addressing school board and administrative concerns about service-learning*. Retrieved July 17, 2005, from Lions Quest Web site: http://www.lionsquest.org/content/Resources/ServiceLearningArticles/slarticle15.htm

Bailey, D. (1991). *What can we do about litter?* New York: Franklin Watts.

Bellanca, J., & Fogarty, R. (1991). *Blueprints for thinking in the cooperative classroom*. Arlington Heights, IL: IRI/SkyLight.

Billig, S. (2004). Heads, hearts and hands: The research on K–12 service-learning. *Growing to greatness* (annual publication of the National Youth Leadership Conference, St. Paul, MN), 12–25.

Billig, S. (2005). *Use research knowledge to advance district-wide service-learning*. Retrieved August 9, 2005, from National Service-Learning Partnership Web site: http://www.servicelearningpartnership.org/site/PageServer?pagename= pub_distlessons3

Boyer, E. (1983). *High school. A report on secondary education in America*. New York: Harper & Row.

Buchen, I. (1995, January). Service learning and curriculum transfusion. *NASSP Bulletin*, 66–70.

Buzan, T., & Buzan, B. (1994). *The mind map book*. New York: Dutton Adult.

Cawood, F. (Ed.). (1996). *The big book of health tips*. Peachtree City, GA: Frank W. Cawood.

Chalofsky, M., Finland, G., Wallace, J., & Klass, I. (1992). *Changing places: A kid's view of shelter living*. Washington, DC: Gryphon House.

Clark, S., & Welmers, M. (1994, September). Service learning: A natural link to interdisciplinary studies. *Schools in the middle*, 11–15.

Clothier, P. (1996). *The complete computer trainer*. New York: McGraw-Hill.

Completing the learning cycle: Service-learning. (n.d.). Retrieved July 21, 2005, from University of New Hampshire Web site: http://unh.edu/teaching-excellence/resources/service-learning.htm

Conrad, D., & Hedin, D. (1991, June). School-based community service: What we know from research and theory. *Phi Delta Kappan*, 743–749.

Counts, G. (1932). *Dare the schools build a new social order?* New York: John Day.

Covey, S. (1989). *The seven habits of highly effective people*. New York: Simon & Schuster.

DeRegniers, B., & Sendak, M. (Il.). (1997). *What can you do with a shoe?* New York: Margaret McElderry Books.

Dewey, J. (1916). *Democracy and education*. New York: Free Press.

Dewey, J. (1938). *Experience and education*. New York: Collier Books.

Diamond, M. (1988). *Enriching heredity: The impact of the environment on the brain*. New York: Free Press.

Dillon, H. (1995). *The flower garden: A practical guide to planning and planting* (Wayside Gardens Collection Series). New York: Sterling Publications.

Disalvo-Ryan, D. (1991). *Uncle Willie and the soup kitchen.* New York: William Morrow.

Donatelle, R., & Davis, L. (1997). *Access to health.* Needham Heights, MA: Allyn & Bacon.

Dunitz, R. (1992). *Street gallery: Guide to 1000 Los Angeles murals.* Los Angeles: RJD Enterprises.

Eberly, D. (Ed.). (1995). *Building a community of citizens: Civil society in the 21st century.* Frederick, MD: University Press of America.

Eksterowicz, A., Cline, P., & Hammond, D. (1995). *American democracy: Representation, participation, and the future of the republic.* Upper Saddle River, NJ: Prentice Hall.

Ellyatt, W. (2003). Exercising body and brain. *Montessori International, 67,* 8–9.

Everett, F., Castor, H. (Eds.), & Gower, T. (Il.). (1995). *The monstergang.* Springfield, IL: E. D. C.

Fiske, S. T., & Taylor, S. E. (1984). *Social cognition.* Reading, MA: Addison-Wesley.

Fogarty, R. (1997a). *Brain-compatible classrooms.* Arlington Heights, IL: SkyLight.

Fogarty, R. (1997b). *Problem-based learning and other curricular models for the multiple intelligences classroom.* Arlington Heights, IL: SkyLight.

France, M. D., et al. (1996). *Pooh's little fitness book.* New York: E. P. Dutton.

Fredericks, L., Kaplan, E., & Zeisler, J. (2001). *Integrating youth voice in service-learning.* Retrieved June 9, 2005, from Education Commission of the States Web site: http://www.ecs.org/clearinghouse/23/67/2367.htm

Furco, A. (n.d.). *Service-learning: A balanced approach to experiential education.* Retrieved July 21, 2005, from Florida Compact Web site: http://www.floridacompact.org/pdf/resources/SL-ABalancedApproach.pdf

Gladwell, M. (2002). *The tipping point.* New York: Back Bay Books/Little, Brown.

Goleman, D. (1995). *Emotional intelligence: Why it can matter more than I. Q.* New York: Bantam Books/Doubleday.

Goodlad, J. (1984). *A place called school.* New York: McGraw-Hill.

Greenberg, J., Dintiman, G., & Oakes, B. (1996). *Wellness: Creating a life of health and fitness.* Needham Heights, MA: Allyn & Bacon.

Hall, M. (1991, June). Gadugi: A model of service-learning for Native American communities. *Phi Delta Kappan,* 754–757.

Hanna, P. (1937). *Youth serves the community.* New York: Appleton Century.

Harris, M. (1986). *Museum of the streets: Minnesota's contemporary outdoor murals.* St. Paul, MN: Pogo Press.

Hart, L. (1975). *How the brain works: A new understanding of human learning.* New York: Basic Books.

Hill, D., & Pope, D. C. (1995, April). Establishing a beachhead: Service learning at Stanford: Are school-university-community partnerships worth the struggle? *Service Learning: A Case Study.* Paper presented at the annual meeting of the American Educational Research Association, San Francisco.

Hoff, A. (1997). *Thrift score: The stuff, the method, the madness.* New York: HarperPerrenial.

Holdsman, K., & Tuchmann, D. (2004, December 9). The Philadelphia story: A guide to service-learning building. *District Lessons, 2.* New York: National Service Learning Partnership.

Honnet, E. P., & Poulen, S. J. (1989). *Principles of good practice for combining service and learning* (Wingspread Special Report). Racine, WI: Johnson Foundation.

Jacobsohn, R. (1994). *The reading group handbook: Everything you need to know, from choosing members to leading discussions.* Westport, CT: Hyperion Press.

Jensen, E. (1995). *The learning brain.* San Diego, CA: Turning Point.

Jensen, E. (1996). *Completing the puzzle: The brain-based approach.* Del Mar, CA: Turning Point.

Jensen, E. (2000). *Brain based learning: The new science of teaching and training* (rev. ed.). San Diego, CA: Brain Store.

Johnson, D. W., Johnson, R., & Holubec, E. (1994). *Cooperative learning in the classroom.* Alexandria, VA: Association for Supervision and Curriculum Development.

Johnson, M. (2001). *The lessons learned about service-learning: Voices of experience about urban service-learning in Saint Paul public schools.* Retrieved July 17, 2005, from American Association of School Administrators Web site: http://www.servicelearning.org/lib_svcs/lib_cat/index.php?library_id=4547

Joyce, D. (1996). *The complete container garden.* Cincinnati, OH: Reader's Digest Books.

Kilpatrick, W. (1918, September). The project method. *Teachers College Record,* 319–335.

Lankard, B. A. (1995). *Service learning, trends and issues alerts.* Washington, DC: Office of Educational Research and Improvement.

Larson, D. (Ed.). (1996). *Mayo Clinic family health book.* New York: William Morrow.

Lazear, D. (1999). *Eight ways of teaching.* Arlington Heights, IL: SkyLight.

Leedy, L. (1991). *The great trash bag.* New York: Holiday House.

LeVitus, B. (1997). *Mac OS 8 for dummies.* Foster City, CA: IDG Books Worldwide.

Lewis, B. A. (1995). *The kid's guide to service projects.* Minneapolis, MN: Free Spirit.

Lewis, B. A. (1996, February). Serving others hooks gifted students on learning. *Educational Leadership,* 70–74.

McClurg, R. S. (1995). *The rummager's handbook: Finding, buying, cleaning, fixing, using and selling secondhand treasures.* Pownal, VT: Storey Communications.

McMahon, S. (Ed.). (1997). *The book club connection: Literacy learning and classroom talk.* New York: Teachers College Press.

Nathan, J., & Kielsmeier, J. (1991, June). The sleeping giant of school reform. *Phi Delta Kappan,* 739–742.

Newmann, F. (1975). *Education for citizen action: Challenge for secondary curriculum.* Berkeley, CA: McCutchan.

Nielsen, S., & Boles, T. (Il.). (1993). *Trash! trash! trash! (target earth).* Minneapolis, MN: Abdo & Daughters.

Nisbett, R. E., & Ross, L. D. (1980). *Human inference: Strategies and short-comings of social judgment.* Englewood Cliffs, NJ: Prentice Hall.

Parry, T., & Gregory, G. (1998). *Designing brain-compatible learning:* Arlington Heights, IL: SkyLight.

Physician Task Force. (1985). *Hunger in America: The growing epidemic.* Middletown, CT: Wesleyan University Press.

Quezada, P., & Kim, S. (1996). *Chicano graffiti and murals: The neighborhood art of Peter Quezada.* Oxford: University Press of Mississippi.

Rappoport, A., & Kletzien, S. (1996, May). Kids around town: Civics lessons leave impressions. *Educational Leadership,* 26–29.

Rathbone, A. (1997). *Windows 95 for dummies* (2nd ed.). Foster City, CA: IDG Books Worldwide.

Rochester, J. B., & Rochester, J. (1993). *Computers for people.* Burr Ridge, IL: Richard D. Irwin.

Ross, R. (1996). *Returning to the teachings.* New York: Penguin.

Roth, S. (1995). *Better Homes and Gardens complete guide to flower gardening.* Des Moines, IA: Better Homes and Gardens.

Rubin, B. (1997). *A citizen's guide to politics in America: How the system works and how to work the system.* Armonk, NY: M. E. Sharpe.

Russell, P. (n.d.). *How to mind map.* Retrieved June 15, 2005, from Pete Russell Web site: http://www.peterussell.com/MindMaps/HowTo.html

Sagor, R. (1996, September). Building resiliency in students. *Educational Leadership,* 38–43.

Sams, J. (1990). *Sacred path cards: The discovery of self through native teachings.* New York: HarperCollins.

Service-learning delivers what Americans want from schools. (n.d.). Retrieved June 8, 2005, from National Service-Learning Partnership Web site: http://www.learningindeed.org/tools/other/sldelvrs.pdf

Shaw, R. (1996). *The activist's handbook: A primer for the 1990s and beyond.* Berkeley: University of California Press.

Shirley, L. (1996). *Pocketguide to multiple intelligences.* Clemson, SC: National Dropout Prevention Center.

Silcox, H., & Leek, T. (1997, April). International service learning: Its time has come. *Phi Delta Kappan,* 615–618.

Smith, A. (2005). *What are brain breaks?* Retrieved June 6, 2005, from Alite Web site: www .alistair-smith.co.uk/information/brain_breaks.htm

Sousa, D. (2001). *How the brain learns: A classroom teacher's guide* (2nd ed.). Thousand Oaks, CA: Corwin Press.

Stanton, T. K., Giles, D. E., Jr., & Cruz, N. I. (1999). *Service learning.* San Francisco: Jossey-Bass.

Sylwester, R. (1995). *A celebration of neurons: An educator's guide to the human brain.* Alexandria, VA: Association for Supervision and Curriculum Development.

Sylwester, R. (2000). *A biological brain in a cultural classroom.* Thousand Oaks, CA: Corwin Press.

Titlebaum, P., Williamson, G., Daprano, C., Baer, J., & Brahler, J. (2004). *Annotated history of service learning.* Retrieved June 15, 2005, from University of Dayton Web site: http://www.servicelearning.org/article/archive/36

Tomlinson, C. A. (1999). *The differentiated classroom: Responding to the needs of all learners.* Alexandria, VA: Association for Supervision and Curriculum Development.

van Hook, B. (2003). *The virgin and the dynamo: Public murals in American architecture, 1893–1917.* Athens: Ohio University Press.

White, R. (n.d.). *Interaction with nature during the middle years: Its importance in children's development and nature's future.* Retrieved July 29, 2005, from White Hutchinson Leisure and Learning Group Web site: http://www.whitehutchinson.com/children/articles/nature .shtml

Wigginton, E. (1985). *Sometimes a shining moment: Twenty years at Foxfire.* Garden City, NY: Anchor Press/Doubleday.

Wolfe, P. (2001). *Brain matters: Translating research into classroom practice.* Alexandria, VA: Association for Supervision and Curriculum Development.

Wright, J. (1997). An administrator's guide to service learning. Clemson, SC: National Dropout Prevention Center.

Yang, L. (1995). *The city and town gardener: A handbook for planting small spaces and containers.* New York: Random House.

Index

Academic learning, xxii, xxv
  alignment, service/educational goals
    and, xxiv, 7–8
  content-knowledge assessment, 13
  graduation requirements and, xxii
  mastery-level attainments and, 7
  monitoring strategies, 9–10, 10 (figure)
  See also Service learning
    curriculum model
Alignment concerns, xxiv, 1–2, 7–8
AmeriCorps program, xxii, 47
Analysis/prioritization skills, 123–124
Assessment techniques:
  assessment plans, 13, 14 (figure)
  celebration of learning, 16–17
  evaluation conferences, 13–14
  needs assessment, 2, 118–119, 120
  observation checklists, 12–13, 12 (figure)
  portfolios, content-knowledge
    evaluation, 13
  project evaluation rubric, 2–3,
    4 (figure), 188
  report cards, 16
  service evaluation checklists, 189–190
  teamwork evaluation rubric, 13
  writing evaluation rubric, 191
Association for Supervision and
    Curriculum Development (ASCD), xxii
Authentic community service, xxii

Base teams, 23–24
Boyer, E., xxi
Brain-compatible learning, xxiii, xxvi, 179
Brainstorming, xxiii, xxvii, 11
Broken windows theory, 165
Buying-in to a project, 17, 122, 181–182
Buzan, B., 46
Buzan, T., 46

Celebration of learning, 16–17
Clean streets/green streets project:
  alignment, service/educational goals
    and, 32–35, 34 (figure)
  assessment/evaluation of, 37–38
  base team in, 23–24
  community partners in, 25–26, 31
  description of, 23–26
  focus of, 27–31
  KND charts and, 24
  portfolio contents and, 25, 37, 38
  project evaluation rubric, 28–29,
    28 (figure)
  project management plan for, 35,
    36 (figure)
  reciprocity, community of learners
    and, 33–35
  record-keeping and, 24–25
  reflective learning and, 35, 37
  reflective logs, templates for, 39–41
  risk assessment, safety/health protocols
    and, 26–27, 31
  school-community connection,
    development of, 30–31
  student responsibilities, curricular areas
    and, 32–33
Communication skill refinement, xxiii, xxvi
Community improvement. *See* Clean
    streets/green streets project;
    Community vision project; Main Street
    gardens project
Community partners, xxiv, xxv
  safety/health protocol
    development and, 5
  selection of, 5–6, 9
Community vision project:
  alignment, service/educational goals
    and, 163–165, 164 (figure)
  assessment/evaluation of, 167–168
  broken windows theory and, 165
  community partners in, 154, 162
  description of, 153–157
  focus of, 159–160
  Northern Latitude Visions project
    example, 157–158, 162–163
  portfolio contents and, 156, 167–168
  project evaluation rubric, 160, 160 (figure)

197

project management rubric for, 165,
166 (figure)
reciprocity, community of learners
and, 165
record-keeping and, 156–157
reflective learning and, 165, 167
reflective logs, templates for, 169–170
risk assessment, safety/health protocols
and, 158–159
student responsibilities, curricular areas
and, 163–164
working-group prototypes and,
155–156, 157
Computer tutors project:
alignment, service/educational goals
and, 125–127, 126 (figure)
assessment/evaluation of, 129–130
community partners in, 120, 124–125
description of, 117–122
focus of, 122–123
needs assessment activities, 118–119, 120
portfolio contents and, 122, 129–130
project evaluation rubric, 123, 123 (figure)
project management plan for,
127, 128 (figure)
reciprocity, community of
learners and, 127
record-keeping and, 119–121
reflective learning and, 129
reflective logs, templates for, 131–132
risk assessment, safety/health protocols
and, 122
school-community connection,
development of, 124
student responsibilities, curricular
areas and, 125–127
Consumer education. *See* Hygiene
tree project
Cooperative learning/work, xxiii,
xxiv, 8–9
Covey, S., 54
Curriculum model. *See* Service learning
curriculum model
Curriculum standards, xxiv, 8

Deep understanding, xxvi–xxvii
Dewey, J., xxi, xxii
Diverse populations, xxiii, xxvi

Educational goals. *See* Academic learning;
Service learning curriculum model
Ellyatt, W., 176
Evaluation. *See* Assessment techniques;
Project evaluation rubric

Experience, xxi, xxii
academic learning and, xxiv
growth through, xxvi–xxvii
reciprocal experiential learning
and, xxii, 7
reflection and, xxii
Expert knowledge, 15

Family education. *See* Soup troop project
Feedback, 9–10, 10 (figure), 11
Fogarty, R., 1, 179
Foster care holiday boxes project, 47
Funding sources, 15–16, 62–63,
82, 102, 136, 142, 171, 174

Gladwell, M., 165
Goodlad, J., xxi
Graphic organizers, 179

Health. *See* Hygiene tree project; Lending
locker project; Safety/health protocols;
Soup troop project
Hygiene tree project:
alignment, service/educational goals
and, 67–71, 70 (figure)
assessment/evaluation of, 73–74
community partners in, 62, 67
description of, 61–65
focus of, 66–67
funding for, 62–63
portfolio contents and, 65, 73–74
product purchase excursion, 63
project evaluation rubric, 67, 68 (figure)
project management plan for, 71,
72 (figure)
reciprocity, community of
learners and, 69–71
record-keeping and, 65
reflective learning and, 71–73
reflective logs, templates for, 75–77
risk assessment, safety/health
protocols and, 66
rubric-building process and, 64–65
school-community connection,
development of, 67
student responsibilities, curricular
areas and, 68–69

In-context learning, xxvi–xxvii
Instructional technology. *See* Community
vision project; Computer tutors project;
Voice of the people project
Intentional academic learning, xxii
Internal locus of control, xxvi

International Conference on Service-
Learning Research, xxii
Internet resources:
  book reviews, 86
  community partners, 67
  cooperative learning, 9
  government activities information,
    136, 144
  health/safety protocols, 5
  landscape design, 172–173
  project selection, 31
  public art, 153, 154
  service learning ideas, 2
  tutoring programs, 125

Johnson, M., xxiii, 10, 27, 31, 71, 119, 125
Johnson, President L. B., xxi

Kelling, G. L., 165
Kennedy, President J. F., xxi
Kilpatrick, W., xxi
KND charts, 24
Kolb, D., xxii

Language arts. *See* Computer tutors project;
  Reading pals project
Learning cycle theory, xxii
Learn and Serve, 2
Lending locker project:
  alignment, service/educational goals
    and, 51–54, 53 (figure)
  assessment/evaluation of, 54, 56
  base team in, 44
  community partners in, 44, 49–51
  description of, 43–47
  focus of, 48–49
  portfolio contents and, 45–47, 56
  project evaluation rubric, 49, 50 (figure)
  project management plan for, 54,
    55 (figure)
  reciprocity, community of learners
    and, 52–53
  record-keeping and, 44–45
  reflective learning and, 54
  reflective logs, templates for, 57–59
  risk assessment, safety/health protocols
    and, 48
  school-community connection,
    development of, 49
  student responsibilities, curricular areas
    and, 52
Liability concerns, 16
Library technology. *See* Community vision
  project; Voice of the people project

Life skills, 7–8
Life skills project. *See* Reading pals project

Main Street gardens project:
  alignment, service/educational goals
    and, 179–181, 180 (figure)
  assessment/evaluation of, 182, 184
  community partners in, 171, 177–178
  description of, 171–174
  focus of, 176–177
  funding for, 171, 172, 174
  portfolio contents and, 174, 184
  project evaluation rubric, 177,
    178 (figure)
  project management plan for,
    181–182, 183 (figure)
  reciprocity, community of learners
    and, 181
  record-keeping and, 173–174
  reflective learning and, 182
  reflective logs, templates for, 185–186
  risk assessment, safety/health protocols
    and, 175–176
  school gardens project example, 175
  student responsibilities, curricular
    areas and, 179–181
  visual patterning and, 179
Management plan. *See* Project
  management plan
Manpower Development Internship
  Program, xxii
Mapping possibilities, 29–30, 46
*Michigan Journal of Community Service-
  Learning*, xxii
Mind mapping, 46
Monitoring strategies, 9–10, 10 (figure)
Motivation to learn, xxvi-xxvii
Multiple intelligences strategies:
  absent teammates, missed work and,
    161–162
  analysis/prioritization skills
    and, 123–124
  large muscle movement, brain breaks
    and, 176
  management plans and, 18
  mapping possibilities and, 29–30
  mind mapping model and, 46
  music/rhythm, learning and, 106
  rubrics, design of, 64–65
  storyboarding the project and, 147
  storytelling in nature and, 90
  structuring learning teams and, 8–9
  visual patterning and, 179
Murals. *See* Community vision project

National Center for Service-Learning, xxii
National Service-Learning Clearinghouse
(University of Minnesota), xxii, 2
National Service-Learning
Partnership, 2
National Student Volunteer Program
(NSVP), xxii
Needs assessment, 2, 118–119, 120
Northern latitude visions project,
157–158, 162–163

Observation checklists, 12–13, 12 (figure)
Organic education-experience
relationship, xxi

Partnerships. *See* Community partners
Passing the referendum project, 137–138
Peace Corps, xxi
Peer-partner sharing, 11
Performance management grid, 18
Personal experience. *See* Experience;
Reflective engagement; Service
learning
Physical education. *See* Lending
locker project
Planning process. *See* Project
management plan
Portfolio contents, 13, 25
*The Principles of Good Practice
for Combining Service and Learning,* xxii
Prioritization/analysis skills, 123–124
Problem solving:
opportunities for, xxiii, xxiv
skill development, xxvii, 123–124
Professional development, 15
Progressive education movement, xxi
Project evaluation rubric, 2–3,
4 (figure), 188
Project management plan, xxiv, xxvii
components of, 9–10
feedback, evaluation/reflection
guide, 10, 10 (figure)
KND charts, 24
mapping possibilities and, 18
monitoring progress, 9–10
performance management grid and, 18
preparation phase, 9
safety/health protocol development, 5
storyboarding the project and, 147
See also Service learning curriculum
model
Public art. *See* Community vision project;
Main Street gardens project

Ramsey, W., xxii
Reading pals project:
affective processing and, 84
alignment, service/educational goals
and, 90–93, 92 (figure)
assessment/evaluation of, 95–96
community partners in, 88–90
description of, 81–85
focus of, 86–88
funding for, 82
materials acquisition and, 83–84
portfolio contents and, 81, 83–84,
85, 95–96
project evaluation rubric, 88, 88 (figure)
project management plan for, 93,
94 (figure)
reading comprehension tests and, 81, 85
reading partners and, 82, 83, 84
reading strategies survey and, 81–82, 84
reciprocity, community of learners
and, 92–93
record-keeping and, 82–83
reflective learning and, 93, 95
reflective logs, templates for, 97–99
risk assessment, safety/health protocols
and, 85–86
school-community connection,
development of, 87–88
session formats and, 83, 84
student responsibilities, curricular areas
and, 90–91
writing/sharing science books and, 86–87
Real-world skills, xxiii, xxvi, xxvii
See also Life skills
Reciprocal experiential learning, xxii, 7
Reflective engagement, xxi
deep understanding/transfer of learning
and, xxvi-xxvii
experiential education programs and, xxii
learning strategies for, 11
reciprocal experiential learning
and, xxii, 7
self-evaluation and, 9–10, 10 (figure)
service goals/content standards and, xxiv
tools/techniques for, xxiv-xxv
written reflection logs and, 11
Report cards, 16
Representative portfolios, 13
Reproducible masters:
project evaluation rubric, 188
service evaluation checklist, 189–190
writing evaluation rubric, 191
Resilience, xxvii

Resources, xxii
funding, 15–16, 62–63, 82, 102, 136, 142, 171, 174
See also Internet resources; Reproducible masters
Risk assessment, 4–5
Risk taking, xxvi
Rubric-building process, 64–65

Safety/health protocols, 4–5, 16
Science. *See* Clean streets/green streets; Main Street gardens project
Self-evaluation, 9–10, 10 (figure)
Service learning, xxi
academic learning and, xxii, xxiv
brain-compatible learning and, xxiii, xxvi
elements of, xxiv-xxv
history of, xxi-xxii
key stakeholders in, xxv-xxvi
program development, reference sources and, xxii
rationale/benefits of, xxii-xxiv
reciprocal experiential learning and, xxii
student learning opportunities and, xxii-xxiii, xxvi-xxviii
value-added component in, xxii
See also Project management plan; Service learning curriculum model
Service learning curriculum model, xxii
alignment, service/educational goals and, xxiv, 7–8
assessment/evaluation techniques in, 12–14, 14 (figure), 16–17
challenges, management of, 14–17
community partners, selection of, 5–6
content-knowledge assessment, 13
elements of service learning and, 1–11
funding sources and, 15–16
liability concerns and, 16
multiple intelligences, team assignments and, 8–9
need for service, analysis of, 2
observation checklists, 12–13, 12 (figure)
portfolio contents, 13
project evaluation rubric, 2–3, 4 (figure), 188
project management, components of, 9–10, 10 (figure)
reciprocity, community of learners and, 7
reflective learning strategies, 11
risk assessment, health/safety protocols and, 4–5

student benefits in, xxvi-xxviii, xxviii (figure)
student buy-in and, 17
teacher professional development and, 15
teamwork evaluation rubric, 13, 189–190
time for planning process and, 15
written reflection logs and, 11
See also Project management plan
Sigmon, R., xxii, 7
Smith, A., 176
Social consciousness, xxvii
Social studies. *See* Clean streets/green streets; Voice of the people project
Soup troop project:
alignment, service/educational goals and, 107–110, 108 (figure)
assessment/evaluation of, 112–113, 189–191
community partners in, 101, 102, 107
cooperative student teams and, 102
description of, 101–103
focus of, 104–105
food handling issues in, 102
funding for, 102
length of service and, 101–102
portfolio contents and, 103, 112–113
project evaluation rubric, 105, 105 (figure)
project management plan for, 110, 111 (figure)
reciprocity, community of learners and, 109–110
record-keeping and, 103
reflective learning and, 110, 112
reflective logs, templates for, 114–116
risk assessment, safety/health protocols and, 103–104
school-community connection, development of, 104–105
site location and, 102
student responsibilities, curricular areas and, 109
Standards, xxiv
Storyboarding the project, 147
Students, xxv-xxvi
analysis/prioritization skills and, 123–124
brain-compatible learning and, xxiii, xxvi, 179
buy-in/ownership of project, 17, 122, 181–182
communication/cooperation skills and, xxiii
multiple intelligences, team assignments and, 8–9

project planning and, xxvii
real-world skills and, xxiii, xxvi, xxvii
self-esteem/self-confidence and, xxii-xxiii
self-evaluation, 9–10, 10 (figure)
social consciousness, development of,
    xxvii
See also Reflective engagement; Service
    learning curriculum model

Teachers, xxv-xxvi, 5, 15
Team assignment:
    absent teammates, missed work and,
        161–162
    base teams, 23–24
    structuring learning teams, 8–9
Teamwork evaluation rubric, 13, 189–190
Technology. *See* Community vision project;
    Computer tutors project; Internet
    resources; Voice of the people project
Transfer of learning, xxvi-xxvii, 7, 8

Value-added component, xxii
Viability evaluation, 2–3, 4 (figure), 188
VISTA (Volunteers in Service to
    America), xxi
Visual arts. *See* Community vision project;
    Main Street gardens project
Visual patterning, 179
Voice of the people project:
    alignment, service/educational goals
        and, 143–145, 144 (figure)

assessment/evaluation of, 149
buddy groups in, 136
community partners in, 136, 141–142
description of, 135–139
focus of, 140–141
funding for, 136, 142
Passing the Referendum project
    example, 137–138
portfolio contents and, 138, 149
project evaluation rubric, 141,
    142 (figure)
project management plan for, 145,
    146 (figure)
reciprocity, community of learners and,
    144–145
record-keeping and, 138–139
reflective learning and, 148
reflective logs, templates for, 150–151
risk assessment, safety/health
    protocols and, 140
school-community connection,
    development of, 141
student responsibilities, curricular areas
    and, 143
survey construction/use in,
    137, 138–139

Wigginton, E., xxi
Wilson, J. Q., 165
Wingspread Conference, xxii
Writing evaluation rubric, 191